The 2000s

The
2000s

Bob Batchelor

American Popular Culture Through History

GREENWOOD PRESS
Westport, Connecticut • London

Library of Congress Cataloging-in-Publication Data

Batchelor, Bob.
  The 2000s / Bob Batchelor.
        p. cm. — (American popular culture through history)
  Includes bibliographical references and index.
  ISBN 978–0–313–34912–6 (alk. paper)
  1. United States—Civilization—1970–   2. United States—Civilization—21st century.
3. Popular culture—United States.   I. Title.   II. Title: Two thousands.
E169.12.B323   2009
973.93—dc22   2008027464

British Library Cataloguing in Publication Data is available.

Library of Congress Catalog Card Number: 2008027464
ISBN: 978–0–313–34912–6

First published in 2009

Greenwood Press, 88 Post Road West, Westport, CT 06881
An imprint of Greenwood Publishing Group, Inc.
www.greenwood.com

Printed in the United States of America

The paper used in this book complies with the
Permanent Paper Standard issued by the National
Information Standards Organization (Z39.48–1984).

10   9   8   7   6   5   4   3   2   1

With all my love
to my wife Kathy and our daughter, Kassandra Dylan,
the single best thing to happen to us in the new millennium

Contents

Contents

Introduction

America-the-dream is the self-conscious invention that has molded a
huge population with varying, local folkways into a national culture.
—Russell Duncan and Joseph Goddard (2005)

Welcome to Pop Culture 2.0!

In the new millennium, we are all members of "Generation eXposure,"
whether that means using social media Web sites, such as LinkedIn.com to
make business connections or keeping in touch with high school friends via
Facebook. Every minute of every day, millions of people are using the Internet to connect. Today, regardless of a person's age, the explosion of Internet-
based innovations essentially eliminates communications boundaries. Even
for people who do not use social media sites on a personal basis, the fact
that more and more corporations are using the channel to reach consumers is pulling them into the online conversation. A blue-haired grandma,
for example, might receive coupons for products she buys via e-mail. At
the same time, her tattooed granddaughter surfs MySpace searching for
downloadable singles from the hottest emo band. Perhaps for the first time
in human history, the old adage "it's a small world" is actually true.

The combination of technological innovation, economic factors, governmental forces, and cultural dynamics has created a new world—generation
eXposure—in which nearly everyone manages a public image (the fastest
growing segment of the population using MySpace, for example, consists
of people over 30 years old). On a social network, like Facebook or MySpace,
users create a persona that is both spectacle and truth in some odd
amalgamation, which enables autonomy (if desired) and self-promotion
simultaneously.

One of the most popular features on Facebook, for example, allows people to display what mood they currently exhibit, whether melancholy or looking forward to the weekend. When the user changes her mood, a new "Mini-Feed" alert is posted, so that "friends" (real or virtual) get nearly instant access to that new detail, spread by a news feed across the site. As a result, one's every impulse can be made public knowledge. Social media networks, whether designed for entertainment, business, or pleasure, provide users with a voice and a public persona that they can share across the street or around the world.

Scholars Stanley J. Baran and Dennis K. Davis explain the dramatic change taking place in the new millennium, saying, "We are in the midst of a revolution in communication technology that is transforming social orders and cultures around the world. Each new technological device expands the possible uses of the existing technology."[1] At the heart of this transformation is the American people, or as *Time* magazine dubbed its 2006 Person of the Year: You. "It's a story about community and collaboration on a scale never seen before," said journalist Lev Grossman, in outlining the magazine's rationale, "It's about the cosmic compendium of knowledge Wikipedia and the million-channel people's network YouTube and the online metropolis MySpace. It's about the many wresting power from the few and helping one another for nothing and how that will not only change the world, but also change the way the world changes."[2]

POP CULTURE AT WHAT PRICE?

Every revolution inevitably contains a dark side and the spread of the Web is no exception. With the advent of social media and Web-based communications, many young people find that it is not enough to merely imitate Britney Spears or Paris Hilton. Following celebrity trends is done from the keyboard and a short trip to the nearest Target provides knockoffs that mimic designer brands. More important, technology gives everyone a platform to launch his or her own 15 minutes of fame. In the new millennium, Andy Warhol's famous maxim transformed the public yearning for fame into a spectator sport.

The negative aspect of this elusive search is that the fixation on self and celebrity acts as a diversion from more serious challenges the nation faces, including President George W. Bush's "War on Terror" and a myriad of economic and socioeconomic problems that prevent millions of people from having any real share of the American Dream. Moreover, the same innovations that enable people to interact online also enable corporations to connect to consumers in a whole new way, extending their reach into people's wallets.

In the new millennium, however, popular culture is also at the heart of many national debates. For example, the wars overseas sharply divided the country, after a period of unity in response to the 9/11 terrorist attacks, which destroyed one of the world's most recognizable buildings. Our collective culture helped people process and interpret the world around them, from dramatic feature films to music and literature that addressed the national trauma head-on. Also, in the early years of the new century, the country watched as interest rates dropped to historic lows, but by late-decade "subprime" became one of the most searched terms on Google as the nation teetered on recession.

The low interest rates from that earlier era helped bring in an era focused on "big" like never before. Seemingly overnight, people across the country could buy or build their own McMansion—a giant-sized slice of the American pie. The fascination with the bigger the better not only had influence on supersized homes, but gargantuan fast food meals became commonplace, new plasma and LCD televisions grew to epic sizes, and people themselves (or at least their waistlines) seemed to grow bigger and bigger.

Whereas one part of pop culture centered on big, electronics and transportation advances proved that good things also came in increasingly smaller packages. Apple's iPod reinvented how people interacted with music and hybrid automobiles changed thoughts about fuel efficiency as a gallon of gas topped $4.00 and threatens to head much higher. And cell phone usage (many plans with "unlimited" minutes) ballooned in an "always on" society, while physically shrinking to the size of a deck of cards. Yes, Pop Culture 2.0, which pundits predicted would some day arrive, burst onto the scene: always on—me-centric—and ultimately transforming the way we interact with one another and the world around us.

WHAT IS POPULAR CULTURE TODAY?

What is American popular culture? At the turn of the previous century, the answer seemed more straightforward. An awkward giant, the United States rode the presidency of Theodore Roosevelt to a position as world military and economic leader. The nation took these first aching steps toward global hegemony, however, still firmly rooted inward, a society dominated by its local outlook and nature. For most people, popular culture existed in a 10-mile radius from the place they were born or grew up.

During the twentieth century, the national outlook grew increasingly global. Overseas wars took Americans to the four corners of the world. Presidents and political leaders orchestrated a sea change in diplomacy, pushing the country into a role as the world's police force. Military supremacy prompted the expansion of cultural hegemony as the far reaches of the globe suddenly grew smaller.

In the midst of the new millennium, national and international borders are blurred, particularly as cultures blend and technology enables instant communications. Today, popular culture unites and intertwines technology, economics, and power relations—the epic forces shaping the modern world. The resulting tapestry enables people to situate themselves within society, among family, friends, neighbors, and communities.

As a result, despite being difficult to define because of its amorphous nature, popular culture is a type of unifying system. Using popular culture as a guidepost, people navigate among one another. We use its symbols, representations, and ideas to make sense of the world around us. The large-scale influences on people's lives are often difficult to understand or interpret, but popular culture provides a common language. The hottest television show or hit movie, for example, is a sort of guide or handbook that enables people to interact.

The power of popular culture today transcends discussions of low or high culture, which dominated interpretations of the topic for decades. As a fusing and interlacing force, popular culture allows for discussion that transverses barriers based on class, race, profession, wealth, or education. Of course, there are still societal breakdowns, especially in times of crisis. The aftermath of Hurricane Katrina, for example, reveals much about the fabric of society stitched together under the banner of popular culture. Under regular circumstances, however, popular culture seems to be a uniting influence. Perhaps it is during crises that the nation experiences the limitations of using popular culture as such a tool.

DAWN OF A NEW ERA

At one point in the recent past, observers held out hope that the Internet would serve as a democratizing force, allowing greater equality among users in a heated race toward greater information, education, civility, and wealth. The 2000s, though, have revealed a growing fracture in this idea—access issues actually contributed to a "digital divide" between those who could afford connectivity and those who could not.

The notion that popular culture is realized as a series of milestones in one's life is particularly vital in a world that can easily slip out of control or seem altogether frenetic. Still, popular culture holds remarkable power. The words, images, and communication vehicles that deliver this power have the potential to change the world. Bob Dylan's 1963 lyrics, imploring that "the times they are a-changin" remain significant, just as the artist himself is still important over a career spanning more than 45 years. Yet, when we look back at the hope and aspirations of those times, we see that the revolution failed. The "flower power" kids are now running the world. They morphed into their elders as they aged, replacing idealism with conservatism, and conducting a land-grab for all they could accumulate. Still, Dylan's words, and the dreams of a new and better day live on.

The new millennium is a microcosm of the ways popular culture can be orchestrated to both impose order and initiate change. Discussing the aspirations of celebrity-obsessed online chatters, journalist David Samuels says, "A good number of readers seem to write in the openly delusional (yet not entirely impossible) belief that if their post is sincere or hateful enough, the walls separating their own lives from the lives of celebrities will dissolve, transporting them from the backlit world of their LCD screens to the super-pollinated atmosphere of the media daisy chain."[3]

The American Dream and popular culture are deeply knotted in the national psyche. Perhaps late in any decade, one senses that some cataclysmic change has either just taken place or is bound to occur in the near future. This feeling in itself is wholly American—continually assessing the past for lessons and guideposts, while simultaneously peering into the future for glimpses of what may soon come. At this time, in this decade, the national mood is one of apprehension and menace.

The economic picture is cloudy and talk of recession mounts, despite the consolidated efforts of the Bush Administration, Congress, and various federal monetary agencies. Moreover, the United States is in the midst of a debilitating overseas war that seems to have no positive outcome. People long for good news from the real estate industry, but each new indicator leads to further concern. And, at the same time, the gap between wealthy individuals and the rest of the nation grows exponentially. All this leads to a volatility that, although not unprecedented, is far astray from what most people assume to be the American Dream.

So where is popular culture in this new era? My view is that popular culture is central not only to what Americans believe but how they interpret the world. The challenge is that many people use these forces to willingly allow themselves to be blinded to reality. If one is consumed by the latest films, television, or celebrity gossip, it is easier to put off thoughts of war, economic disparity, and melancholy. Thus, popular culture—literally the study of what influences people as they conduct their daily lives—can be a force for reinterpreting and changing the world. Or, it can mask reality in favor of a Hollywood version of life that emphasizes happy endings and rainbows. Wake up or tune out—the choice is yours.

Timeline of the 2000s

2000

February   Stock market jitters turn into widespread panic, signaling the end of the dot-com boom.

May   Computers around the world are infected with the "I love you" virus attached to spam e-mail.

September   Six-year investigation into the Clintons regarding Whitewater allegations ends with no indictments.

November   Presidential election pitting Vice President Al Gore against Texas Governor George W. Bush is gridlocked over turmoil regarding outcome of Florida vote. The recount is hindered by fraud allegations and legal wrangling. Bush is later declared winner by 537 votes.

December 12   The Supreme Court votes 5–4 to halt presidential election recounts, essentially declaring Bush the winner.

2001

January   George W. Bush sworn in as nation's 43rd president.

June   President Bush advocates and Congress passes $1.35 trillion tax cut over 11 years.

September 11   Islamic terrorists under the direction of al-Qaeda leader Osama bin Laden hijack four passenger airliners in the United States. They deliberately crash them into the World Trade Center in New York City and the Pentagon in Washington, DC. The fourth plane crashes in a rural area outside Shanksville, Pennsylvania, while thought to be headed for the White House or U.S. Capitol. The attack on the

World Trade Center destroys the buildings and inflicts major damage to the surrounding areas. Overall, 3,000 people are killed.

October   Nation terrified by anthrax scare after drug-laced letters sent to
                media and governmental figures.

                In response to 9/11 attacks, the United States and British armies
                invade Afghanistan to find bin Laden, to destroy al-Qaeda terrorist
                camps, and to overthrow the Taliban government.

December 2   Enron files for bankruptcy in a spectacular flameout after years of
                winning critical acclaim from the media for its successes in corpo-
                rate America.

2002

January   In his State of the Union address, President Bush labels Iraq, Iran,
                and North Korea an "axis of evil" that threatens world peace.

                Dave Thomas, founder of the fast food chain Wendy's, dies. He
                gained widespread fame from starring in the company's television
                commercials.

March   The Homeland Security Advisory System is introduced. The color-
                coded scale links the threat against the United States based on a
                five-point range, from red ("severe") to green ("low").

                Fox airs the show *Celebrity Boxing*, pitting celebrities against one
                another in the ring. The first program featured former child actors
                Danny Bonaduce versus Barry Williams and former Olympic ice
                skater Tonya Harding versus Paula Jones, a woman infamous for
                alleging an affair with Bill Clinton.

                At the 74th Academy Awards, actress Halle Berry becomes the first
                African American female to win the "Best Actress" award.

April   Lisa "Left Eye" Lopes, a prominent female rapper and member of
                the hip-hop group TLC, is killed in La Ceiba, Honduras, in a car
                accident while on vacation.

May   FBI agent Robert Hanssen is sentenced to life in prison without pa-
                role for selling secrets to Russia over a 22-year period in exchange
                for money and diamonds.

July   Baseball great Ted Williams dies. After his death, his family battled
                over his remains, with his son eventually having the body placed
                in cryonic suspension.

October   Former president Jimmy Carter wins the Nobel Peace Prize.

                A series of shootings takes place in the greater Washington, DC
                area; 10 people are killed and 3 more critically injured. The gunman
                is labeled the "beltway sniper." Residents are urged to use caution
                and stay away from some areas. Two men orchestrated the attacks,
                which they had carried out earlier in the South and West. In total,
                they are known to have killed 16 people.

Congress votes to authorize President Bush to use force, if necessary, to disarm Iraq.

2003

February 1   The Space Shuttle *Columbia* explodes on reentry. All seven astronauts inside are killed.

March   President Bush says in a primetime news conference that he is prepared to go to war against Iraq, with or without United Nations or other international support.

The United States launches a predawn missile attack in Iraq, targeting sites of "military importance," according to President Bush. Saddam Hussein appears on Iraqi television to denounce the attacks and rally his people.

Dixie Chicks lead singer Natalie Maines sets off a national controversy when at a London concert she exclaims that the group members feel "ashamed" that President Bush is a fellow Texan.

April   Allied forces rescue Army Pfc. Jessica Lynch, a prisoner of war held at an Iraqi hospital.

After the fall of Baghdad and Tikrit, the Pentagon declares an end to major fighting in Iraq and begins withdrawing troops, warships, and aircraft from the Gulf region.

May   President Bush signs $350 billion tax cut bill.

September   Federal and local authorities raid the Bay Area Laboratory Co-operative (BALCO) offices owned by Victor Conte. The raid sets in motion the investigation of professional athletes with ties to BALCO.

2004

February   The CIA admits that no imminent threat from weapons of mass destruction existed before the 2003 invasion of Iraq.

The city of San Francisco begins issuing marriage licenses to same-sex couples.

March   Dove launches "Celebrating Curves" campaign, featuring real women as models in print and television ads, in contrast to young, waiflike models that dominated most advertisements.

June   Former president Ronald Reagan dies in his Bel-Air, California, home at the age of 93.

October   The Boston Red Sox win the World Series. The victory breaks the supposed "Curse of the Bambino," said to haunt the franchise since it last won a title and then later sold the rights to Babe Ruth in 1918 to the New York Yankees.

November
After a long investigation and trial, a jury finds Scott Peterson guilty of the murder of his wife Laci and unborn son Conner. The case dominated the news headlines after Peterson reported his wife missing on Christmas Eve in 2002.

2005

January
The United States and other countries around the world donate supplies and assist with relief efforts after a tsunami devastates 11 Asian nations.

Jennifer Aniston and Brad Pitt announce their separation, setting off a media frenzy.

February
NHL Commissioner Gary Bettman cancels the season after owners and players fail to reach agreement on a new contract and salary cap for players.

March
Lifestyle celebrity Martha Stewart is released from a West Virginia prison.

Terri Schiavo, a woman in a persistent vegetative state for 15 years, serves as a political lightning rod after her husband decides to remove the feeding tube keeping her artificially alive. While activists argue the morality of such a decision, the House and Senate vote to allow a federal court to rule on the case. Federal judge James Whittemore refuses to order that her breathing tube be reinserted. The U.S. Supreme Court does not hear the case. Schiavo died on March 31, 13 days after the tube is removed. An autopsy revealed that she had no chance for recovery.

The House Government Reform Committee holds hearings to investigate steroids use in baseball. Ten players testify, including Mark McGwire and Sammy Sosa.

May
Pfc. Lynndie England pleads guilty to seven criminal counts related to her role in torturing Iraqi prisoners of war held in Abu Ghraib.

W. Mark Felt reveals that he is the famous "deep throat" informant who leaked information regarding Watergate to Bob Woodward and Carl Bernstein.

June
An audit released by Democratic legislators reveals that the Pentagon disputed $1 billion in bills submitted by defense contractor Halliburton for work performed in Iraq.

Pop singer Michael Jackson is acquitted of 10 charges, including molesting a child, conspiracy, and providing alcohol to minors, in a California courtroom.

July
Sandra Day O'Connor, the first woman on the U.S. Supreme Court, retires after serving for 24 years.

Musicians in nine countries hold Live 8 concerts to raise money and awareness in the global fight against poverty in Africa.

August	Hurricane Katrina ravishes part of Florida, Louisiana, and Mississippi. The storm surge causes the levees to break in New Orleans, resulting in widespread damage, as 80 percent of the city is flooded. The Bush administration is criticized for its slow response and mismanagement of disaster relief efforts.
September	Millions of people are left homeless or displaced as a result of Hurricane Katrina. Thousands of stranded people are evacuated to the Astrodome in Houston. President Bush signs emergency $10.5 billion relief bill for the region.

2006

May	Former Enron executives Ken Lay and Jeff Skilling are convicted of conspiracy and fraud for their roles in the company's downfall.
July	For the first time in his presidency, President Bush uses his veto power, declining legislation that would have expanded federal financing for stem cell research.
September	Bob Dylan's *Modern Times* album debuts at Number One on the Billboard chart, his first work to hit the top spot since 1976's *Desire*.
November	The Democrats gain control of the House and Senate in the midterm elections.
	Technorati, the first blog search engine, estimates that there are 28.4 million blogs online.

2007

January	After the Democrats win a majority of seats in the 2006 midterm elections, California Democrat Nancy Pelosi becomes the first woman Speaker of the House of Representatives.
February	Harvard University names its first female president when historian Drew Gilpin Faust takes over for embattled former leader Lawrence Summers.
	Two articles by *Washington Post* reporters Dana Priest and Anne Hull that investigate medical negligence at Walter Reed Army Medical Center in Washington set off a national controversy over treatment of returning and injured American soldiers who fought in Iraq.
April	Shock jock Don Imus sparks a national controversy after making derogatory racial remarks about the Rutgers University women's basketball team. The fallout includes Imus losing his CBS Radio and MSNBC television shows. By December, however, he is back on the air with different networks.
	A lone gunman goes on a killing rampage on the campus of Virginia Tech University. He kills 32 people.

June   The final episode of the HBO hit drama series *The Sopranos* airs.
            Fans and critics debate the open-ended finale.

            Price Is Right host Bob Barker retires from the show at age 83 after
            35 years of hosting the show. Barker is replaced by comedian Drew
            Carey.

            Apple Computer launches the iPhone, a high tech cell phone that
            enables users to easily surf the Web and download music with a
            sleek black design and virtual keyboard.

            "I Got a Crush on Obama," a YouTube video posted by "Obama
            Girl" Amber Lee Ettinger, gains wide popularity. Although Barack
            Obama criticizes the video, it gets more than 3 million viewings by
            the fall.

August   A bridge spanning the Mississippi River outside Minneapolis col-
            lapses, killing 13 people and injuring hundreds more. The tragedy
            begins a national conversation regarding bridge safety.

            San Francisco Giants slugger Barry Bonds hits his 756th homerun
            to pass Henry Aaron as the all-time homerun king. Many consider
            Bonds's feat tainted by allegations that he used steroids.

            Atlanta Falcons' star quarterback Michael Vick pleads guilty to
            charges of operating a dog fighting operation and participating in
            killing dogs.

September   Britney Spears lip-synchs and dances awkwardly through a live
            performance at the MTV Video Music Awards show. Her hopes for
            a "comeback" are foiled, but the shoddy performance keeps her in
            the celebrity news cycle.

            Former football star and actor O. J. Simpson is arrested in Las Vegas
            and charged with robbery with a deadly weapon and other charges
            after attempting to steal some of his sports memorabilia items.

            A panel of international experts upholds the decision to strip the
            2006 Tour de France title from Floyd Landis, an American cyclist
            accused of doping violations.

October   Fueled by the Santa Ana winds, a wildfire rages across southern
            California. The flames scorched more than 400,000 acres, destroyed
            2,000 homes, and forced the evacuation of 1 million people before
            being contained.

December   Former Vice President and Senator Al Gore wins the Nobel Peace
            Prize for his work on global climate change.

2008

January   Presidential primary race is officially underway with Iowa cau-
            cuses. Democrat Barack Obama and Republican Mike Huckabee
            win in Iowa. In the New Hampshire primary, Democrat Hillary
            Clinton is victorious, as is Republican John McCain.

Louisiana Republican Bobby Jindal becomes the first Indian-American governor in the United States.

President Bush proposes a $145 billion economic stimulus package in response to the sluggish economy, including the housing market crisis and rising oil prices. The plan features rebate checks for individuals. The House votes 385 to 35 in favor of the plan.

The Federal Reserve cuts interest rates by .75 percent, the largest single-day reduction in Fed history.

February   The Senate votes 81 to 16 in favor of the revised $168 billion stimulus package.

The Senate votes 68 to 29 to extend for six more years a law passed in August 2007 that permits government eavesdropping on telephone and e-mail conversations of American citizens and people overseas without a warrant. The bill also provides immunity to telecommunications companies that assist the government in its eavesdropping efforts.

A strike that began in November 2007 between Hollywood production companies and the Writers' Guild of America ends. The strike is estimated to have cost the industry more than $2 billion and forced an overhaul of the television season.

A lone gunman opens fire on a classroom at Northern Illinois University, killing six students and himself and wounding 15 others.

March   Propelled by primary victories in Texas, Vermont, Rhode Island, and Ohio, John McCain wins the Republican presidential nomination.

New York Governor Eliot Spitzer admits to his role in a prostitution ring. A former state attorney general, Spitzer gained fame as a crusader against white collar crime.

May   Neil Diamond, 67 years old, becomes the oldest performer to reach Number One on the Billboard album chart with *Home Before Dark*, produced by music impresario Rick Rubin.

Citigroup Chairman Win Bischoff predicts that "we're through the worst" caused by the collapse of the subprime mortgage market. Citigroup, the largest bank in the United States, booked more than $40 billion in credit losses.

June   Illinois Senator Barack Obama becomes the presumptive Democratic presidential nominee when he passes the 2,118 delegates mark needed to win the nominee. New York Senator Hilary Clinton suspends her campaign and endorses Obama, after a long battle between the two. Obama becomes the first African American to become a presidential candidate of a major political party.

Part One
Life and Youth During the 2000s

The 2000s

1

Everyday America

It's better to think of America's pop-culture choices not as a monolithic State of the Union address but rather as a mix CD we make every year. The tempo and tone don't always mesh. Some of the songs have a direct message; some have emotional meaning; and some, in gimlet-eyed retrospect, make you wonder why you ever picked them in the first place. . .But then you play that CD back on the stereo, a few older, fatter years later. Your toe taps. A memory comes back. And you realize that in that nonsensical mess of cotton-candy lyrics and throwaway choruses, you somehow managed to write down your life.
—James Poniewozik (2002)

In the twenty-first century, American popular culture is omnipresent. Sometimes it flows like a mighty river, slowly rolling along, but with powerful currents just under the surface. In other instances, pop culture spills over its banks, sweeping away everything in its path.

Popular culture comes alive at the juncture of the entwined forces of mass communications, technology, political systems, and the economy. The industry that developed to support and disseminate culture requires a seemingly endless supply of fact, fiction, gossip, illusion, and misinformation. Add a dash of national tragedy or smidge of political or economic intrigue and the pot boils over. The popular culture machine shifts into high gear, whether that means the evening news team at ABC or a citizen journalist posting a grainy video on YouTube. The result of countless pop culture impressions over the course of a lifetime produces a permanently heightened sense of sensationalism, chased with healthy doses of societal angst.

The 2000s have been a decade of popular culture explosions, from the September 11, 2001 terrorist attacks and the nation's military response to natural and humanmade phenomena, such as the devastation of Hurricane

Katrina and Wall Street's implosion at the hands of the real estate mess. These are serious issues that forced action, reaction, and interpretation, which then helped citizens comprehend the world around them.

After 9/11 the somber national mood led some experts to declare the end of popular culture based on irony and satire. Others wondered if future films and television shows would ever be able to feature exploding airplanes or buildings. Over time, however, popular culture played dual roles: first, helping the nation mentally transition through the aftermath of terrorism, and second, calling into question the rationale for war and the long-term occupation of foreign nations. Perhaps this ability to examine the actions of the government and other institutions of power is the most positive aspect of popular culture, although one could certainly argue that the fascination with pop culture diverts attention from important challenges the nation faces and serves as a kind of placebo, enabling people to feel good about the world around them without really confronting issues directly.

Many contend that popular culture is about individuals from across the celebrity spectrum, perhaps mainly because people interact with it from the standpoint of their favorite actor, band, or television shows. Others counter with the notion that culture is actually about the larger influences that drive society, such as technology, government, economic structures, and national ethos. For example, technology, economics, and innovation combine to produce culture-shifting products, such as the iPod and computers. These goods then set in motion a shift in popular culture as these products influence people far beyond their intended functions. In turn, users come to define themselves by them—the kinds of music they download, the movies they watch, and television shows they record via TiVo. Each of these larger forces acts like the wind on our climate—transforming the weather without really being seen, or often, even felt. All the roots of popular culture trace back to technology, governmental system, economic influences, and culture.

TECHNOLOGY

Technology is a critical component of popular culture, weaving through virtually every aspect of society. Although the Internet is a major factor in how pop culture develops, technology goes beyond the Web. For example, plasma and high definition (HD) televisions are changing the way people watch programs and buy content. Cell phones seem to constantly evolve, not only getting smaller, but adding new capabilities that expand far beyond linking users by voice.

The Internet

U.S. Internet activity reflects and expands on what is happening in the offline world. Perhaps one could argue that there really isn't even much of a distinction between the real world and virtual world at this point. Unique visitors as political Web sites, for example, jumped 35 percent between December 2006 and December 2007 to 8.38 million. Furthermore, while pundits debated whether or not the nation sat in the midst of a recession, 31 percent more Web users visited online classifieds and career training and education sites over the same timeframe. In addition, Craigslist.org, which features both classifieds and job ads, increased unique visitors by 74 percent to reach 24.5 million.[1]

The search market continued to grow at an astronomical clip in 2007. Total searches eclipsed 113 billion for the year, with Google gaining a 56 percent market share. In December 2007 alone, Google recorded 5.6 billion searches, up 30 percent from a year earlier. Yahoo! sites accounted for 2.2 billion searches, but dropped 4 percent from its mark 12 months earlier.[2]

The downside of more widespread Internet activity is that the number of scammers, spammers, and cyber criminals multiplied as well. The battle against hackers and others who hope to exploit people's personal identity is like a vicious cycle, with government agencies, corporations, schools, and organizations spending greater time and effort putting up firewalls and installing antispyware software. The bad guys, however, are working just as hard to thwart these systems.

According to several observers, the number of records lost, such as credit card or social security numbers, increased 300 to 400 percent from 2006 to 2007. For example, the San Diego-based Identity Theft Resource Center estimates that the number of records compromised jumped from 20 million to 79 million over that period. One of the highest profile cases involved discount retailer TJX Cos., which admitted that hackers accessed some 46 million customer credit card numbers. After further examination, however, banks involved in this fraud estimated that the number of records actually reached 94 million. TD Ameritrade, the online broker, had its records hacked as well, resulting in 6.3 million customer files breached.[3]

Dot-com "Revolution"

The dot-com "revolution" referred to the period spanning from the late 1990s through the spring of 2000 when Wall Street, corporate America, the general public, and the media caught a wave of euphoria generated by the Internet and the use of advanced technology for business purposes. Numerous factors all came together to create an "Internet bubble" of market speculation and frenzied investment, primarily small investors who could use Web-based trading sites to easily buy and sell stocks online.

The ensuing stock market boom revolutionized the way businesses operated by providing the capital to invest in new technology. Perhaps more important, the dot-com revolution fundamentally changed the way people communicated through Internet-based technologies, such as e-mail, message boards, chat rooms, and others. Thus despite the failure of most dot-com companies, the transformation continued through the use of technology and the Internet for business purposes.

In its broadest sense, the dot-com revolution served as a massive growth engine for the American economy. For the first time in recent history, the power and mystique of small, entrepreneurial companies began to dwarf that of established corporations. Given the public's willingness to invest in Internet-based startups, their valuations soared.

Finally given the chance at riches gained from stock options and participation in initial public offerings (IPO), workers flocked to dot-coms, despite the risk involved. Added to the possibility for quick riches, the quirky, decentralized culture of Web companies drew Generation X (born 1965 to 1980) workers in droves. The media added fuel to the mass exodus from the Fortune 500 by reveling in stories of office foosball tournaments and game rooms, company-sponsored espresso machines, and a constant state of "business casual" clothing. Tech entrepreneurs were also able to promote work as a way of achieving a more spiritual or fulfilling state, which appealed to the sullen masses of workers awash in endless rows of drab, gray cubicles in the nation's large companies. Startups were seen as antiauthoritarian and laid back, mirroring the lifestyle exuded in northern California since the 1960s. Some of the early companies included PayPal, pets.com, eToys.com, dot-com "incubator" Internet Capital Group, and a slew of service firms to publicize and advertise these entities, such as Organic Online, Scient, and USWEb/CKS.

Dot-com mania reached a peak in the late 1990s when venture capitalists started funding dot-coms based on the ability to take the company public, thus cashing in on the IPO shares. Seemingly ludicrous businesses started getting millions of dollars in seed money from a variety of investors, despite having little more than a bright idea. The list of now defunct dot-coms reads like a comedy sketch, ranging from fashion site Boo.com, which "burned" through its $135 million investment before declaring bankruptcy, to online toy retailer eToys, online newspaper LocalBusiness.com, and the self-descriptive FurnitureAndBedding.com. Online grocer Webvan may be the biggest failure in Internet history, burning through an estimated $1 billion before shutting down.

Soon, large companies started to get in on the rush. Corporations such as America Online, Cisco Systems, Sun Microsystems, and Oracle began publicizing their Net wares and purchasing startups that could add innovative technology to their portfolios. Microsoft, which had been slow to grasp the importance of the Web, debuted its Internet Explorer, MSN Web sites, and an online service. Fortune 500 corporations also rushed to implement e-commerce capabilities, put up Web sites, and searched for methods to sell their products and services online.

The dot-com revolution coincided with and was stimulated by the Year 2000 (Y2K) problem that gripped businesses worldwide. The necessity for purchasing and updating computer systems hinged on the belief that computers would not function properly when the New Year changed from 1999 to 2000. Although the switch did not cause global panic, greatly increased expenditures on corporate information technology systems added to the rationale for Internet spending.

Dot-com Bubble Bursts

The companies that flamed out at the tail end of the New Economy bubble were like kindling for the recession wildfire that gripped the United States at the dawn of the new century. Over the course of one month (March 10, 2000 to April 6, 2000), the Nasdaq stock market lost $1 trillion in value, the figure then jumped to nearly $1.8 trillion by the end of the year.[4] The tsunami destroyed the dreams of many dot-coms in its wake and startled tech investors back to reality. For employees at startups, from the CEO on down, stock options ended up "under water," worthless scraps of paper that would never regain their luster. Suddenly, the casual attire and office perks did not look so enticing.

Today, economists contend that people should have seen the downfall coming sooner. Flying in the face of multiple warning signs, too many people still sought a shot at Web wealth and glory, unable to pass on the gamble, despite the long odds. Even after Nasdaq crashed in spring 2000, investors rushed in to buy shares of depressed stocks, many of which would rebound slightly before falling for good. The media (fueled by business cable stations, like CNBC, which turned Internet CEOs into celebrities, and the plump ad-soaked tech magazines) made folk heroes out of people like Amazon.com's Jeff Bezos and Yahoo's Jerry Yang. So many Internet legends were tales of rags-to-riches glory or college students coming up with an idea in their dorm rooms that by focusing on them, the media made it seem easy.

By the end of 2001, thousands of dot-com companies went bankrupt and countless tens of thousands of employees lost their jobs. The massive failure of the New Economy and the subsequent trickle of new investments in technology companies, combined with corporate governance scandals and the September 11 terrorist attacks, sparked a recession that plagued businesses in the early years of the century. High tech centers, such as Silicon Valley, San Francisco, Austin, TX, Washington, DC, and New York were especially hard hit by the failure of the dot-com revolution.

Despite the meltdown, the high tech revolution continued, although on a more modest scale, as traditional businesses used e-commerce and the Internet to meld online and physical storefronts. Companies used Web-based services and technologies to become more efficient and profitable. It is nearly impossible to find an industry that has not been improved through Internet-based technology, whether it is in education and nonprofits or financial services and manufacturing.

The dot-com revolution ended in early 2000, but innovation continued to propel companies into novel areas that mix business and the Internet. According to data released by the United Nations, there were 655 million registered Internet users worldwide in 2002 and global e-commerce topped $2.3 billion, doubling the figure from 2001.[5]

BIG MEDIA

The Internet did not remain the "Wild West" domain that many observers imagined in its early days. Small companies and startups continued to drive innovation, but most often they would grow to a certain size and prominence, then a large corporation came in and gobbled it up. In the new millennium, much of the consolidation took place among media conglomerates, which had the stock price and cash reserves to purchase upcoming technology-based firms. The trend continued from the mass empire building that took place in the wake of the Telecommunications Act of 1996, which loosened ownership regulations across mass media. With the federal government more lenient, large organizations had the freedom to buy up additional channels in various markets.

The traditional fear is that a handful of media moguls will wind up owning the majority of the "voice" that consumers hear across radio, television, newspapers, and the Web. Rupert Murdoch, the founder and CEO of the global corporation News Corp., is the living embodiment of critics' fears, owning Fox Broadcasting, the *New York Post,* London's *The Times,* and the *Wall Street Journal.* He purchased the *Wall Street Journal* in December 2007 for $5 billion, adding its 2 million readers worldwide to his global news network.

Although Murdoch's vast reach is symptomatic of the challenge of monopolistic ownership, harkening back to earlier barons, such as William Randolph Hearst, in today's media world about a dozen corporations own about 33 percent of the nation's 1,400 daily newspapers, according to journalist Samantha Levine. The largest is Gannett Co., which owns *USA Today,* followed by the Tribune Company.[6] Gannett revenue surpassed $8 billion in 2006 among its 20 TV stations, approximately 100 daily newspapers, magazines, and Internet properties.

One of the most intriguing and mind-boggling media conglomerates is Time Warner. Through a series of high-profile mergers and acquisitions, the company built a network of television networks, a cable system, movie companies, magazines, and Internet companies. In 2006, the company ranked number one in the media business with $44.2 billion in revenues, up from $37 billion in 2005. Despite its size and reach, however, Time Warner never lived up to its $164 billion acquisition of AOL in 2001, ranking as the largest media deal in history.[7]

By mid-decade, it became evident that the company renamed "AOL Time Warner" could not take advantage or even exploit the "synergies" inherent in the merger. Executives struggled to find a strategy. Not helping matters, the company combated the triple-whammy of an economic recession, the dot-com implosion, and the terrorist attacks on America and the subsequent war on terror; however, no one cried for AOL Time Warner, especially when the combined entity dropped in value to become worth less than the sum of its own parts. Stockholders were left holding the bag; they watched as more than $100 billion in shareholder value dropped off the board.

In 2008, media watchers project that new chief executive Jeff Bewkes will slice and dice the company, selling off many units and spinning off AOL. Drastic measures are necessary given that company shares rose a meager 13 percent in the preceding five years. A former business executive at HBO, Time Warner's highly successful premium cable network, Bewkes discussed his vision for the company, stating: "I believe strongly in trial and error, and Time Warner needs to move faster, take more risk and change course more often."[8] The parts of the Time Warner puzzle most frequently rumored for sale are its cable business, AOL's access division, along with a significant number of magazines.

GOVERNMENT

If one thought in early 2000 that the polarizing force of the Clinton administration would dissipate and lead to a friendlier political atmosphere post-Clinton, they would have been sorely mistaken. The 2000 presidential election fractured the nation even further as Al Gore and George W. Bush squared off. The contentious environment peaked in the weeks after the hotly contested election, in which Gore won the popular vote by about 540,000 votes, but Bush won the Electoral College by a vote of 271–266.

The furor over voting ignited in Florida, where officials disputed the outcome of the election and who should win its critical 25 electoral votes. The inconsistencies in results included the now-famous "hanging chads," or partially punctured voting cards. In the end, the court battles over recounts took 35 days past election day. In his first speech as president-elect shortly after Gore's concession, Bush said, "I know America wants reconciliation and unity. I know Americans want progress. And we must seize this moment and deliver. Together, guided by a spirit of common sense, common courtesy and common goals, we can unite and inspire the American citizens."[9]

In the 2004 presidential election between President Bush and Massachusetts Senator John Kerry, both political parties and affiliated groups supporting them took part in a race that became increasingly divisive and mean-spirited. In the end, the election was again so close that one state determined the outcome. Ohio's 20 electoral votes went to President Bush, giving him a 286 to 252 win in the Electoral College, to go along with his 62 million to 59 million win in the popular vote (51% to 48%).

A personal bitterness developed between the two candidates, the political parties, and special interest groups that did not exist in the 2000 campaign. The supposed moral gulf between the two candidates fueled a great deal of this acrimony. Much of the rhetoric that developed during the contest centered on what would happen in the "war on terror" depending on who won the election. Some of the barbs were direct, such as Bush's labeling Kerry a "flip-flopper" and "Massachusetts liberal." Both terms painted the challenger as someone who would not be tough enough to lead during wartime. Another example of the personal attacks that characterized the 2004 election is the work of a group called the Swift Vets and POWs for Truth. In a national television campaign, the members called Kerry's military service and combat medals he won into question. Summing up the Bush victory, historian Eric Foner said, "I suspect that the attacks of September 11 and the sense of being engaged in a worldwide 'war on terror' contributed substantially to Bush's victory. Generally speaking, Americans have not changed Presidents in the midst of a war. The Bush campaign consistently and successfully appealed to fear, with continuous warnings of imminent and future attacks. Land of the free? Perhaps. Home of the brave? Not anymore."[10]

GEORGE W. BUSH

Rarely do historians garner the headlines the way Sean Wilentz did in early 2006 when he rhetorically questioned whether President George W. Bush could be considered "The Worst President in History" in a headline that appeared on the cover of *Rolling Stone* magazine with a caricature of the president sitting in a corner with a dunce cap on. The Princeton University professor ignited a media frenzy, including countless blog posts, and television appearances. Wilentz cited a 2004 survey of 415 historians by the nonpartisan History News Network (HNN) that revealed 81 percent considered the Bush administration a "failure." And as Wilentz notes, HNN took the pulse of America's historians before the "debacles over Hurricane Katrina, Bush's role in the Valerie Plame leak affair and the deterioration of the situation in Iraq."[11]

The Plame affair, for example, occurred when Vice President Dick Cheney's aide Lewis "Scooter" Libby leaked Plame's name to newspaper columnist Robert Novak, who then outed her as a CIA officer.[12] Libby slipped the information to Novak in retaliation for the role Plame's husband, former ambassador Joseph C. Wilson IV's highly publicized op-ed in the *New York Times* claiming that the Bush administration relied on shoddy information to support its theory that Iraqi officials purchased uranium from Niger. A jury convicted Libby, but others thought that the blame should have reached Bush strategist Karl Rove or other high-ranking members of the administration. President Bush commuted Libby's prison term in June 2007.

Wilentz's article and the resulting multimedia firestorm point to Bush's role as a polarizing force in American society. Soon after the terrorist attacks on 9/11, for example, the president received the highest approval ratings in history, reaching about 90 percent. As the Iraq war dragged on with no end in sight after 2006, his ratings dropped to historic lows, hitting 26 percent in mid-2007.[13] Wilentz sees the downturn as the culmination of Bush's "disastrous domestic policies, foreign-policy blunders and military setbacks, executive misconduct, crises of credibility and public trust." Moreover, the historian explains, "He has also displayed a weakness common among the greatest presidential failures—an unswerving adherence to a simplistic ideology that abjures deviation from dogma as heresy, thus preventing any pragmatic adjustment to changing realities."[14]

Despite his flagging numbers during his last four years in office, Bush remains upbeat and convinced of the correctness of his strategic initiatives and administration, from its handling of the economy to the wars in Iraq

President George W. Bush in the documentary No End in Sight *(2007). © Magnolia Pictures. Courtesy of Photofest.*

and Afghanistan. As he prepared for his final State of the Union address to Congress in 2008, Bush borrowed from the playbook of Ronald Reagan, another lame duck Republican president who faced falling approval ratings. He focused on what he still had left to accomplish, including a $150 billion economic stimulus package.[15]

Historians will debate the Bush presidency far into the future, but they will be forced to acknowledge the wins in his early years in office, including tax-cutting measures and his support of the "No Child Left Behind" education plan. The narrow victory over Massachusetts Senator John Kerry in 2004 and the disastrously executed handling of the Hurricane Katrina disaster in the Gulf region in 2005, however, started a chain reaction that weakened public support for programs at home and abroad and enabled the Democrats to win back Congress in the midterm elections of 2006.[16]

The ultimate turning point for the Bush administration took place when the president ordered the invasion of Iraq based on what was later found to be faulty (and perhaps fabricated) intelligence that outlined Saddam Hussein's potential nuclear capabilities and the now-infamous "weapons of mass destruction," which could be turned on the United States. Many political and military experts believe that by drawing Iraq into the "War on Terror" and linking Hussein to Al Qaeda, Bush and members of his cabinet, including Vice President Dick Cheney and Defense Secretary Donald Rumsfeld, took the country in a direction that committed America to a military quagmire that cost the nation more than $870 billion to conduct (as of July 2008). After the public learned of the faulty rationale for the war in Iraq and as further atrocities came to light, such as the torture of Iraqi prisoners in Abu Ghraib and Guantanamo Bay, Bush's approval ratings dropped like a rock.[17]

SEPTEMBER 11, 2001

In the blink of an eye, the terrorist attacks that took place September 11, 2001, transformed the Bush presidency. In responding to Al Qaeda and its leader Osama Bin Laden, the president directed a massive retaliatory attack on Afghanistan to root out the terrorist group and topple its power.

The terrorist attacks on the World Trade Center in New York took place on a beautiful morning, marked by clear blue skies and bright sunshine. No one could have imagined that on such a morning, 19 Al Qaeda operatives set out on four separate planes to launch a coordinated attack on New York and Washington, D.C. Before the morning ended, three planes had crashed into American landmarks, and another—potentially heading for the nation's capital—would be brought down in a Shanksville, Pennsylvania, field before it could reach its target. Nearly 3,000 people died in the attacks.

Aftermath

Immediately after the 9/11 attacks, the nation turned more patriotic, and firefighters and police officials across the nation became heroic figures, lauded for their bravery and willingness to serve the nation. President Bush, with the backing of Congress, launched a series of military and economic programs designed to eliminate terrorist cells worldwide, particularly against members of Al-Qaeda, the organization headed by Osama bin Laden. The efforts culminated in the October 2001 military invasion of Afghanistan and its Taliban government, known partners of the terrorists. Despite the success of the military operations and overthrow of the Taliban regime, however, the United States could not capture bin Laden.

The Bush administration also initiated a series of domestic security programs designed to ease the public's fear regarding future terrorism on American soil. The president authorized the creation of the Department of Homeland Security and named former Pennsylvania Governor Tom Ridge as its first leader. Next, the administration worked with leaders in Congress to pass the USA Patriot Act (2001), which gave the federal government far-reaching power to carry out surveillance activities to weed out potential terrorism threats.

Homeland Security officials began a national alert status indicating potential threats, ranging in colors from red (severe risk) to green (low risk). Early in the system, the nation often found itself in orange (high risk) or yellow (significant risk) status. The new federal regulatory agency also set out to make the nation's borders safer, including its ports. Critics immediately questioned the resources it would take to inspect the millions of cargo containers arriving and departing the country's waterways. No terrorist activities, however, have taken place in this area of potential weakness.

In response to the attacks, the nation rallied around President Bush, officials in New York, including Mayor Rudy Giuliani, and the families of victims there and in Washington. Both Bush and Giuliani made high-profile appearances at "Ground Zero" amid the remains of the World Trade Center. Ground Zero transformed into a sacred area, with visitors later flocking to the site to pay their respects. And, "United We Stand" became a rallying cry for Americans, as well as a variety of peace symbols, including a "Support Our Troops" ribbon affixed to automobiles.

In the immediate years after 9/11, the anniversary of the event dominated the airwaves. Television programming came to a standstill and refocused the viewing public on the tragic day. In 2002, CBS aired a documentary filmed inside the World Trade Center on 9/11, watched by more than 39 million viewers. "All broadcast and many cable networks tossed out their normal programming schedules (and their advertising) on the anniversary," explained journalist James Poniewozik, "as if supersaturating the airwaves—turning Sept. 11 into a virtual national holiday—could magically confine the terrible events to history, never to be repeated. There was mawkishness, anger, finger pointing, navel gazing, bathos, pathos— every possible response except forgetting."[18]

In response to questions about intelligence failures leading up to the terrorist attacks, Congress created a 10-member National Commission on Terrorist Attacks on the United States in November 2002. The Bush Administration fought the creation of such a panel, although the president eventually signed the bill into law. On July 22, 2004, the group released its public report,[19] which created a media spectacle of finger-pointing and accusations. In preparing the report, the panel interviewed more than 1,200 people in 10 countries and inspected 2.5 million pages of documents, including classified national security briefs. The report recommended significant changes to the national security model, which included greater shared resources and interaction between agencies.

In December 2004, the passage of the Intelligence Reform and Terrorism Prevention Act reorganized the American intelligence community, although critics have observed that the results of the bill have not fundamentally transformed the disparate groups for the better. According to Jack Devine, a former CIA acting deputy director of operations, the centralized power created by the bill diminished the role of the CIA, which he believes has actually weakened national security, although the budget for security has grown to $43 billion. More important, he says, American agents have not penetrated the terrorist organizations that pose the greatest threats: Iran, North Korea, Russia, China, and Pakistan.[20]

AMERICA AT WAR

On March 20, 2003, the United States and a multinational coalition force invaded Iraq with the intent of stopping Saddam Hussein's building of weapons of mass destruction, as well as terrorism threats Iraq posed, which President Bush linked to the 9/11 attacks. In May, aboard the U.S.S. *Abraham Lincoln*, the president declared victory in Iraq, a swift win in an overwhelming battle between good and evil. The rhetoric of the event ran at an all-time high, given that Bush flew onto the aircraft carrier on a jetfighter and stood before a televised audience in a Navy flight suit with a banner in the background blazing the now infamous phrase: "Mission Accomplished."

The reality of the situation, however, emerged and the public saw that the country was far from finished in Iraq. Many political observers believe that the victory declaration touched off a downward spiral for the Bush Administration. According to one journalist, "As American casualties mount and bombs shake Baghdad, the image of Bush's flight suit strut under a banner proclaiming 'Mission Accomplished' is so discordant, his opponents believe, it says more about the administration's arrogance and incompetence than any stump speech could."[21]

According to a survey conducted by the Pew Research Center, some 72 percent of Americans viewed the military efforts in Iraq as the "right decision" in early 2003 and 88 percent saw the war going "very/fairly well." This early support is accentuated by the president's reelection in 2004 and the many symbols of national unity that sprung to life in support of the war, from patriotic "Support Our Troop" car magnets to a rise in the number of American flags purchased. In the post-9/11 world, no politician, civic leader, or business executive could leave the house without an American flag lapel pin.[22]

In the ensuing five years, more than 4,000 American soldiers lost their lives in the fighting, and 29,500 have been wounded. Most of the most recent 1,000 to die were killed by an improvised explosive device (IED), the most sinister piece of jargon to emerge from the War on Terror. According to journalists Lizette Alvarez and Andrew Lehren:

The year 2007 would prove to be especially hard on American service members; more of them died last year than in any other since the war began. Many of those deaths came in the midst of the 30,000-troop buildup known as "the surge," the linchpin of President Bush's strategy to tamp down widespread violence between Islamic Sunnis and Shiites, much of it in the country's capital, Baghdad. In April, May and June alone, 331 American service members died, making it the deadliest three-month period since the war began.[23]

The fallout from the War on Terror in both Afghanistan and Iraq threatens to continue pulling at the feelings of national unity experienced after 9/11. Certainly, as the war grew more hotly contested, President Bush suffered an extraordinary drop in his personal approval rating. Furthermore, the Democrats were able to use discussion of a war with no end in sight to regain control of the House of Representatives and the Senate after the 2006 midterm elections. The Democratic Party's election triumph not only swept them into power, but led to the election of Nancy Pelosi as the first woman to serve as Speaker of the House.

The national approval rating for the war in Iraq dropped to a low of 47 percent in February 2005 and remained below 50 percent until rebounding slightly to 54 percent three years later. In early 2008, 48 percent of Americans surveyed declared that the war in Iraq was going very/fairly well, but the same number said that the effort continued either not too/not at all well. These figures indicate that the war in Iraq continues to be a divisive issue.[24]

Troubles for Vets Back Home

The challenges facing veterans who served in the war on terror remained virtually hidden after the warfare ensued. Most commentators remarked that the national feelings of patriotism resulting from the terrorist attacks would ensure that people would not treat these veterans with disdain, as many Vietnam vets were treated. In early 2007, however, *Washington Post* reporters Dana Priest and Anne Hull exposed the horrific treatment many wounded and ailing veterans received at the Army's top medical facility, the Walter Reed Army Medical Center in Washington, D.C. For penetrating the secretive world of the army facility, the article received a 2007 Pulitzer Prize.[25]

The article by Priest and Hull provided graphic details of black mold, cockroaches, mouse droppings, rotten ceilings, and other horrible conditions that caught the nation's attention. At the heart of the investigative work, however, stood a more sordid story of the neglect that faced the wounded soldiers, from bureaucratic logjams to overcrowded conditions that forced the less wounded to care for their more sickly comrades. According to the journalists, "The soldiers say they feel alone and frustrated. Seventy-five percent of the troops polled by Walter Reed last March said their experience was 'stressful.' Suicide attempts and unintentional overdoses from prescription drugs and alcohol, which is sold on post, are part of the narrative."[26]

Since the conditions at Walter Reed surfaced, veterans groups have kept up the pressure on the federal government. Two nonprofit organizations filed a class-action lawsuit that went to trial in April 2008 against the U.S. Department of Veterans Affairs claiming that the federal agency is not doing enough to prevent suicide among returning soldiers or providing adequate medical care. Statistics that came to light during the pretrial investigation revealed that an average of 18 military veterans commit suicide each day, including five under VA care. In addition, a RAND Corp study released in early 2008 estimated that 300,000 troops, or 20 percent of those deployed in the war on terror, suffer from depression or posttraumatic stress disorder after serving in Iraq or Afghanistan. In response, the VA counters that the number of claims have grown tremendously, from 670,000 in 2001 to 838,000 in 2007, primarily from veterans aging, not the current war efforts. Regardless of who wins the lawsuit, such claims continue to tug at the national conscious and call into question the postwar status of the heroes who return home after serving overseas.[27]

HURRICANE KATRINA AND THE AFTERMATH

On August 29, 2005, Hurricane Katrina slammed into the Gulf Coast as a Category 5 storm. Many areas of Louisiana, Mississippi, and Alabama suffered mightily, but New Orleans could not withstand the onslaught. Levees designed to protect the city broke, which inundated the area with devastating flood waters. An estimated 1,836 people died in the storm and its aftermath, which also caused $81.2 billion in damages, the most costly hurricane in the nation's history.

Hurricane Katrina caused devastation across the Gulf Coast, including New Orleans. iStockphoto. © Chad Purser.

The national tragedy of Katrina soon took on a life of its own as a barometer of race relations in the United States. Critics quickly placed blame on the Bush Administration and Federal Emergency Management Agency (FEMA) Director Michael D. Brown for not responding quickly enough to help those without the means to escape the terror.

As a result, desperate citizens, primarily African Americans, took shelter in the Louisiana Superdome—the "Crown Jewel of the New Orleans Skyline"—which quickly became a cesspool of waste and sewage. More important, people died while at the Superdome. The city's poor who flocked there for relief had no food, running water, or air conditioning. The ill-equipped emergency shelter, like the nearby Convention Center, became a symbol of the storm's devastation and the Bush administration's failure to aid the people suffering in the drowned city.

The news media scurried to broadcast the lurid tales of mayhem amid the flooded ruins. The plight of disadvantaged African Americans left behind to virtually fend for themselves in the wake elicited a national outcry. Millions of viewers sat spellbound as the news of the city filtered out. Rapper Kanye West summed up the private thoughts many dared not speak publicly, proclaiming that "George Bush doesn't care about black people" on a nationally televised hurricane relief program. Katrina put race back on the national agenda.

Mike Myers, left, and Kanye West appear on Saturday Night Live *(NBC), October 1, 2005, satirizing their controversial appearance at a televised Hurricane Katrina fundraiser.* © *NBC. Courtesy of Photofest.*

Unfortunately, many Americans are quick to dismiss racism as simply a defective character trait or a sign of overt stupidity. But many believe it runs deeper, straight to the heart of the country's national fabric. Historian John Hope Franklin told the Associated Press, "The New Orleans tragedy speaks in a loud but eloquent voice that racial inequities in the United States persist. As far as race in America is concerned, Katrina was just another example of the failure of the people of the United States to come to terms with a centuries-old problem . . . and make a forthright effort to solve it."[28] Simply by being born an American, a person is infused with race and the legacy of slavery, and America's continued inability to solve the race issue is its most crippling defect and exacerbates most, if not all, societal ills.

The chaos in New Orleans revealed the depths of racism that exists in the United States, but many hoped the catastrophe would touch off a renewed national dialogue on racism and possibly eliminate it once and for all in the post-Katrina America. When the immediate chaos and governmental finger-pointing devolved into a post-storm bureaucratic nightmare of red tape, and after the sensationalist images and stories disappeared, however, so did the discussions of racism.

Some observers note that Americans are so ashamed of the heritage of slavery and the current state of those living in poverty that the nation can only examine race if it comes from the mouths of cartoon characters (think of Token Black, the African American on South Park), standup comics like Chris Rock and Dave Chappelle, or rap musicians. But although West's audacious claim touched off a media frenzy, frank dialogue never really materialized, and today, even though Barack Obama has won the Democratic nomination for president, most observers believe that America is not much closer to solving its race problem.

Looking back, the failure of a national dialogue regarding race to materialize proves West's point yet again. Race slipped from the national agenda in part because George W. Bush did not keep the issue at the forefront. Of course, politicians going back to the Founding Fathers have failed to adequately address race. Bush, however, had the opportunity to use the Katrina tragedy to reinvigorate the race discussion on a national level.

RACE IN AMERICA

Although President Bush is criticized for routinely flubbing multisyllabic words, he is a master of modern American corporate speak, in which a CEO is applauded for focusing on looking to the future without ever acknowledging current or past errors. For example, the president played up his post-Katrina discussions with NAACP CEO Bruce Gordon without conceding any slip-ups on the part of his administration: "We talked about the challenges facing the African American community after that storm. We talked about the response of the federal government. And most importantly, we talked about the way forward. We talked about what we can do working together to move forward." At another point in the speech, he revealed the real reasons he finally addressed the organization: "You must understand I understand that racism still lingers in America. It's a lot easier to change a law than to change a human heart. And I understand that many African Americans distrust my political party. I consider it a tragedy that the party of Abraham Lincoln let go of its historic ties with the African American community. For too long my party wrote off the African American vote, and many African Americans wrote off the Republican Party."[29]

As striking as the language is, especially coming from Bush, the key word in his statement is vote. The Republican Party sees little difference between its success at winning over former Democratic voters in strongholds like western Pennsylvania, Michigan, and Ohio and capturing the black vote. Republicans see an opportunity to win back black voters.

So the speech wasn't about healing wounds deep within the national fabric; the appearance was to win the African American vote.

Political strategists assert that the black vote could be critical in the 2008 presidential race. Bush, however, won the southern vote across the Dixie South (and subsequently both elections) by appealing to white southerners with "coded" language, including his "tough on crime" stance.

Despite his lip service and political pandering in this speech, Bush has done little to help African Americans. According to NAACP statistics, blacks are twice as likely as whites to be unemployed, significantly less likely to own homes (75 percent for whites compared to 48 percent for blacks), and have an average median net worth of $10,000 versus $81,700 for whites.

Many experts agree that a president who cares about African-Americans would look out on the nation and be disgusted by what is happening in black communities. He would place race on the national agenda. If the weight of the office can push terrorism and security to the top of the agenda, then it can do the same for racism. Although the Bush administration has "czars" for everything from cyberterrorism to AIDS, there's no czar for racism, no money behind completing the "unfinished story of freedom." The National Priorities Project estimates that the war in Iraq has cost more than $300 billion, yet poverty-stricken Americans at home slip further into despair.

But as easy as it is to blame the president for the current state of racism in America, the lack of leadership within the African American community must be cited as well. The fact that West—a musician—stood as the most significant black political figure to emerge from the devastation in New Orleans reveals the paucity of leadership among blacks.

No black leader today wields enough influence to rise above the political fray and put racism on the national agenda, even with Barack Obama's run for the Democratic nomination for president. Prominent black leaders, such as Jesse Jackson and Al Sharpton put too much faith in the political process. Like the American labor movement, African Americans since the 1960s have been co-opted by the Democrats, virtually handing over power to an organization that is more concerned with winning office than standing up for ideals. There is merit in sustained voter registration drives and raising money for candidates, but these tactics have not brought racism to the forefront.

Because politicians are predominantly concerned with getting elected rather than defending principles, it seems unlikely that the leadership needed in today's conditions will come from an African American senator or congressperson, even the wildly popular Barack Obama, who won the Democratic nomination for president. The early presidential campaign against Republican candidate John McCain has already revealed itself as more "politics as usual," despite Obama's call for change and bipartisanship. Is it Pollyannaish to wonder when the next Martin Luther King, Jr. or Malcolm X will appear? Neither held political office or aligned too closely with a political party. They drew from religious backgrounds and followings but were able to bring their causes to the national stage. Ultimately, racism is more than a political issue that can be fixed through party affiliation.

For the good of the nation, racism must be quashed. Spike Lee's highly publicized documentary, *When the Levees Broke,* showed the nation that building a better world means retaining our collective humanity. Lee's provocative film revealed that in today's polarized society, racial equality may seem out of reach, but it is an attainable aspiration.

THE ECONOMY

Innovation fuels America's power and culture. Yet the constant demand for "more" and "faster" ratchets up anxiety as well. In the new millennium, general nervousness about the economy spreads a bit more each day. Little signposts signal large problems on the horizon. Soaring gas prices, for example, serve as a daily yardstick. For-sale signs and the empty homes they mock fill the nation's streets, cul-de-sacs, and suburban enclaves, constantly reminding hard-working (but scared) citizens that the other shoe could (and soon may) drop.

Despite individual stress, however, the country stands as the world's capital center. The United States chugs along with the strongest economy. People benefit. The gain is felt across age, sex, demographics, and race. In 2007, for example, about 50 percent of all law and medical students were women, up from merely 10 percent in 1970. These kinds of socioeconomic changes pull up the nation as a whole. Approximately 24 percent of adults in their prime working years live in households earning at least $100,000 annually. Between 1983 and 2004, median family net worth doubled from $49,700 to $99,300.[30]

On the downside, individual happiness has not kept pace with the technological innovation and abundance of consumer goods available.[31] In many respects, access and speed made life less enjoyable. Americans are not working fewer hours, living healthier, worrying less, or taking smaller quantities of medicines for smaller numbers of ailments. As employers search for ways to squeeze every penny out of overhead, increasing healthcare premiums for workers is an easy fix. By 2005, the average household spent $8,300 annually on health insurance and out-of-pocket health expenses annually.[32]

At mid-decade, many individuals and families floated their consumer habits on a sea of credit and debt. Historically low interest rates enabled homeowners to refinance, taking money out of their homes to use for other things, whether that meant renovations or buying a new plasma television.

Across the nation, homeowners essentially gambled on pumped up home values and traded debt for greater debt, but at a lower interest rate. Banks and mortgage companies contributed to the system by offering subprime loans and other "creative" financial packages that allowed people to buy a home with little money down and subsequent low payments over a set period of time. Many people, particularly those who are not financially savvy or have shaky credit reports, did not realize that once the introductory period passed, the loans could increase significantly.

At the heart of the mortgage fiasco is people losing their homes, which for most is still synonymous with attaining the American Dream. Government reports indicated that in the yearlong period from July 2006 to July 2007, foreclosures jumped 93 percent nationwide. Nearly 180,000 foreclosures took place in July 2007 alone, an astonishing 1 filing for every 693 households. Nevada led the foreclosure market with 1 filing for every 199 homes. Taken as a whole, five states made up almost half the total foreclosures in the nation: California, Florida, Ohio, Michigan, and Georgia.[33]

Credit card debt also reached epidemic proportions in the new millennium. In the early 1970s, households carried about $600 in credit card debt in real dollars. In 2006, the average household balanced topped $7,300, a 1,200 percent increase.[34] Two years earlier, the Federal Reserve Board reported that revolving debt in the United States reached $800 billion, the majority composed of credit card balances.

Recession Debate and the Teetering Economy

By later 2007 and early 2008, the subprime mortgage crisis placed an anchor around the neck of an otherwise teetering American economy already groping under the weight of a costly overseas war. Recession, the dreaded r-word, crept back into the national conscious. While the experts debated whether or not the country had already entered a recession, politicians devised "stimulus packages" designed to force spending money into the pockets of cash-strapped Americans. On a daily basis the news never seemed to improve, ranging from massive layoffs at various global financial corporations to declining numbers of jobs created. People who turned to Wall Street for some indication of the nation's economic status found themselves in the midst of rollercoaster swings.

As with most other aspects of popular culture, perception soon became reality. The more the media reported on the recession, the more steam the idea gained. People's fears about their jobs, the economy in general, and an unsettled situation in Iraq and Afghanistan made them apprehensive about spending money. Historically, when consumers turn off the spigot, the national economy is in big trouble. The gloomy national economic outlook forced President Bush to address the situation, saying, "Obviously the housing market is creating deep concern. And one of the real problems could be that people, as a result of their value of their homes going down, kind of pull in their horns."[35]

A poll conducted by the Associated Press in February 2008 revealed that 61 percent of the public believed that the United States stood in the midst of its first recession since 2001. The facts provided evidence to the national mood. In 2007, the economy had its weakest year overall since 2002, expanding a mere 2.2 percent. The real estate fiasco triggered the anemic growth, with builders dropping their spending by almost 17 percent. People also took home less pay in 2007, with average weekly earnings actually falling 0.9 percent when adjusted for inflation.[36]

Despite mounting hard evidence, many economists joined President Bush in stating that the American economy was not in a recession. The threat of more fiscal challenges on the horizon, however, led Congress and the president to work on an economic stimulus package that would provide tax rebates for individuals and tax cuts for businesses. In the rush to "solve" the nation's monetary problems, however, relatively few people questioned how we would pay for the $168 billion rescue package.[37]

The World Is Flat

America remains the center of world finance, but its dependence on foreign nations to finance its growing national debt, Middle Eastern oil reserves, and Chinese imports reveals the shaky nature of that position. *New York Times* columnist Thomas L. Friedman coined the phrase "the world is flat" to describe the consequences of globalization on the United States in his 2005 bestseller The *World Is Flat: A Brief History of the Twenty-First Century.*

After visiting India, Friedman astutely realized that globalization provided global nations a level playing field economically and removed many barriers to foreign trade that previously existed. For example, one of Friedman's examples is the outsourcing trend occurring in corporate America. Companies sent jobs to overseas knowledge centers, which saved them money, instead of offering the same services using American employees. Companies like Dell, Microsoft, Citigroup, and many others outsourced information technology and customer service functions to India, China, and other Far Eastern nations. Despite the backlash against such practices, outsourcing provided a greater return on investment.

The International Association of Outsourcing Professionals estimated that American companies spent $4.2 trillion on outsourcing in 2006, up from $3.1 trillion just three years earlier. Obviously, with trillions of dollars being put into outsourcing, the trend is not going to stop. Rather, the question for U.S. corporations is how best to use it strategically. For example, some organizations are moving away from India, the traditional power base in the field, to places such as Russia, the Philippines, and Mexico.

Any nation with a workforce strong in software and engineering and English-language skills is a potential hotbed for outsourcing.[38]

Enron and Corporate Crooks

From the mid-1990s until its financial collapse in late 2001, Enron stood as a darling of the business media, ranging from one of *Fortune* magazine's "World Most Admired Companies" to a corporation studied in business schools nationwide for its innovation and success. Enron, led by chief executive Jeff Skilling and chairman Ken Lay, also fooled finance professionals, receiving glowing reports from analyst firms that bought and sold enormous blocks of stock for investors, retirement funds, and 401Ks. Billions of dollars were at stake in these decisions and Enron duped all the major players in perhaps the largest Ponzi scheme in history. Enron's stock, which at one point traded for $90 a share, plummeted to 50 cents a share, not really even worth the price of the certificate it would have printed on.

When the Enron collapse began, it unraveled faster than anyone could have imagined. Bankruptcy and mass layoffs took place quickly, and some employees lost their retirement funds in the meltdown. On May 25, 2006, a jury found Lay and Skilling guilty of conspiracy and fraud. For journalists Bethany McLean and Peter Elkind, who helped break the Enron fraud, the guilty verdicts had "positive implications," including offering "a measure of consolation—or retribution—for those employees who lost everything in Enron's bankruptcy. And it reinforces a critical notion about our justice system: that, despite much punditry to the contrary, being rich and spending millions on a crack criminal defense team does not necessarily buy freedom."[39]

At the heart of Enron's criminal activity was the deliberate manipulation of company stock to make the company more valuable on paper than in reality. Top executives then sold millions of dollars of essentially worthless stock for profit, when they knew the price was a sham. The unfortunate aspect of every underhanded financial plot is that someone is left holding the bag. In this case, it turned out to be Enron employees and investors.

The Enron scandal serves as the most shocking downfall in an era of high-profile corporate collapses. The others spanned a variety of industries and included some of the more prominent corporations in America. Like Enron, these were considered topnotch businesses. Accounting firm Arthur Andersen fell apart in the wake of serving as Enron's public accounting agency. Although the company collected revenues of $9.3 billion in 2001, some 85,000 Andersen employees either left the firm or lost their jobs in the downfall.

Adelphia Communications, founded by the Rigas family, grew into the fifth largest cable company in the United States. Members of the Rigas family hid debt and essentially allocated themselves millions of dollars in undisclosed loans. John and Timothy Rigas were found guilty of securities violations after federal officials determined that they stole $100 million in company money. Other stunning disintegrations included Tyco chief executive Dennis Kozlowski and WorldCom founder Bernard Ebbers. Both leaders, seen as innovative leaders before the scandals, ended up in jail for bilking investors. Ebbers, for example, had $400 million in undisclosed loans.[40]

The outcome of Enron and other corporate shenanigans is that the public and government officials are less likely to give business leaders a free pass. In March 2008, the House Oversight and Government Reform Committee called to task executives largely responsible for the real estate bust for their roles in the crisis. Chief executives testifying before the committee included Angelo Mozilo of Countrywide Financial, Stanley O'Neal formerly of Merrill Lynch, and Charles Prince formerly of Citigroup. Rep. Henry Waxman, D-Calif., chairman of the committee, called the CEOs to task for their lavish compensation packages.

In 2006, on average, these leaders at the nation's largest 500 corporations made $15.2 million. Countrywide, which is well known for its television commercials and Web advertising pushing home financing, paid Mozilo a $1.9-million salary and $20 million in stock awards based on performance, while he sold another $121 million in stock options. This took place as the company lost $1.6 billion in 2007 and its stock dropped 80 percent. Mozilo told the committee, "As our company did well, I did well." While Waxman viewed the disparity between company results and CEO compensation as "a complete disconnect with reality."[41]

The Workplace

Americans have a love-hate relationship with work and the workplace. From an early age people are taught to strive for the American Dream, which places notions of hard work and meritocracy at the heart of one's cultural being. On the flipside, however, the constant agonizing over work- and money-related issues produces a nation full of uptight employees, basically unhappy with their status, wages, and position within workplace politics. Ironically, work provides a route to happiness and material comfort, while at the same time shackling individuals to their jobs and limiting freedoms.

Cubicles across the nation are littered with Scott Adams's Dilbert cartoons. Adams turned the "cubiclization" of the workplace into a multimillion dollar industry. In essence, people lampoon themselves by tacking up the Dilbert episodes that seem to mirror their own lives as workers, but also express a degree of personalization. Others load their office space with knickknacks. Outside of family photographs, tchotchkes, or knickknacks, are perhaps the most common feature in America's "cube farms." Many tchotchkes are adorned with the company logo, such as miniature desk clocks and acrylic plaques touting the latest inner-office recognition.

Retaining personal space within a corporate setting gives workers a feeling of empowerment in a somewhat dehumanizing and powerless aspect of their lives. Surrounding themselves with the merchandise covered in logos shows a sense of pride in where one works but the tacky displays scream of a mutated individualism allowed within the structured corporate setting. The company owns the cube, but employees individualize it as it becomes an extension of who they are.

There may be no better indicator of the duality of the corporate world than e-mail, a piece of technology that has the potential to make one's job infinitely easier, but at the same time adds additional work to already long weeks. Basex, Inc., a research firm in New York, estimates that 35 million e-mails are sent each day, which take up 2.1 hours daily for white-collar workers. This drain costs businesses money. In total, 28 billion hours are spent annually on e-mail, with a price tag of $650 billion. Other efficiency experts place the figures even higher, with studies reporting that corporate workers get 50–100 e-mails a day, some even placing the total sent daily at upwards of 142 billion.[42]

Another technology that is actually sapping efficiency is online video. A study released in early 2008 by Nielsen Online revealed that online video sites, such as market leading YouTube and others, receive most use on weekdays at lunchtime, usually between 12 P.M. and 2 P.M. The number of online videos consumed during the workday is astronomical: YouTube users accessed 674 million video streams in January 2008, Yahoo had 157 million, and Fox Interactive Media nearly 93 million.[43]

Carriage Services Inc., a funeral services company in Houston, for example, told the *Wall Street Journal* that it "discovered" that 70 percent of 125 workers in the company headquarters watched online videos about an hour a day. As a result, the information technology executive blocked access to both YouTube and MySpace. But Carriage Services is just one of many companies confronting workers' Internet use while on the job. Most corporations implemented policies against using work computers for personal e-mail, instant messaging, streaming music, and accessing inappropriate content.[44]

Another organization, Catholic Charities of Santa Clara County in San Jose, California, blocked video access so that its network would not crash, ultimately leading to costly computer outages and potential loss of sensitive information. "It's a real issue when a network can't handle demand," said William Bailey, the nonprofit's IT manager. "Too much media, particularly video, is usually the reason why."[45]

Across the nation in Atlanta, a mid-size real estate company grappled with similar issues but decided to block video sites because of bandwidth concerns. Without blocking the sites, the company faced a costly network upgrade—a difficult expense to swallow during a challenging real estate downturn. The downside of such decisions, however, is that employees may actually turn against management, particularly if they feel entitled to visit these sites during lunch breaks. "I know our people will say we're acting like Big Brother," explained another IT administrator. "But those pipes belong to the company. If management says we need to protect our resources, then that's what happens."[46]

Downsized. . .

If the real estate collapse and credit crunch did not do enough to make Americans fearful, corporations added to their anxiety through downsizing. In February 2008, employers laid off 63,000 workers, the highest figure since 2003. In the perverse world of unemployment calculations, however, the national rate actually dropped from 4.9 percent in January to 4.8 percent, since the Labor Department does not count those individuals who simply drop out of the job search altogether or drop off the role of people collecting unemployment checks. As a matter of fact, the national unemployment rate is further skewed by the simple quantitative formula used to establish the number. There is no system in place to measure the real loss of a middle manager in Cleveland who earns $85,000 annually versus the addition of a fast-food clerk in Florida who makes $8.50 an hour.[47]

The industries suffering the most widespread losses indicate the state of the overall national economy: construction, financial services, manufacturing, retailing, and business services. The snowball effect of the housing crunch, combined with costly overseas wars, is stretching the economy's effort at stability. In an increasingly unstable environment, executives react by cutting overhead, which usually results in massive job losses. Repeated efforts by the Federal Reserve to manage the economy through interest rate cuts and other cash-infusion measures have little consequence on individual households affected by layoffs, credit challenges, and real estate woes.

The February 2008 job cuts followed about 22,000 losses in the previous month, setting 2008 on a record course for layoffs. The last time the nation suffered back-to-back cuts occurred in May and June 2003. At that time, the United States struggled to regain its footing after the 2001 recession. The Federal Reserve predicts a difficult year for workers in 2008, estimating that the unemployment rate will jump to 5.3 percent, versus an average of 4.6 percent in 2007. These figures are low compared with other difficult economic times in modern American history, but the jobless rate has taken on a more important psychological role in the 2000s. The panic that would ensue if the jobless rate reached double-digits, as it did in the 1980s, would devastate the economy and begin a spiraling effect that would choke off consumer spending and corporate expansion, thus resulting in further job losses and eroding confidence.[48]

Some observers view the actions taken by the Federal Reserve as ineffective. Steven Lehman, an analyst at Federated Investors, explained, "There is a profound lack of understanding of markets and economies, and there is still persistent lingering faith that the authorities effectively have a magic wand they can wave to make everything fine. Economies and markets do go down—particularly after a multidecade credit boom."[49]

LIVING CONDITIONS

In the 2000s, much of the national conversation about living conditions takes place in the context of marriage and the family. The public debate regarding gay marriage, for example, is wrapped within a wider discussion about marriage in general. Much of the talk follows a pessimistic viewpoint, either lamenting the decline of traditional marriages or questioning how the union can retain its sanctity, given the possibility of nontraditional marriages.

In 2007, a survey conducted by the Pew Research Center showed that the public's perception of a happy marriage changed dramatically from an earlier study done in 1990. The most telling information is that the perception of kids as a source for marital bliss dropped significantly, from 65 percent in 1990 to 41 percent in 2007, ranking eighth out of nine categories. At the top of the survey were faithfulness (93%) and a happy sexual relationship (70%). Interestingly, "sharing household chores" ranked third, reaching 62 percent, versus 47 percent in 1990. In all, 53 percent of respondents claimed "adequate income" as a necessity in a successful marriage.[50]

The Pew researchers considered the 24-point drop in the children question and the jump for more day-to-day activities indicators of an overall shift in the way people view a happy marriage. When it comes to children, people are more open to unwed couples raising kids, adoption, and blended families then at any time in the past. "In the United States today," the report says, "marriage exerts less influence over how adults organize their lives and how children are born and raised than at any time in the nation's history."[51]

Picking Apart the Generations

Americans often define themselves (or are defined by cultural critics, corporations, marketers, and other entities) by generation. The 2000s are noted for two interrelated events: the retirement of the Baby Boomers and coming of age of Generation eXposed (also known as Generation Y or Millennials) group. In 2008, the first wave of Baby Boomers (born between 1946 and 1964) turned 62 years old, while the early Echo Boomers (born between 1977 and 1994) turn 31.

The sheer size of these generations spurs much of the resulting national culture, from what products are manufactured and marketed to the kind of television shows and films that get aired. Some 78 million people were born during the Baby Boom alone. The "echo boom" that defines their children refers primarily to the period between 1989 and 1993 when birthrates eclipsed 4 million per year.[52]

In some cases, it seems as if entire industries are devoted to selling to one of these two age groups. Certainly much of the television lineup, from the major networks to specialized cable stations, is geared toward these demographic segments. For example, TV shows like *The Office* and *How I Met Your Mother* appeal to and focus solely on Echo Boomer audiences; *Without a Trace* and *CSI* are designed to attract all audiences, but are favorites of Baby Boomer audiences.

Recent studies reveal that Baby Boomers watch more television than younger segments of the population. In 2006, adults ages 45 to 64 watched 37 hours and 38 minutes of television each week. In contrast, those between 18 and 34 tuned in for just over 27 hours. For marketers, the positive aspect of this information is that Baby Boomers often watch shows targeted at younger viewers, such as *Grey's Anatomy* and *Desperate Housewives.*[53]

The power of the Boomers is in their immense size (nearly 24% of the population, or about 78 million) and their buying power (estimated at $3 trillion). Most of the nation's political and corporate leaders fall into this category, such as Hillary Clinton and Bill Gates, but marketing efforts to treat the demographic like one big happy family do not work. Marilynn Mobley, senior vice president at Edelman, a communications firm that conducted an extensive study of Boomers, explains, "Baby boomers have always been considered the 'me-generation,' and that doesn't change with age. We're still just as self-centered and we want things very customized."[54]

Using Technology

One of the most glaring disparities between older and younger people is in how they use technology. In general, for someone in their later fifties or sixties, just being online is a sign of being hip, whereas for someone under the age of 25, sending e-mail is somewhat passé, as is waiting for more than a couple seconds for a Webpage to load. Furthermore, although some people still resist owning a cell phone, the number of those holdouts is rapidly decreasing. It seems as if everyone, whether a senior citizen or middle school student, is connected.

One of the common denominators, according to journalist Chad Lorenz, is e-mail. In his interactions with a younger niece, it dawned on him that e-mail, what seems like a necessity for those older than 25, really is not part of younger people's lives. His niece, "was too busy sending IMs and text messages to bother with e-mail," he explains. "That's when I realized that my agility with e-mail no longer marked me as a tech-savvy young adult. It made me a lame old fogey."[55]

For a generation of people raised (and raising themselves) on Facebook and MySpace, e-mail simply is not fast enough and requires too much work. While older people are firing away at their keyboards, the typical 20-year-old is writing on a friend's Facebook wall, texting via cell phone, and all the while blogging on WordPress. According to Lorenz, teens are sending about 50 messages a day via cell phones, while being logged in to Facebook and/or MySpace during all hours outside of school. "When everyone's online," he explains, "kids never have to leave the company of their pals. If you're not constantly plugged in, they say, you start to feel left out."[56]

One could merely chalk this behavior up to teens being teens. Is there really a difference between chattering away on Facebook and talking for hours a day on the telephone, like older people did when growing up? There is a reflective quality of e-mail that is falling by the wayside. Certainly composing an e-mail should not be equated with writing the next great American novel, but it is still considered more serious and considerate than the text message, with its clipped content and reliance on shorthand.

Another disconnect that younger users face is the transition from the dorm room to the workplace, where e-mail still dominates. A young employee cannot simply turn on an understanding of etiquette when it comes to communicating with co-workers and bosses. One of the cutting-edge tools that Google introduced to combat this challenge is Gmail, which mixes e-mail with IM. This may be a future state for corporations as they cope with young workers who feel e-mail is too archaic to be part of the workplace of tomorrow.

The New Religious Zeal

Religion plays a critical role in American popular culture, just as pop culture exerts a significant influence on religion. On the conservative side, pop culture is something to be derided for its Hollywood (read "bad") morals and permissiveness. On the left, religion is the culprit, a codeword for the "simple" and "average" people that liberals look down on. Undeniably, both conservatives and liberals make assumptions about the spirituality of the other based more on stereotype than experience. And, like any issue that they can exploit, the mass media use religion as a tool to sell television programs, newspapers, and magazines.

The most comprehensive information available about religion in the United States comes from the 2008 Pew Forum on Religion & Public Life *U.S. Religious Landscape Survey* based on interviews with 35,000 American adults. The report indicates that the primary characteristics of American religion are fluidity and diversity. In all, 28 percent of those surveyed left the faith that they were raised in and either chose another affiliation or left religion altogether. The number jumps to 44 percent if those who switched groups within Protestantism are included.[57]

Another 16 percent of people claim that they are unaffiliated with any particular faith, including 25 percent of those ages 18 to 29. These figures are surprising if one were to follow the political discussion of religion and its consequences on voting. Liberals paint a portrait of extreme right-wing religious zealots running the Republican Party, whereas the right sees the left as godless. In fact, only 4 percent of those surveyed fall into the agnostic (2.4%) or atheist (1.6%) categories.[58]

The other major tenet of American religion is its fluidity. According to the study, "Constant movement characterizes the American religious marketplace, as every major religious group is simultaneously gaining and losing adherents. Those that are growing as a result of religious change are simply gaining new members at a faster rate than they are losing member." For example, the Catholic portion of the adult population has been around 25 percent for the past several decades; however, the undercurrent is those who have left the Catholic Church. Thirty-three percent of those raised in the faith no longer describe themselves as Catholics. The survey explains that "roughly 10% of all Americans are former Catholics." The losses do not look more severe because of the large number of immigrants coming into the United States who are Catholic.[59]

2

World of Youth

You might peek into your kid's room, and your kid is on MySpace and they're talking on the phone and they're texting and IMing and there's music coming from the iPod—basically, you're seeing kids who are so technologically adept that parents don't quite know what to do about it.

—Larry D. Rosen (2007)

The traditional nuclear family rarely exists in America today. First, fewer people are marrying. In 1970, for example, 90 percent of women were married by the time they reached age 30. In the intervening three decades, that figure fell to 60 percent. People are marrying later in life and divorce remains commonplace. As a result, just 7 percent of all households in the nation consist of a married couple with children, where the father works and mom stays at home. When more specifically looking at households headed by a married couple, only 13 percent are traditionally nuclear. Another 31 percent are families with two working parents. In contrast, the number of married couples who both work but do not have children is 25 percent. In 2000, the average household size shrunk to 2.59 people, and the people per family fell to 3.14. These basic changes in household composition have significant consequences on children in the new millennium.[1]

It is not simply the impact of the environment that they are born into that is shaping young people. Other large societal trends are similarly influencing today's youth. One major force is the pervasiveness of technology, which on one hand provides them with access to greater amounts of information than any previous generation on earth. The dark side, however, is that technology also brings with it an "always on" mentality that makes kids as harried as their overworked and overstressed parents.

In the new millennium, as technology mixed with young people's celebrity obsession and the popularity of reality television, the result was a strange concoction. Suddenly, America's youths morphed into "generation eXposed," providing the world with their most intimate thoughts and feeling through online profiles used on social networking sites and Web logs, such as Facebook, MySpace, Blogger, and LiveJournal. Where young people bare their souls, they are vulnerable to predators eager to prey on youth's naivety.

Many observers contend that children face a more dangerous world in the new millennium. In response to this perception, parents (primarily baby boomers and gen Xers) are more vigilant in monitoring their children and are certainly raising them in a manner much different from the one they found themselves in as youths. The terms *hovering* and *helicopter parents* grew out of this sense of control. Today's young people, consequently, are carted from one event to the next on a tight schedule, watched over by their increasingly concerned parents. Whereas parents in the past let their children's challenges work themselves out, today's parents stand at the ready to fight their battles for them and, if necessary, browbeat, cajole, and bully until they get their way.

BREAKING STEREOTYPES OR CREATING NEW ONES?

Young people in the new millennium are using technology to create their own environments, away from the prying eyes of parents. The level of sophistication they use is mind-boggling for their often hapless parents. These efforts show a kind of maturity; today's youths live in a world that is often cruel and sometimes dangerous. The use of social networking sites, instant messaging, and texting via phones has given rise to "cyber-bullying," where the bully uses technology to more quickly and pervasively spread disinformation about others. Although young people understand how to circumvent parental control through text messaging and use computers at a much younger age than preceding generations, they are not capable of fully understanding the implications of their decisions. Children are still children and teenagers are still rebellious souls, despite the ever-present cell phone and technological wizardry.

The challenge for experts today is figuring out what makes young people tick in an age where they are much more connected through the virtual ties that bind them together. What studies are showing is that today's young people are collectively much different from the preceding generations, but they also hold an interesting mix of traits inherited from the baby boomers and generation Xers.

Technology is a defining factor in enabling young people to define themselves as separate entities. Just like earlier generations used telephones and cars to break away from their parents, kids today use online and cell technology to establish new boundaries. Researchers predict that online mobility, both using cell phones and accessing the Web through them, will continue to increase. In 2005, 53 percent of people ages 5 to 24 owned a cell phone, but that figure is expected to reach 81 percent by 2010. Sherry Turkle, a professor at the Massachusetts Institute of Technology, explains the social impact of cell phones: "For kids it has become an identity-shaping and psyche-changing object. No one creates a new technology really understanding how it will be used or how it can change a society."[2]

The challenge that lies ahead for parents and their children is how to integrate mobile communications with the face-to-face interactions that society demands. One dad, who owns a restaurant in Portland, explains the divide, saying: "I see kids text under the table at the restaurant. They don't teach them etiquette anymore." As a result, young people "don't know that's the time to carry on a conversation. I would like to walk up to some tables and say, 'Kids, put your iPods and your cell phones away and talk to your parents.'"[3]

Narcissism or Healthy Self-Worth?

The Pew Research Center grabbed headlines with a 2007 report titled *A Portrait of "Generation Next."* Among the most telling findings were that respondents ages 18 to 25 said getting rich (81%) and being famous (51%) were important for members of their generation. The report also dubbed these young people the "Look at Me" generation based on their extensive use of social networking sites.[4] Other observers have made similar conclusions, including Jean M. Twenge, a professor at San Diego State University and frequent television commentator, who wrote the book *Generation Me: Why Today's Young Americans Are More Confident, Assertive, Entitled—and More Miserable Than Ever Before* (2006).

Twenge studied 1.3 million young people over a 13-year period to develop a generational view of Americans born in the 1970s, 1980s, and 1990s. She sees this group as confident, assertive, and possessing the uncanny belief in themselves and their ability to do great things. There is a downside to the "me first" mantra of today's young people, however. They are leaving college and facing a difficult world that does not share their view. Consequently, the rigors of the everyday world, from rent payments to electric bills, bring disappointment, disillusion, and depression. Under these conditions, it is little wonder that more and more twenty-somethings find themselves living at home with their parents, thus returning to a more nourishing environment.

Twenge pinpoints the narcissistic trait on millennials in a study published in 2008 by the *Journal of Personality.* After studying data on 16,000 college students conducted between 1979 and 2006, she concludes that narcissism and entitlement have increased dramatically. Although Twenge's data reveal the truth on one level, one simply needs to look at the behavior of college-age individuals on a slew of reality television shows, or more acutely, walk through a crowded mall near a university to witness the me-first attitude of today's young people. "What we really have is a culture that has increasingly emphasized feeling good about yourself and favoring the individual over the group," Twenge explains. "And that has happened across the board, culturally, and it's showing no signs of slowing down." She even sees it in her own home: "I have a 14-month-old daughter, and the clothing available to her has 'little princess,' or 'I'm the boss,' or 'spoiled rotten' written on it. This is what we're dressing our babies in."[5]

Boys

The 2007 comedy *Superbad* grossed more than $169 million worldwide, revealing the enduring interest in teen boys and the search for booze, parties, and girls. The rollicking story follows three teenagers as they

Poster art for the hit teen movie Superbad *(2007). Columbia Pictures/Photofest. © Columbia Pictures. Courtesy of Photofest.*

attempt to buy alcohol to impress a girl who is throwing a party. Although the popularity of the film is attributed to its universal truths about boys as they prepare to leave high school for college, certainly its reliance on stereotypes is a key as well. The subject of teen boys on the make for girls and booze has been at the heart of youth-oriented films from the *Revenge of the Nerds* franchise in the 1980s to the *American Pie* trilogy (1999–2003).

The popular image of what drives young men has validity, just like many stereotypes. A recent study, however, reveals that the true nature of boys is different and more complex than generally imagined. Andrew Smiler, a professor at the State University of New York at Oswego, questioned tenth-grade boys to determine their views on females. When asked why they pursued a relationship, 80 percent answered that they "really liked the person," followed by physical attraction and wanting to get to know them better. Conversely, only 14 percent answered wanting to lose their virginity.[6]

Smiler's study confirms a nationwide survey of 1,500 college students in 2007 that asked the reason why they have sex. Both men and women had the same top answer: "I was attracted to the person." As for Smiler, he thinks that pushing the hormonal-driven stereotype on boys is detrimental. "The stereotype reduces boys to one-dimensional beings who just want sex and nothing else. But there are certainly other things boys want," he explains. "They want to play baseball. They want good grades and to go to good colleges. But if we insist all boys want is sex, in any context, it really limits boys and how we think of boys."[7]

Girls

A double-edged sword exists when examining how girls break traditional stereotypes in the new millennium. Although statistics show that female students are making great strides to equal, and in many cases, overtake males in math, science, and engineering, girls are also succumbing to dangers usually associated with boys, such as drinking, drug use, and smoking. Several recent reports indicate that teenage females drink alcohol, smoke, and use drugs as much (if not more) than boys. James Garbarino, a professor at Loyola University in Chicago, says, "When you take off the shackles, you release all kind of energy—negative and positive. By letting girls loose to experience America more fully, it's not surprising that they would absorb some of its toxic environment."[8]

The challenge for parents and others who would be repelled by the antics of teenage females is getting them to open up and then find the root causes for such behavior. Some experts have indicated that society sees girls differently now and that is taking root. Whatever wholesome, nostalgic vision of early female life people formerly held has now mutated into the repeated scandals, meltdowns, and arrests of celebrity bad girls Britney

The Hills (MTV) Season 1, 2006, Shown from left: Audrina Patridge, Whitney Port, Lauren Conrad, Heidi Montag. © Steven Lippman. Courtesy of Photofest.

Spears, Lindsay Lohan, and Paris Hilton. These are the images and role models that young women confront each day. "Teenagers are surrounded by a mix of messages," says journalist Lori Aratani. "On one hand, their parents and teachers tell them not to drink, smoke or do drugs, but on the other hand, music and such television shows as Gossip Girl and The Hills showcase teens indulging in just such behavior."[9]

CREATING TOMORROW'S CONSUMERS

American teenagers spend more today than at any other time in history. In 2005, for example, teens spent $159 billion. One reason for this mind-boggling statistic is that teens have greater access to money. Ten percent of teenagers own credit cards and about 20 percent use debit cards, while another 20 percent get money whenever they ask for it from their parents. In some respects, the out-of-control spending taking place among young people mirrors the extravagant buying spree most adults have been on in the 2000s. In general, baby boomer parents are not doing enough to teach their children financial literacy, according to a study by the Charles Schwab Foundation, a nonprofit arm of the financial services company. The study revealed that the average teen owes $230, and 25 percent of those ages 16 to 18 are more than $1,000 in debt.[10]

In the defense of teenagers, however, credit card companies aggressively market to them, particularly as young college students away at school where parental supervision is less likely to occur. The giant corporations willingly pursue teens with credit cards but, on the flipside, do not work as diligently on educating them regarding credit and personal finance issues. Every major financial institution has special college student checking account packages that are tied to debit and credit cards. As a result, it is nearly impossible to walk across a college campus today without seeing a myriad of advertisements for credit cards, from bulletin board flyers to tables set up and staffed by company representatives.

Washington Post financial writer Michelle Singletary explains, "Don't think for a second the companies marketing these cards have our children's best interests in mind. They have one goal—to hook a customer as early in life as possible."[11] Consequently, the typical undergraduate has four credit cards and owes more than $2,000. Some college students are putting their entire tuition on credit cards, then making minimum payments, virtually ensuring a lifetime of debt. In 2004, Massachusetts-based education lender Nellie Mae surveyed college students who received credit cards and found that 76 percent had their own cards. Of these respondents, 43 percent opened the account in their freshman year, but less than 25 percent had the same card before going to college.[12]

Teenagers have no shortage of options in spending money, particularly when the Internet is added to the equation. In many respects, teens are a godsend to marketers continually hawking products, from the latest iPod to new fashions that fulfill young people's desire to be like their favorite celebrities. The Center for a New American Dream, a nonprofit devoted to responsible consumerism, estimated that the ad industry spent $15 billion in the teen market in 2006. Juliet B. Schor, a Boston College professor and author, says: "Contemporary American tweens and teens have emerged as the most brand-oriented, consumer-involved and materialistic generation in history."[13]

HEALTH

Although high-profile accounts of young people using drugs or excessively drinking grabs headlines, youth drug use actually declined from 2001 to 2007, according to the Office of National Drug Control Policy. The organization estimates that the use of any illicit drug dropped 24 percent over the period, marijuana decreased 25 percent, steroid use fell by one-third, and ecstasy and methamphetamine usage both plunged by more than 50 percent.[14]

The most obvious reason for the drop in teen drug use is that the outreach efforts on a federal, state, and local level that began in the 1980s have worked well, although the fight continues. In addition, more comprehensive law enforcement efforts have curbed drug use among young people. According to Steve Pasierb, CEO of the New York-based nonprofit Partnership for a Drug-Free America, which produced the famous "This is your brain on drugs" public-service announcements, "It becomes this idea of unselling a product. Instead of driving up perception of benefit, we drive perception of risk. Instead of driving up social acceptance, we drive social disapproval. And what you find is you literally move consumers away from your product."[15]

The relationship today's young people have with their parents also plays a role in the drop in drug use, particularly in narcotics. Children who have grown up with a closer relationship with their parents are less likely to turn to drugs or alcohol. In addition, many outreach and education programs target both teens and parents, starting as early as elementary school.

Childhood Obesity

One of the most important challenges facing the United States in the twenty-first century is childhood obesity. The problem is a national epidemic in the eyes of many healthcare experts, including Acting Surgeon General Steven K. Galson. There are numerous explanations for why kids today are so overweight, from the rise of video games and more sedentary lifestyles to the way fast food restaurants targeted children with commercials and marketing campaigns, such as theme-driven "kid meals."

In early 2008, researchers from the Johns Hopkins Children's Center released a report published in the *Journal of Pediatrics* that targeted the seemingly limitless number of fast food commercials on Spanish-language television for the dramatic increase in childhood obesity in the Hispanic community, which has the highest rates in the nation. Examining peak programming segments when children would be most likely watching Univision and Telemundo, which reaches 99 percent and 93 percent, respectively, of Hispanics in the country, the study found that a third of all the food commercials aired were aimed directly at children.

About half of all the food ads were for fast food, and more than half the drink commercials featured soda and high sugar drinks. Darcy Thompson, a pediatrician at Hopkins and lead investigator on the project, explained, "While we cannot blame overweight and obesity solely on TV commercials, there is solid evidence that children exposed to such messages tend to have unhealthy diets and to be overweight."[16]

In response to the findings, the research team concluded that young children should not be allowed to watch more than two hours of television each day and that those younger than two should not be allowed to watch any. In addition, they recommended stronger parental supervision and dietary education, as well as a more direct role for pediatricians caring for Hispanic children.

The national childhood obesity problem is a primary focus of Galson and his staff at the Department of Health and Human Services. In a speech in early 2008, Galson outlined the magnitude of the epidemic, explaining, "Childhood overweight prevalence has nearly tripled for children ages 6 to 11 years since 1980. Today, approximately nine million children over the age of 6 are considered overweight in this country. Imagine . . . the population of New York City is 8.6 million people." The outlook for changing this condition in the short run is not good either, as the physical activity rates among school-age youths is also declining. Only 25 percent of high school students are moderately active for 30 minutes a day, five days a week, half the time necessary for young people to thwart potential weight problems.[17]

To combat childhood obesity, Galson initiated a "Healthy Youth for a Healthy Future" program designed to educate local communities, particularly (implementing 9/11 language) "first responders" in the fight: parents, caregivers, schools, public health leaders, the food industry, and local community leaders. A part of the campaign includes working with the food, sports, beverage, and entertainment industries to limit the kinds of calorie-laden things children consume. In Austin, Texas, for example, this work meant prohibiting the sale or distribution of carbonated beverages, candy, and other foods that are considered having "minimal nutritional value." Another facet centers on a series of public service announcements created by the NFL, Ad Council, and the federal government urging young people to get 60 minutes of exercise each day.[18]

Smoking

For decades the image of a cool teenager with a cigarette hanging from his lips served as a kind of symbol of teen life. Recent studies, however, reveal that the stereotype is on the decline. Drug education programs, state tax initiatives, and peer pressure are combining to drop teen smoking rates to historic lows.

In Massachusetts, a 2008 study by the state's education and public health departments found that high school smoking dropped between 2005 and 2007, from 20 percent to 18 percent. Since 1995, teen smoking in the state dropped by 50 percent. According to Jeffrey Nellhaus, the acting commissioner of the Massachusetts Department of Education, "The results here attest to the success of state agencies, schools, communities and families working together to prevent tobacco use among adolescents."[19]

Fewer New York City teens smoked in 2006 than in 2002, with just 11 percent of high school students claiming to be smokers. Mayor Michael R. Bloomberg indicated that he believed the decline took place in part due to higher cigarette taxes, which raised prices out of reach for many teens, and a ban on smoking in the workplace. City researchers reported that the number of high school students who smoked at least one cigarette in the last month dropped from 23 percent in 1997 and 18 percent in 2001 to reach the 11 percent figure.[20]

The New York City report also found that students in poorer neighborhoods were less likely to smoke, overturning a long-held stereotype about disadvantaged youths. Areas like the South Bronx, Harlem, and parts of Brooklyn fared poorly when examined for general health challenges, but the researchers did not find widespread teen smoking among them. White students rated highest among smokers (29%), followed by those living on Staten Island (23%), and girls (12%). Bloomberg discussed the travails of smoking, explaining, "I used to smoke as a young man, so I know how strong the addiction is and how hard it is to beat it—but it can be beat, and of course the best way to beat it is never getting hooked in the first place." He added, children "are bombarded each day with messages, both subtle and overt, encouraging them to smoke."[21]

Violence

The Office of National Drug Control Policy released a special report on teens, drugs, and violence in mid-2007. The study revealed that teens who engage in drug use are more likely to resort to violent behavior, steal, abuse drugs, and join gangs. Violence is the outward manifestation among teens who use drugs. They end up hurting themselves and others at a much higher rate than drug-free youth.

Twenty-seven percent of those who use drugs, for example, attacked another person with intent to harm. About one in six teens who fought at school or work said that they used illegal drugs; most were between 13 and 15 years old. The overall violence that permeates society increases greatly when drug use is involved. According to the study, "Adolescents represent approximately 14% of the general population, yet they comprise about 31% of the victims of violence, and teens are twice as likely as any other age group to be victims of violent crime."[22]

Teenagers ages 12 to 17 who smoke marijuana, the most widely used illegal drug by young people, are more than four times more likely to join gangs, which leads to increased criminal activity and substance abuse versus teens who do not use the drug. Most gang members are male, composed of 49 percent Hispanics and 37 percent African Americans, and usually between 15 and 17 years old. The transition from middle school to high school at around age 15 is when most young people join gangs. Although a teen's reasons for joining a gang vary greatly, from protection to developing a sense of belonging, experts agree that the more risk factors a young person is exposed to the more likely he is to join a gang.[23]

GENERATION EXPOSED

Young people in the new millennium are the first to grow up with the Internet in their lives, and the numbers of teens who sign on each day is staggering. By the end of 2004, 87 percent of those ages 12 to 17 used the Web daily. As a result, these youth have integrated instant messaging, social network sites, text messaging, and cell phones into their everyday balance of family, friends, school, and work. They are comfortable using and interacting through this broad mix of communications devices; however, many lack the wisdom to understand potential dangers they could face.

For example, a 2006 study conducted by California State University, Dominguez Hills professor Larry D. Rosen reveals that 83 percent of teens feel that MySpace is safe, compared with 83 percent of their parents who worry about sexual predators on the site. In contrast, only 35 percent of the teens surveyed admitted concern about sexual predators on MySpace, whereas 46 percent believe that there are "some, but not too many" predators using the site.[24]

From his extensive interviews with teens and their parents, Rosen, however, is not deeply concerned with the ways in which most teens under the age of 18 are using MySpace. "Overall, while MySpace may have some negative aspects, it can provide a forum for teenagers to develop a sense of their personal identity through communication with friends and strangers," he says. "The bottom line is that MySpace is not inherently scary or dangerous. In fact, it is helping teens develop an all-important sense of their identity." Rather than assume the sensationalist media portrayals of social networking sites are the end of the world, Rosen suggests that parents take a more active role in explaining the right and wrong way to use MySpace, as well as more actively monitoring their online usage.[25]

Online Safety. . .Or Lack of Safety?

In early 2007, a Texas judge dismissed a $30 million lawsuit against MySpace brought on by the family of an underage girl sexually assaulted by an older man she met on the social network site. Only 13 years old, the teen created a MySpace page claiming her age to be 18. She met a 19-year-old man, who contacted her via the site, then later spoke to her on the phone. After several weeks, the two met, and the man sexually assaulted the girl.

The lawsuit charged that MySpace did not have the proper safeguards in place to protect younger users. In ruling for the company, U.S. District Judge Sam Sparks explained, "If anyone had a duty to protect Julie Doe [victim's alias], it was her parents, not MySpace."[26]

Despite the judge's opinion, MySpace and the dozens of other social networking sites dominated by young people face ongoing scrutiny regarding users' safety. In today's Web-based world, this kind of predatory scenario is constantly on the minds of parents. Most find it nearly impossible to fully police how their children use the Internet. To make matters worse, the predators are using technology to their advantage as well. The cat-and-mouse game pits countless predators against overworked and understaffed local and state police authorities and the FBI.

In Buffalo, New York, the FBI arrested a 48-year-old male cafeteria worker who posed as a 20-year-old to lure young teens into sending him nude pictures. In all, police suspect that more than 100 area teens may have sent the man photos. Stefan Perkowski, who works with young sex crime victims at Child & Adolescent Treatment Services of Western New York, says, "They're not bad kids; they're victims of seduction by an adult. And they're growing up in an age when you have an explosion of role models like Paris Hilton telling them that this kind of behavior is not only acceptable, but something they should aspire to."[27]

Predators using the Internet to bait vulnerable children into dangerous situations has also found its way into mainstream popular culture featured on television shows like *Law and Order: Special Victims Unit*. The sole premise of *Dateline NBC's* "To Catch a Predator" series is luring potential sexual predators into on-air confrontations with host Chris Hansen after they arrive at the stakeout location of an undercover police officer posing as an underage female. The NBC show alone resulted in hundreds of arrests.

The media portrayal of the potential threat of online predators has brought an important subject to the forefront, but the sensationalist aspects also serve as a primary source of misinformation. In early 2006, a group of House of Representatives members called the Suburban Caucus introduced the Deleting Online Predators Act (DOPA), which requires schools and libraries to block access to Web sites that enable strangers to contact children. Michael Fitzpatrick, a Republican from Pennsylvania, explained: "One-in-five children has been approached sexually on the Internet. Child predation on the Internet is a growing problem."[28] The challenge is that many people use the 20 percent figure as a benchmark when there is not verifiable data to back it up. It sounds good in a sound bite, so it gained traction, regardless of its authenticity.

EDUCATION

By mid-decade, 90,000 American elementary and high schools enrolled more than 50 million young people. This figure surpassed the late 1960s enrollments when the last of the baby boomer generation filtered through the school system. About 10 percent of children are enrolled in private schools, and approximately 1 student in 50 is schooled at home. Schools in the new millennium are struggling to keep up with the sheer numbers of students entering the system. Also adding to the challenge is the influx of immigrants, many who require additional resources, particularly in English as a Second Language (ESL) studies.[29]

Preparing students who do not speak English at home is a predicament for today's schools. In 2000, 47 million Americans (18%) spoke a language other than English at home, a 47 percent increase in 10 years. In Fairfax County, Virginia, a near-suburb just west of Washington, D.C., it costs an additional $2,500 a year more to teach an ESOL student.[30]

The real burden for educating students falls into the laps of the nation's 3.2 million teachers. The strain against limited resources, low pay, and state-mandated proficiency test is relentless. In response, many up-and-coming teachers simply opt out of the system—this at a time when experts predict that the country needs to recruit 2.8 million teachers between 2008 and 2016 to replace retiring baby boomers, anticipate turnover, and meet enrollment growth. According to journalist Claudia Willis, "Research suggests that a good teacher is the single most important factor in boosting achievement, more important than class size, the dollars spent per student or the quality of textbooks and materials."[31]

No Child Left Behind

In 2002, the No Child Left Behind (NCLB) law placed federal guidelines around standardized testing, making schools responsible for student outcomes on these exams. The legislation requires individual states to establish standards in key subject areas and test children in grades 3 through 8 each year. The goal is for all students to be "proficient" by 2014. A key piece of President Bush's platform when he ran for high office, NCLB created a high-stakes poker game between state boards of education and teachers. The new law also permitted the state or a private entity to take over schools that did not meet performance goals, dubbed "Adequate Yearly Progress (AYP)." Bush and other proponents believed NCLB would hold schools accountable for student performance, which the federal and state agencies would back up with financial resources.[32]

Owing to the consequences for America's children and the educational system in general, NCLB immediately drew both praise and criticism. On the positive side, observers found that the law enabled them to closely examine schools that were failing and find means for improvement. In some cases, because of lackadaisical administrators and/or teachers, underperforming schools simply needed an overhaul. Other schools, especially those in poor districts, used NCLB to focus on basic skills and build school pride. For example, after implementing a rigorous testing program to help build reading skills, James G. Blaine Elementary (pre-K to eighth grade) in the Philadelphia city school district saw its reading scores for fifth- and eighth-graders reading at grade level jump from 13 percent to 36 percent. President Bush sees NCLB fighting "the soft bigotry of low expectations."[33]

Other reviews have been mixed regarding the effectiveness NCLB, although educators themselves routinely disparage the program. The most damning critique of NCLB is that it forces teachers to teach to the specifics of a standardized test, rather than creating lesson plans and activities based on knowledge, experience, and creativity. "Teach to the test" is a common shorthand phrase used to outline this position. According to University of Tampa professor Theoni Soublis Smyth, "Educators have discovered that the plan is flawed, developmentally inappropriate, ill funded, and leaving more students, teachers, and schools behind than ever before."[34]

The wider criticism about NCLB is that the rigorous preparation and testing program is creating a generation of students so focused on getting the right score that they lose invaluable critical thinking and creative skills. In addition, there are important areas not tested that can sometimes fall to the wayside in a school's march toward lifting test scores, such as writing, science, and social studies.

A real challenge for schools and federal agencies who enforce NCLB is helping students who fall by the wayside in traditional standardized testing, including students from low socioeconomic status, minorities, special needs students, and students who speak a language other than English at home. The big business aspect of NCLB, however, makes it a high-stakes part of today's educational system. The U.S. General Accounting Office estimated that the program would cost between $1.9 billion and $5.3 billion from 2002 to 2008.[35]

Emerging evidence reveals that a key facet of NCLB is not working—school restructuring. Research conducted by the Center on Education Policy in Washington, D.C. showed that in the 2006–2007 school year only 33 of more than 700 California schools in restructuring made enough progress to leave the program, a meager 5 percent. There are many options available for schools who do not meet AYP, but each one of them is divisive—from contracting with an outside organization to take over the school to replacing the staff or forcing existing teachers to reapply for their jobs. In California and other states across the country, the education challenge is intensified by a lack of financial resources, both for the schools and the states in general. California projects its state budget deficit to hit $14 billion by 2009.[36]

Another challenge for NCLB is that the budget crunch most states face is placing undue strain on education. As a result, more marginal schools are slipping into restructuring. In California, the number of schools jumped from 701 in 2006–2007 to 1,013 in 2007–2008. More distressing, the number of suburban schools forced into restructuring grew by 35 percent in the same period. The problems in California, which is a progressive education state, are replicated across the nation and should be used as a guideline in fixing the gaping holes in NCLB.

The Homework Conundrum

Homework is a battleground in the new millennium, but not the traditional fight to get young people to do it before turning on the TV or computer games. Rather, the argument in the twenty-first century is whether or not children have too much homework and if it is actually hurting them over the long term, leading to depression, anxiety, and stress. For example, homework doubled over the past 20 years for youngsters in first and third grade, going hand-in-hand with an increase in more complex subject matter and more emphasis on standardized tests. By the time these students get to high school, however, they have slipped below the basic amount of homework a college-bound student should complete. About 30 to 40 percent of high school students say that they have no homework, and most college freshmen report that they did less then an hour per night while in high school. They have also slipped behind their counterparts in foreign nations based on time spent in class. As a result, American students routinely place in the middle of the pack compared with students in other nations.[37]

Despite the statistics that show American students falling behind, a growing backlash against homework is on the rise. Fueled by middle- and upper-income families, activist groups are attempting to change school policy to limit homework. Books, such as *The Case Against Homework* (2006) by Sara Bennett and Nancy Kalish and *The Homework Myth* (2006) by Alfie Kohn, questioned homework's primacy in the modern education system.

To fully understand the modern homework challenge, one must consider the pressure placed on students by corporate and government leaders to raise achievement, primarily through standardized test scores. Because much of the testing begins early in a student's scholastic career, more emphasis is placed on developing skills in first through third grade. The result, says journalist Marcia Clemmitt, is that "some schools also are pressuring kindergarten and preschool teachers to teach academic subjects to 4- and 5-year-olds, who often lack the physical and cognitive skills to handle them."[38]

The trend indicates that the primary increase in workload is taking place in elementary and middle school, but high school students, in general, face less grueling schedules. A 2006 study about how high school students spend their time conducted by researchers at Indiana University revealed that 27 percent spend 10 or more hours each week socializing with friends outside of schools, and another 21 percent said they worked those hours. Laurence Steinberg, a professor at Temple University, does not view high school students working harder. In a similar study, he showed, "A very high percentage of kids in our sample say they do as little as they can without getting into trouble."[39] Actually, only about 21 percent of students complain about having too much homework, along with 11 percent of parents. Seventy-two percent of students and 68 percent of parents say that the amount of homework is appropriate.

COLLEGE

College culture is changing in the new millennium, from the special amenities schools must offer to attract new students to the consequences of the intense testing and test prep that students endure as high schoolers. At the same time, the larger forces of technology, the economy, government, and culture are transforming the way college students view themselves and the world around them. Included in this evolution is the basic change in age of the "typical" college student, no longer just young people 18 to 22 years old. The advent of online degree programs and the constant need for keeping pace with technological innovations lead more people back to school at an older age.

A primary change in today's student versus their generation X predecessors is that young people today see the "college student" label as only part of what defines them. Yes, they are students, but they place a much higher emphasis on full- and part-time jobs, friends, consumerism, and other diversions that draw them further away from a student mindset. In contrast, most gen Xers were students first and everything else second. When a young person in the twenty-first century makes decisions, such as class versus picking up another shift as a bartender at Chili's, classes often lose out because the young person does not identify foremost as a student. More deeply, this attitude obliterates the traditional emphasis on teacher-centric education. If a student considers going to class no more or less important than updating a MySpace page, working, or visiting the nearest mall, then the institution is diminished.

In some ways, schools themselves play into this notion. Competition for students among colleges is a high-stakes game. Thus admissions departments use the same tools that savvy marketers in the corporate world use to sell products. "Our top universities compete for 'market share' and 'brand-name positioning,' employ teams of consultants and lobbyists and furnish their campuses with luxuries in order to attract paying 'customers'— a word increasingly used as a synonym for students," explains Andrew Delbanco, a professor at Columbia University.[40]

While observers continue the never ending debate about the future of higher education in America, an influx of students in the latter half of the decade is straining the nation's college system. Some relief may be in sight early in the next decade, but the age groups preparing to enter are even bigger, ranking as some of the largest in history. They face increasing costs, especially in a shaky economy, which in turn, necessitates students to take out substantial student loans. For example, from 1976 to 2006, public college tuition and fees jumped from $2,200 to $5,800. Private school averages reached $22,200. Some of this money is collected for "technology fees," "energy," and other surcharges designed to lighten the wallet of students, parents, or the banks paying for the student's education.

One thing is for certain in the 2000s—today's college students are stressed out, perhaps more than any preceding generation. According to a survey conducted by The Associated Press and mtvU, the arm of the network directed at colleges and universities, their stresses range from grades and jobs to relationships and chores. In all, 40 percent of respondents claim that they endure stress often, and 20 percent say that they feel it all or most of the time. The result is that college students display classic stress symptoms and wonder about their choices, particularly regarding drinking, going out, and drug use. About 17 percent of those students surveyed said that they have friends who discussed committing suicide in the last year, and 10 percent say they considered it themselves. Another 13 percent say that they have been diagnosed with a mental health condition such as depression or anxiety.[41]

Experts often note the close relationship the current generation of college students has with their families, but the new study on student stress proves the stereotype wrong. A total of 17 percent of white students said they seldom or never feel understood by their families. When considering minority students the numbers soar: 31 percent of Hispanics, 29 percent of Asians, and 28 percent of African American students report these feelings. Obviously, there are holes in the common idea that millennials have a special relationship with their parents that sets them apart from earlier ones. That cell phones, texting, and e-mail enable parents to watch over their college-age children more closely does not mean that these students are isolated from the common fears and stresses of school.[42]

Politics

Although courted by both political parties and various activism groups, college students traditionally have not turned out in sufficient numbers on election day to really play a significant role on the national scene. Each election cycle saw new attempts at increasing participation, from MTV's "Rock the Vote" campaign (begun in 1990) to the 2004 "Vote for Change" tour, featuring Bruce Springsteen, REM, and Pearl Jam. Whether focusing on a particular candidate or on voter registration in general, students did not follow through by actually voting.

The 2004 presidential election, however, energized the college vote. Fifty-four percent of young people ages 18 to 24 cast their ballot in the campaign pitting incumbent Bush against challenger John Kerry. The figure trailed only 1972 (55%) in the percentage of voters from that demographic who voted in presidential election years. The 2004 number also marked a 12 percent jump over the 2000 turnout and a 14 percent increase over 1996.[43]

Although the increased turnout by young people encouraged many observers in 2004, evidence also exists that reveals how little the age group truly cares about voting, particularly in contrast to older demographics. When young people were asked whether they always or nearly always vote, only 35 percent in 2000 and 37 percent in 2004 of 18- to 25-years olds claimed to do so. In comparison, 63 percent of those 26 to 40, 77 percent of those 41 to 60, and 85 percent of those 61 and over claimed the same in 2004. Furthermore, only 42 percent of the younger demographic agree that it is their duty as a citizen to always vote, compared to 62 percent of the public overall.[44]

In 2008, the tide may again be shifting in favor of younger voters, if evidence gathered from the primary season is any indication. College students—too busy for television news or reading a newspaper, like their older counterparts—are turning to social media sites and new technology to get involved in politics. All the major candidates have MySpace pages, with many college students filling the ranks of "friends" on the sites to access the latest information and news about their favorite. Video site YouTube has also been important during the run for the 2008 presidential nominations. Students watch clips (often three minutes or less) whenever it is convenient to them, not on the traditional news cycle. Christopher Kubash, a senior at Grand Valley State University in Michigan, explains, "I have used YouTube to search for debates between candidates. There seems to be an almost endless archive . . . You could probably find a video from any public appearance a candidate has made in the last year."[45]

According to the nonpartisan Center for Information & Research on Civic Learning & Engagement, turnout for presidential primaries and caucuses by people under 30 years old tripled or quadrupled in states such as Florida, Georgia, Tennessee, and Texas, among others. Cherie Strachan, a professor at Central Michigan University, views the use of technology as a deciding factor for renewed involvement among college students. "Technology has made it a lot easier for young people to keep track and send each other links," Strachan says. "They don't feel the need to keep up by reading the paper every day."[46]

Political pundits never could have predicted the interest YouTube would generate. A pro-Obama music video, dubbed "Yes We Can," filled with celebrities that back the Illinois senator and posted by Black Eyed Peas singer will.i.am. accrued more than 7 million views. An important speech Obama gave on the topic of race drew about 4.3 million hits in the first month it was available. Political parties and candidates are well aware of the power of these social media tools and actively recruit donors and campaign workers using the sites.[47]

College Online: A Cyber Myth or Cyber Reality?

Online education is in many respects a two-headed monster. On one hand, the opportunity for studying without being limited by physical space holds great promise for democratizing education like never before. On the other hand, however, there are many disreputable organizations attempting to pass themselves off as academic institutions, acting as virtual "diploma mills," thereby cheapening everyone's diploma. There are also questions of the value of online classes versus the traditional classroom model and ethical issues involved with who is actually on the other end of the computer.

Despite the challenges surrounding online education, there is no doubt that it is popular and growing. In fall 2006 (the latest data available), about 3.5 million students took online courses, up nearly 10 percent from the previous year. According to Jeff Seaman, survey director for the Sloan Consortium, a nonprofit research group, two-thirds of all American colleges and universities offer some form of online classes. The largest growth in online teaching is occurring at community colleges, which makes sense, given the more diverse students and tendency for attracting older and returning adult students who would benefit from the freedom of online classes.[48]

Young people in the new millennium live in a world that is open in a way that previous generations cannot comprehend. Not only are the opportunities for communicating completely changed, but today's youth live in generation eXposure, an environment that more or less forces them into living a kind of billboard-driven existence that is the heart of MySpace, Facebook, and other social media Web sites. Every thought, deed, or emotion can instantly be shared in these virtual worlds, exposing young people to their peers and within the larger culture.

Part Two
Popular Culture of the 2000s

The 2000s

3

Advertising

> Corporations put ads on fruit, ads all over the schools, ads on cars, ads on clothes. The only place you can't find ads is where they belong: on politicians.
>
> —Molly Ivins (2000)

A century ago advertisers plastered American towns and cities with signs, billboards, and brand names. It seemed as if every square inch of the downtown areas contained some directive to potential buyers. Advertisers hoped to entice dollars away from consumers who perhaps for the first time had disposable income and sought new products designed to make their lives easier. At that time, a horse-drawn buggy with the Wrigley logo and slogan painted on the side was cutting edge innovation. Direct mail, such as the Sears catalog, served as the ultimate wish list for millions of families nationwide, particularly those isolated on farms and in rural communities. The advertising profession grew out of this need to connect consumers with goods.

Leap ahead a hundred years and the lives of consumers are filled with similar forces—a constant barrage of commercials, billboards, ad banners, and displays. The primary difference is that physical space is only one dimension of the way advertisers currently ply their trade. Just like in its earlier days, advertising uses advanced technology to reach consumers, which means through television, radio, film, and the Web. Today, advertising is part of the larger discipline of "marketing" or "branding" representing the ubiquity of joining organizations, products, and services with consumers and organizations.

In the 2000s, businesses and manufacturers do not want people to simply buy products; instead they want to form "relationships" with consumers that will keep buyers returning again and again to "trusted" goods and those who provide them. Marketing is at the heart of building this relationship, whether it is redesigning a package to represent a product's place in the market or expounding on a company's social responsibility via a blog. Because of its influence and reach, advertising is a central function in marketing and branding.

DEVELOPING VALUES

Popular culture, technological innovation, and the power of the corporate world are the driving forces dominating American life for the last 150 years. Standing at the intersection of the three and propelling them deep into people's daily lives is *marketing*—the umbrella term used to describe the communications fields of public relations, advertising, and marketing. Marketing has been an important catalyst for the seismic societal transformations that have taken place in modern America, walking hand-in-hand with the nation's increasingly consumer culture. Because corporations speak to the public primarily through communications campaigns, advertising, public relations, and marketing play a critical role in determining how people build their personal value systems.

Historically, the tendency has been to look at marketing as a corporate evil. The idea that companies basically push unnecessary or unwanted products on an unsuspecting public to gain profit seems wholly un-American. Acknowledging the fact that advertisers have a hold over the public somehow robs people of their autonomy or individuality. In addition, the ubiquity of marketing campaigns also works in favor of its critics. Spotting ineffective or crude advertisements is an easy task and the criticism of such work is an industry in itself. The money involved in orchestrating campaigns also makes them convenient targets. One critic, historian Robert W. McChesney, claims: "Modern marketing is clearly the greatest concerted attempt at psychological manipulation in all of human history."[1] He cites the advent of guerrilla marketing in the early twenty-first century as especially egregious. Guerilla marketing is the deliberate attempt to create a relationship with a consumer without the consumer's knowledge that he or she is being marketed to, usually via grassroots, low-cost efforts, although the advent of social media Web sites enables large corporations to launch these campaigns via MySpace, Facebook, or other channels.

A deeper analysis of marketing, however, reveals that there is also an educational aspect of field that enables consumers to make informed, intelligent decisions about the products they purchase. In today's electronic age, for example, public relations keeps the lines of communications open between companies and the public (especially shareholders). Although the system is certainly not perfect, considering that scandals such as Enron still take place, imagine the corruption if public companies were not required to report important financial information such as quarterly earnings. Corporations made this type of financial information available in earlier eras, but in the new millennium it is more readily accessible via the Internet than in previous eras, including the 1990s. Corporate marketing is a polarizing topic, but it deserves a broader examination, especially as it relates to how people use it to determine their own world views.

In the past, one could argue, elites drove much of the interaction between marketers and the public. The pervasiveness of Internet technology, however, is significantly transforming the way the two sides deal with one another. Social media Web sites, such as MySpace, Facebook, and YouTube, have given consumers more power to choose the way they want to interact with those attempting to sell products or services. As a result, corporate America is scrambling to find ways to engage people via these channels.

Shaping Values

By turning on the television for five minutes or glancing through ads in a magazine, one finds countless examples of marketers duping consumers. The most egregious examples seem to be diet- or health-related, the bold print or voiceover pushes a consistent message—"Take this pill and you'll become the thin, beautiful person you've always dreamed of being. You'll live a healthier, happier life and people will love you."

The cultural historian Christopher Lasch believes this thinking represents an addiction to consumption. In his view, advertisers solidify and expand the public's desire for acquiring goods, which makes them feel like they are important, worthy, and accomplished. According to Lasch, "Consumption promises to fill the aching void; hence the attempt to surround commodities with an aura of romance; with allusions to exotic places and vivid experiences; and with images of female breasts from which all blessings flow."[2]

Advertising exists, in other words, to transform people into shopping machines, hell bent on erasing their insecurities through the power of acquisition. Critics of marketing pose a simple question: How can people develop a sense of values or their place in the wider culture if they are little more than ad-driven, brainwashed zombies? According to McChesney, "What such a commercial culture tends to produce—and what the avalanche of commercialism encourages—is a profound cynicism and materialism, both cancerous for public life."[3]

What has changed most dramatically since Lasch's era is that consumption has been subsumed by the public's celebrity obsession. The idea that everyone rightfully deserves their bit of fame is nearly universal in twenty-first century America. Marketers tap into this idea, presenting people with the image of a better, more beautiful self hidden somewhere behind the curtain while they trudge through their daily routines without any of the glamour they view thousands of times a day.

Whether portraying the latest age-resistant facial cream or a new, must-have luxury SUV, advertisements pull at a vein of insecurity that runs deep into the American psyche. While the results of this mindset are numbing, like the plethora of "reality" television shows and hundreds of millions of user-generated videos uploaded to YouTube, MySpace, and a host of smaller social media sites, one cannot understate the impact on popular culture. Despite the popularity of reality television shows, such as *Survivor* and *American Idol,* many contend that these programs are little more than extended commercials and opportunities for seemingly ordinary people to become celebrities. Mark Burnett, the powerful producer of *Survivor,* said that he viewed the show "as much as a marketing vehicle as a television show."[4]

Obviously, despite its long existence at the heart of popular and corporate culture, advertising is much maligned. The field is besieged by an age-old question—is advertising a good or bad thing for society? The notion that advertising influences the way people shape their values and the culture as a whole, however, is now universal. What has changed in recent times is that messages are less likely to be completely driven from the top (agencies/corporations) down. Ideas, issues, and cultural meanings that bubble up from below, such as consumer-generated commercials and content strongly influence how marketers "speak" to audiences.

Marketing as Public Education

Advertising's pervasiveness, in some respects, actually opens doors to public discussion about marketing efforts and one's place in the larger world. People use ads as a barometer for assessing their own values and role as citizens. Consumers also receive a great deal of educational information from companies through marketing campaigns. Bank of America, for instance, launched a new product in January 2005 called SafeSend that enabled Hispanic customers to remit money to Mexico free of charge. Previously, Hispanic consumers had to use costly payday loan establishments or wire transfers to send money back to Mexico, which topped $20 billion in 2005.

In examining Burrell Communications, a large African American-owned advertising firm, communications scholar Irene Costera Meijer sees client work that uses "positive realism" to show black consumers a view of life that is purposely thoughtful, engaging, and well-rounded. A McDonald's ad created by Burrell that showed a successful black father visiting his child's school, for instance, provides "a new story of responsible black male citizenship that can be a source of inspiration and guidance for men and women, whites and blacks."[5]

Meijer sees advertisements like this providing positive social impact. She explains that marketers should consider using positive images "that create so-called win-win situations, images which are good for the market and can change people's ideas about themselves and hopes for society."[6] According to Meijer, advertising can provide valuable stories of what it means to live the good life, which are otherwise hard to find in mainstream media channels. "Such stories should be seen as part of the wide array of practices and technologies with which individuals nowadays have to constitute their sense of self as—among other things—citizens of ever expanding communities."[7]

Of all the disciplines falling under the marketing umbrella, none is more essential to the education process than public relations. As a business function, public relations is driven by the bottom line, but professionals, as opposed to charlatans who do little more than produce spin, fluff, and puffery, conduct themselves ethically. Their goal is to inform consumers about their clients' products and services. Public relations perhaps shines brightest in crises situations, when public education is most critical. The most important crises that public relations professionals handle are community disasters such as plane crashes, fires, explosions, and major workplace accidents.

Public Reaction, Interaction, and Action

Unlike any other sporting event on the planet, the Super Bowl showdown is a spectacle of epic proportions. Many viewers don't even care about the football game itself; they tune in to watch the commercials. The Super Bowl is advertising's annual main event. The buzz about the ads grows to a fever pitch each year, particularly when the price tag is revealed. In 2008, a 30-second commercial spot cost $2.7 million.[8] The stakes are high for corporations willing to hand over that kind of money.

Before the advent of the Web, Super Bowl ads were the hot topic at offices nationwide on Monday mornings, but the impressions had to be drawn from memory of the evening before. Marketers ran their commercials and then waited to get public reaction, perhaps from the morning newspaper. Cultural elites pushed their efforts at the public and received praise or criticism from media elites such as columnists or television news reporters.

With the Internet, however, groups of friends can gather around a computer screen and watch the advertisements over and over again, focusing on each one's strengths and weaknesses. They can also read countless blogs about the winners and losers or post their own thoughts. The Web also provides greater reach for activist groups and industry watchdogs. Suddenly, ordinary people had a hand in determining the success or failure of the commercials.

In 2007, Masterfoods' Snickers Super Bowl spot drew fire from gay rights groups for depicting two burly mechanics accidentally kissing, then reacting by doing "manly" things to prove their straightness, like ripping out chunks of chest hair. Almost instantly, activist groups, such as the Gay & Lesbian Alliance Against Defamation and the Human Rights Campaign, condemned the campaign, which they claimed promoted violence against homosexuals. These groups also criticized a Snickers Web site that ran alternative commercial endings and showed professional football players jeering as they viewed the ad. One ending featured the mechanics hitting each other with wrenches after the inadvertent lip lock.

Years ago, Snickers may have been able to wait out the criticism or quietly cancel the campaign. The fallout may have been minimal, but the firestorm spurred by the ability of people to watch and rewatch the commercials via the Web forced the company to shutter the commercials and the accompanying Web site. In addition, the brand ignited a public relations nightmare. Mike McGuire, research director at Gartner, said: "For good or ill, the Internet dramatically increases awareness and reach. That's difficult to control, and can be very dangerous."[9] The Snickers commercial withdrawal clearly shows that the Internet has changed the way people interact with marketers. Consumers use blogs, Web sites, and videos or podcasts to respond to marketing campaigns directly and may draw audiences as large or larger than the campaign itself.

There is an important link between the marketing message and consumer reaction, interaction, and subsequent action, but it is not straight cause and effect. Advertising scholar Jerry Kirkpatrick bluntly explains: "Advertising can make consumers aware of needs, it can stimulate their wants, it can stimulate demand, and it can make it possible for consumers to enjoy a greater and wider range of tastes. But tastes, needs, wants and demand all originate within the consumer."[10]

The real mystery seems to be where the original thoughts regarding tastes, needs, wants, and demand came from. These ideas are derived from a complex system of establishing one's world view, as much from parents, family members, and friends, as from mass media channels. Jib Fowles sees popular culture playing a critical role, saying: "Based on their exposure to, and discriminating appropriation from, the advertising/popular culture mix, people are then able to purchase the items that give off desired symbols."[11] The flow of information goes both directions—from marketers to consumers and vice versa.

In studying historical case studies on marketing successes and failures, scholar Robert F. Hartley accepts that advertising's value is difficult to determine. Nike's use of celebrity endorsers, ranging from Michael Jordan to Tiger Woods, produces a Nike culture that permeates society, whereas other celebrity pitch campaigns that use those successes as a guide flop unceremoniously. Hartley sees the ultimate power resting in the hands of consumers. "There is no assured correlation between expenditures for advertising and sales success," he explains. "But the right theme or message can be powerful. In most cases, advertising can generate initial trial. But if the other elements of the marketing strategy are relatively unattractive, customers will not be won or retained."[12]

SOCIAL MEDIA TRANSFORMATION

Technology forces change across society. Corporations are often at the helm, pushing innovations out into the wider public. Sometimes, a groundswell of popularity surrounding a new technology bubbles up from below, propelled by users before the business world leaps in and attempts to "monetize" the innovation. This age-old chicken or egg scenario dominates consumer culture, begging the question: What comes first, the new product or the basic want/need for the innovation? In today's tech-heavy environment, the Internet (particularly the Web 2.0/social media craze) is intensifying the push/pull nature of consumer marketing.

Since its launching in 2004, MySpace has attracted more than 100 million members. The MySpace site enables users to create their own personalized Web page filled with music, pictures, and messages. Each day, it receives 1 billion page views, making it one of the top Internet properties in the world. In July 2005, News Corp. CEO Rupert Murdoch bought MySpace for $580 million, at the time a staggering figure, but now considered a bargain.[13]

MySpace fills an interesting void. The site allows anyone with computer access to become the star of his or her own show, a kind of mini-celebrity, attracting "friends," who are then listed on one's page. Journalists have dubbed the most popular users "MySpace celebrities," with some people acquiring more than 1 million friends. Many of these Web friends actually equate more directly as fans, thus the impulse to have as many as possible. Almost like an exaggerated, online version of the high school cafeteria, MySpace provides otherwise ordinary people with a taste of celebrity. Individual users then become their own brand, with friends serving as their enduring fans.

MySpace is also increasingly commercial, not only as a place for marketers to interact with massive numbers of consumers, but for people to find content, whether a video from a little-known indie band or last week's episode of 24. Part of the plan to make MySpace profitable is to build out its advertising function. A number of national advertisers are signed with the site, including Coke, Honda, and Procter & Gamble. An ad on the homepage costs approximately $500,000 a day. Countless corporations have their own MySpace pages, which cost $100,000 or more, including Wendy's and Unilever. Several companies have already run successful viral marketing campaigns on MySpace. P&G, for example, launched a "Miss Irresistible" page for a new Crest toothpaste and drew almost 40,000 friends and more than 3 million page views.[14]

In October 2006, search engine behemoth Google made headlines by purchasing year-and-a-half-old YouTube for $1.6 billion. Although at the time it was wildly popular among teenagers and Web-savvy hipsters, You-Tube was certainly no household name. Critics scoffed at the steep price and wondered if the tech geniuses at Google had finally made a big mistake. Since then, YouTube shows no signs of slowing down. In July 2006, more than 1.6 million U.S. visitors watched 21 million video streams per day. Google, however, is still trying to determine how to make the site profitable.

Given YouTube's vast reach and popularity, marketers have searched for ways to join the phenomenon. At this stage, however, results have been mixed and point to a dramatic change in the way people will accept or reject advertisements. The strongest indication is that it will be on their own terms, not those dictated by the elites running advertising agencies or television networks.

For example, Unilever launched its Dove "Real Beauty" campaign, using real women as models, rather than the typical supermodel or actress that most beauty campaigns use. As part of the campaign, the company placed a video, "The Evolution of Real Beauty," on the site in October 2006 that was an instant hit. The short ad became one of the most popular You-Tube videos of all time, drawing more than 1.8 million views; however, Unilever's next attempt at creating social media buzz for Dove Cream Oil Body Wash fizzled. Unilever bought space for the video on YouTube's front page, which guarantees a large number of hits, but negative reactions ensued, including rebuttal videos discussing how the company does not understand the concept of user-generated video.[15]

The Dove success and failure left marketers shaking their heads and forcing them back to the drawing board in hopes of finding a better way to build brand equity. The challenge is that social media audiences are fickle and have a finely tuned marketing meter. They are quick to label promotional videos "unauthentic" and stand up for the unwritten code that guides such sites. For corporations, viral marketing is a dicey proposition. Companies like Unilever, Coke, or Microsoft spend billions to build its brand. A great deal of equity can vaporize quickly when something like the Dove campaign goes wrong.

A surprising success that points to the breakdown of the wall between marketers and consumers is the user-created commercial. For example, in late 2006, Chipotle Mexican Grill ran a 30-second commercial contest for college students, offering $40,000 in prize money. The company posted the two winning entries on YouTube and received 17 million viewers the first month. Because Chipotle targets 18–34-year-olds, the YouTube exposure hit their primary audience.[16]

Ultimately, high tech has further removed marketers from what they most covet—control. Once a message reaches cyberspace, the corporation/agency no longer wields power over it. Web-savvy consumers satirize ads, develop their own competing messages, and discuss its content without the originator having much, if any, recourse. A mocking image of a corporate logo or unintended use of a product sent out over YouTube or MySpace damages the efforts taken to build the brand. The popularity of these social media sites almost ensures an audience. For some videos that get the magical viral marketing bump, the number of viewers is staggering.

In late 2006, someone leaked a video to YouTube of a Bank of America employee singing a parody of the U2 song "One," but with the lyrics changed to reflect the Bank of America/MBNA merger. The over-the-top shtick and impassioned performance carried the video to Web screens worldwide. No one knows how many views it received, but estimates place it in the tens of millions range. Some even thought that Bank of America purposely leaked the video to create viral buzz. Regardless of how it came into the public eye, the resulting chatter had little to do with the bank's then-marketing slogan "Higher Standards."

Although the available technology gives consumers greater control over how companies market to them, marketers are exploring for ways to use social media to develop deeper relationships. One company, Utah-based Blendtec, a maker of high-powered blenders created David Letterman-like videos of founder Tom Dickson blending a variety of odd items, like marbles and golf balls. Dickson's online grinding of an iPod alone garnered more than 3 million views. The media soon picked up on the company, which received press coverage and a feature on NBC's *Today* show. According to author Paul Gillin, "Online video is the most cost-effective tool ever invented to test and refine ideas and messages. If you're lucky, it may be a bonanza of free publicity."[17]

Gillin believes that public relations practitioners need to concede control if they want to use social media effectively, something that marketers are loath to do. "Once you put your video online, you've lost control of it. People will copy it, modify it, mash it up and have their way with it," he says. "Accept this, and don't try to control what they do. On the contrary, resolve to learn from the changes they make, because there may be a better product or marketing opportunity hidden there."[18]

Consequences

The age-old argument about marketing's role in society is too simplistic in today's media-saturated environment. The interaction between the public and marketers has consequences for society and democracy at large. Neither side can stand on the sidelines and cast stones at the other. Both the traditional corporation/agency (sender) and audience (receiver) of marketing campaigns play a role in determining how the information fuels the creation of values and culture. As shown previously, even the idea of the sender-receiver relationship has undergone tremendous change as the Internet transcends boundaries.

Make no mistake—marketing is at a crossroads. Technology places more power in the hands of the people. This may make each person a kind of mini-activist group able to reach mass audiences in reply to a campaign, a kind of ultra-democracy, where individuals truly work together within campaigns. In the future, perhaps the best scenario is that marketers will view the public as equal partners in the process. Consumers certainly have the tools at their disposal to prove that they are no longer brainless sheep being fed by marketing elites. Communications scholar Jib Fowles explains, "Advertising is not a hail of commercial barbs inflicting damage on huddling consumers and their culture. Advertising is a buffet of symbolic imagery that advertisers hope will prove tempting and lead to the more difficult exchange of money for goods."[19]

The democratization of marketing via the Internet has made the relationship Fowles describes both more tenuous and intimate. Consumers—much more astute than commonly perceived—wander up to Fowles's buffet cautiously and take what they think they need based on deep-rooted values that have in some way been shaped by witnessing a lifetime of marketing campaigns. A person can use technology (think TiVo) to either avoid many of the marketing messages being pushed at him, or choose his/her own method of interaction (think YouTube). The realization must be made, however, that almost everything a person knows or cares about has been filtered through a marketing medium.

POLITICAL ADVERTISING

In the United States, campaign spending is at the heart of getting elected. The largest chunk of the money raised goes directly into advertising. Although the new millennium brought Web-based advertising and marketing to the fore, hundreds of millions of dollars are still spent on television ads. As a result, political candidates place more emphasis on their Web sites, MySpace accounts, and other innovative (and less expensive) tools to reach out to voters, but also rely heavily on television.

With Senator John McCain wrapping up the Republican nomination early, his campaign staff kicked fundraising into overdrive without actually having to spend that much on costly ads. In March 2008, for example, McCain raised $15.4 million. Although he trails the Democratic candidates greatly in terms of finances raised, his lock on the nomination means that he spent only $277,000 on TV ads between March 18 and April 16. In contrast, Senator Barack Obama spent $11 million on television advertisements over the same timeframe, and Senator Hillary Clinton spent

$4.5 million. The Obama campaign raised $40 million in March, 2008, down from $55 million the previous month. Officials from the Clinton camp estimated that it raised $20 million in March.[20]

2004 Presidential Campaign

The most intriguing aspect of the 2004 presidential contest between George Bush and John Kerry is that there may never be a full accounting of the money spent on the battle. Journalist Chuck Todd says, "Billions of dollars were spent . . . on advertising, polls, mailings and campaign stops." Doubtless, as Todd explains, much of that money went toward advertising. The efforts to pay for the campaigns benefited from a change in finance law that allowed individuals to donate $2,000 per candidate, up from $1,000 in earlier elections.[21] The public money a candidate collects is subject to election laws, but the "soft money," or funds from private organizations, such as labor unions, veterans groups, and others, is what makes tallying a total nearly impossible.

One research agency estimated that television ad spending for the presidential campaign from March 3 to October 28 rang in at $575 million, or about $2 million spent for each of the 270 electoral votes needed for victory. More than half the TV money went to five key states: Florida, Iowa, Ohio, Pennsylvania, and Wisconsin. In Ohio, for example, with 20 electoral votes in the contest, the television figures equated to the Democrats spending nearly $3.4 million per electoral vote and the Republicans $1.8 million.[22]

2000 Presidential Election

Republicans enjoyed a 2-to-1 cash advantage in the 2000 presidential campaign, which they used to bolster advertising in key battleground states. In response, labor unions and liberal organizations increased their spending. The soft money financed a great deal of the election efforts. One research firm estimated that the major political parties raised a combined $393 million in soft donations in 1999 and 2000, with the Republicans accounting for about $214 million and the Democrats $179 million. In contrast, traditional donations accounted for another $430 million, with the Republicans outpacing the Democrats: $275 million to $157 million.[23]

With pollsters predicting that the 2000 presidential election would come down to the wire, both parties increased last-minute television ad spending. The Republicans spent $10 million in Pennsylvania, Florida, and California, and the Democrats allocated $9 million in those same battleground states. With dozens of states in the balance—from Washington to Arkansas—both parties increased spending significantly, in addition to the various outside groups pushing for their respective candidates. The AFL-CIO spent $46 million on political activities to get out the vote for then-Vice President Al Gore, and the United States Chamber of Commerce raised $25 million to campaign for then-Texas Governor George W. Bush. Campaign finance experts predicted that the total combined spending for the presidential and Congressional races would exceed $3 billion.[24]

MEGA AGENCIES

What may shock readers is that a mere four multinational conglomerate advertising agencies—Omnicom, Interpublic, Publicis, and WPP—control more than 50 percent of the ad revenues worldwide. This statistic reflects that each one of these mega-firms owns dozens of smaller agencies (ranging from ad to public relations and boutique firms) that conduct business under their own name. For example, the St. Louis-based public relations agency Fleishman-Hillard is owned by Omnicom, as is its competitors Brodeur Worldwide, Ketchum, and Porter Novelli. The consolidation that occurred over the last decade makes this new big-agency era completely different than in the past. The range of choices has diminished, which plays into the public mindset that a small number of nefarious firms control the means for selling goods to innocent consumers.

An unsuspecting business owner, without knowing the background of a firm, might believe that it is a local or regional agency, when in actuality it is a subsidiary of one of the giants. In many cases, whenever a new business pitch occurs, different firms owned by the same mega-agency are competing against one another to win the business.

Omnicom

The 1986 merger of BBDO, Doyle Dane Bernbavck, and Needham Harper formed Omnicom. In that year, combined company revenues hit $754 million. By 2006, the conglomerate posted worldwide revenue of $11.4 billion and a net income topping $864 million. About 43 percent of total revenue came from traditional advertising media, 36 percent from customer relationship management, another 10 percent from public relations, and 11 percent from specialty communications.[25]

The particular talent of the ad firms within the Omnicom umbrella is creativity, demonstrated by BBDO Worldwide, DDB Worldwide, and TBWA Worldwide consistently ranking as the top three most-awarded agency networks globally. Omnicom also benefits from having the resources to invest in cutting edge technology, increasingly demanded by its corporate clients.

At a New York industry summit in December 2007, Omnicom chief executive officer John Wren discussed innovative work conducted for corporate clients General Electric, Target, and Mars that shows the way traditional advertising is changing in the wake of the Web. Rather than talk about television commercials, Wren pointed to efforts that stretched across media channels, including video clips and Web sites.

For example, ad firm BBDO built a Web site (www.becomeanmm.com) for Mars's M&M candies that initially enabled users to insert real photographs into pictures with the brand's animated characters. From there, the site morphed into a place to play online games, make movies, create new animated characters, and send online greeting cards. The highlight of the "Inner M" campaign was that consumers could create an M&M of themselves, virtually melding into the Mars brand. This kind of cross-channel work points to a new kind of advertising that uses technology to extend a consumer's time with the brand. Wren told *AdWeek,* "We earn our fees working for clients by doing what we've always been doing and by pushing it through all sorts of media."[26]

Even a multinational conglomerate like Omnicom faces potential challenges. The firm earns nearly 50 percent of its revenue from its 100 largest clients. The loss of several of these clients, combined with general global cutbacks, could dampen future growth. Geographically, Omnicom generates about 54 percent of its revenue in the United States, with about 21 percent generated in Europe, 11 percent in the United Kingdom, and the remaining 14 percent in other markets such as Asia.[27]

The mega agencies face a future that will most likely reward them for their size and scope, but perhaps also penalize them as well. The news media has responded to the threats it faces from declining readership and classified revenues by retrenching—shifting focus to hyper-local stories and programming. If this movement continues to develop, it is hard to imagine that the big firms will be able to compete in smaller locales scattered all over the nation and all over the world. In the mega agencies' favor, however, is that the transition to interactive, Web-based communications provides them with a way to use their resources to adapt. In addition, the mega agencies have the ability to go out and purchase the kind of expertise needed to thrive in a changing marketplace—in the form of hot startups, innovative firms, and local communications leaders—if necessary.

CELEBRITY ADVERTISING

The most enticing combination of popular culture and celebrity fascination takes place in advertising. Big money, iconic consumer brands, and famous individuals mean serious consequences for all parties involved. In the new millennium, celebrity advertising is growing more important. Even the stars themselves, who once shied away from shilling products in the United States, realize that serving as a spokesperson can have benefits in expanding one's "brand." For example, this kind of thinking takes into account the entire Nicole Kidman brand, or all the aspects of the actress's star power, from films and modeling work to appearances and product endorsements.

Top celebrity spokesperson Nicole Kidman at The 74th Annual Academy Awards (ABC) March 24, 2002. © AMPAS/ ABC. Courtesy of Photofest.

Tiger Woods is one of the world's top celebrity pitchers, hawking everything from Tag Heuer watches and Gillette razors to Gatorade Tiger sports drink and his own line of Nike golf clubs and accessories. Other top celebrity spokespeople include Kidman, Jessica Simpson, and Justin Timberlake. Some celebrities are less likely to appear in a commercial but will still be heard; for example, George Clooney lends his voice to promote Budweiser.

A change in the 2000s is that advertising agencies, companies, and celebrities now view the relationship as a partnership, each hoping to benefit from the association with the other. Bill Cosby and Michael Jordan served as early innovators in this regard. Consumers actually liked them more after seeing them in commercials, whether for Gatorade or Jell-O. "Over the years the trend has slowly shifted from using models to celebrities to endorse products because regardless of what's going on in the world of luxury, celebrities sell," explains Ryan Schinman, president of Platinum Rye Entertainment, a firm that negotiates talent buys for companies and advertising agencies. "Of course, each celebrity has their own characteristics, so their image and lifestyle has to be in tune with the brand. Some are hits, some are misses."[28]

Kidman's work with Chanel No. 5 symbolizes the way a celebrity can transform a brand. The company made the actress the face of the fragrance in 2004 for $12 million. She later starred in a commercial directed by film-maker Baz Luhrmann, shot for an estimated $46 million, making it one of the most expensive ads in history. The gamble paid off—as revenues jumped 16 percent after Kidman joined. Her appeal as a celebrity opened the fragrance to a different, younger demographic and translated into sales. The partnership certainly has a significant financial component, ac-cording to journalist Nicola Ruiz, "Endorsement money is key to a star's bank account. Celebrities, many of whom make between $10 million and $20 million for months of work on a movie set or while on a yearlong concert tour, are cashing in on ad campaigns that can pay as much as $3 million for a day's work."[29]

Another indicator of America's star-craze is that even most bad publicity does not really hurt the products celebrities promote. A 2006 survey by the Luxury Institute revealed that 42 percent of respondents said that a dam-aged celebrity image would not have a negative effect on future purchases. Perhaps this rationale explains why infamous celebrities, such as Pamela Anderson, Paris Hilton, Martha Stewart, and others, continue to receive endorsement deals even after their reputation hits the skids.[30]

THE FUTURE OF ADVERTISING

Although advertising and marketing play a critical role in getting prod-ucts and services in the hands of consumers, advertising is still at the mercy of broader financial considerations such as the looming recession late in the decade. As businesses respond to the growing crisis in the consumer real estate industry, many are pulling back ad expenses. This decision, however, is fraught with complications. For many executives, the move to Web-based ads is a way to hit their target demographics, but this comes at the expense of traditional mediums, such as newspapers, magazines, and radio.

According to Robert J. Cohen, senior vice president and director of fore-casting at Universal McCann, ad spending reached $283.9 billion in 2007, a less than 1 percent gain over the previous year. This increase is the small-est since a recession rocked the industry in 2001. Between 2005 and 2006, for example, ad spending growth reached nearly 4 percent. If there is a bright spot in the storm, Internet expenditures grew by 20 percent from 2006 to 2007.[31]

Another bonus for the advertising industry is the dual-headed monster of the 2008 primaries and presidential election and the Summer Games Olympics in China. Steve King, worldwide chief executive at ZenithOpti-media, estimates that the Olympics will add an additional $3 billion in the global ad economy. He also sees another $2 billion derived from spending by the political candidates.[32]

Ultimately, corporations will push into every area they can—if they feel that it will help them build the brand or sell products. Some of the iconic brands attempting to sell via social media sites have basically nothing to do with the Internet, such as Pepperidge Farm cookies, but that does not mean that savvy marketers won't attempt to use new technology. Pepperidge Farms targeted women in its online campaign, emphasizing a message that cookies help women reconnect with their friends. On the other side of the spectrum, underwear and clothing company Jockey focused on young men. These disparate examples provide a glimpse into the future of advertising, one in which the push of an ad is replaced by the lure of a conversation and the excitement of interaction.

4

Architecture

When industries are competing at equal price and functionality, design is the only differential that matters.
—Mark Dziersk, Industrial Designers Society of America (2000)

Architecture is towering skyscrapers of twisting steel, gleaming glass facades stretching over multiple stories, and a rainbow of colors, shapes, and designs used to make buildings interesting. From another viewpoint, architecture is how a home fits into a subdivision, the type of roofing materials used based on locale, and the size of individual rooms. In other words, architecture encompasses a wide variety of topics that influences people's lives each day, ranging from their own home or apartment to the buildings where they work, shop, eat, and go for entertainment.

The biggest news in architecture in the 2000s was the explosion of the real estate market. As interest rates fell to historic lows, suddenly people all across the nation could buy and/or build their dream homes. Architects and homebuilders responded by changing the way residential homes looked. Big was in—"great" rooms, large chandeliers, oversized entryways, multicar garages, giant picture windows, and other features dominated the "McMansions" of the day.

Then the real estate market crashed back down to earth and effectively took the national economy with it. What seemed like a minor correction in 2005 and 2006 suddenly took on epic proportions. The fall triggered widespread alarm and cast a shadow on every industry even loosely affiliated with real estate.

As the decade nears its end, no one is confident that the real estate business will turn around any time soon. Optimists point to 2009, but as each succeeding month reveals more mortgage defaults and foreclosures nationwide, the doom-and-gloom scenario looks even worse. Other observers predict that the housing market will never recover or gain back the value it lost in 2007 and 2008. Certainly there are millions of Americans experiencing foreclosure, bankruptcy, and increased debt that are barely holding on. Some of these people will never recoup their losses or rebound from the black mark this debacle places on their credit history.

TRENDS

The United States is not one big architectural science lab churning out the same products over and over again. Instead, trends unfold regionally, meaning that what is taking place in New York may or may not resonate in Los Angeles, Atlanta, or Boston. What one is more inclined to find, actually, is diversity and microtrends based on a variety of factors, from the local economic picture to population density. As a result, Pittsburgh's focus may be on redesigning part of its waterfront based on new professional football and baseball stadiums recently built, while in San Francisco efforts concentrate on new public spaces and museums.

Celebrity architects, such as Frank Gehry and Renzo Piano will always attract international attention and significant media coverage, but in most markets it is the smaller design firms that act as change agents. These local and regional architects are the ones designing and building new public buildings, educational centers, company headquarters, and perhaps the most influential architectural work, people's homes and apartment buildings.

So there is a balance in American architecture between the big-name architects usually working in the large metropolitan areas and the lesser-known activities taking place in the rest of the country. Even within these categories, however, important influences cross boundaries, so one finds Gehry designing a new business school at Case Western Reserve University in Cleveland and a building spree taking over Clearwater, Florida, which is changing the way people interact with the waterfront and beaches. In Los Angeles, local architects and designers are re-creating the city's former industrial areas, while at the same time , celebrity architects work on iconic public and private buildings.

City Trends

Many cities in the United States face a similar challenge: how to deal with the limitations of expansion. The large urban centers across the nation were built on waterways and at transportation hubs that now restrict how they grow. For example, Los Angeles's problem in the new millennium is urbanism. People continue to move into the city, but Los Angeles can no longer continue to gobble up surrounding areas and its western edge is the Pacific Ocean. Consequently, the city is redefining itself and taking measures to confront the challenges.

In a city notorious for sprawl, Los Angeles is taking steps to reconnect people. One effort is studying potential mass transit options that will alleviate the traffic on the intricate highways surrounding the city. Another is creating shared spaces, such as the plaza at the Nokia theater, which allows for interaction and spontaneous growth.

Chicago, the birthplace of the modern skyscraper and stomping grounds of Frank Lloyd Wright, confronts a series of urban issues that have little to do with big-name architects. Rather, the city is in the midst of building community-centered projects, such as John Ronan's Gary Comer Youth Center. These buildings must take into account the needs of a diverse clientele who have specific needs. Another problem Chicago and other cities across the nation face, according to journalist Blair Kamin, is the boom in often drab condominiums. "These are the buildings that are killing cities," he says, "and giving us this problem of density without urbanity."[1]

Tremendous growth in Atlanta forced city planners and developers to react to the city's changing face. The trendy Buckhead area, which used to be a near-suburb, essentially morphed into another part of the city. A local developer, Novare Group, purchased a nine-acre site in the area to build retail stores, offices, and luxury condos. Catherine Fox, an architecture critic and journalist, says, "The architecture isn't great, but the project shows the ambitions of the developer."[2]

Whereas many cities start and stammer to confront transportation issues, Atlanta is building BeltLine, a 22-mile transit line that wraps around the city to connect 45 neighborhoods. Included in the transit system are a series of parks, bikeways, and plazas. Developers are gobbling up areas near the BeltLine, which holds great potential in revitalizing the already rejuvenated city core. "The BeltLine could become the city's civic symbol, linking the past and present even as it shapes the future," Fox explains. She is concerned, however: "There is no coherent design vision. The question now is: Will the BeltLine be more than just a transportation project?"[3]

As of early 2008, BeltLine is in the midst of a $60 million capital campaign to raise money toward its projected $2.8 billion price tag over 25 years. The Georgia Supreme Court ruled that school property tax money could not be used in building the transit system, however, eliminating $850 million that city officials expected to come from future school taxes. Atlanta Mayor Shirley Franklin and other civic leaders remain committed to the BeltLine, but the court decision makes implantation more difficult.

Homeownership Trends

The Joint Center for Housing Studies of Harvard University assesses the nation's housing situation with support from a variety of public and private sources, including the National Association of Home Build-ers, Freddie Mac, and the National Association of Realtors. Despite the gloomy news emerging from the real estate meltdown and credit crunch, it expects the long-term growth of homeownership between 2005 and 2015 to reach about 19.5 million units, compared to 18.1 million between 1995 and 2005. The factors contributing to this growth range from pro-jected healthy income growth to the influx of immigrants and resulting boom in their native-born children.[4]

Although the forecasted figures are encouraging, the report's analysis of housing affordability is not. In a single year, the number of households that spent more than 30 percent of total income on housing jumped by 2.3 million. Overall in 2005, 37.3 million households fell into this category, a new record. Once similar figures are released for the years since, then that record will surely fall as well. Income growth for most Americans simply cannot keep pace with home expenses, including insurance, taxes, and other components that make up the monthly mortgage payment.[5]

On the positive side of the equation, time is on the side of the housing market. In the next decade, baby boomers will enter a phase when many will purchase second homes and the echo boomers (born 1981 to 2001) will recharge the market as they enter prime home buying years. Immi-gration is expected to continue its growth patterns and the offspring of recent immigrants will look to their slice of the American dream. In the new millennium, immigrants accounted for 14 percent of purchases, and another 18 percent of foreign-born renters stand poised to enter the real estate market.[6]

The real estate boom that ended in the mid-2000s essentially put a halt to the nation's rapid economic growth since the 2001 recession. According to the Harvard study, "The drop in home building was so drastic that it shaved more than a full percentage point off national economic growth in the latter half of 2006. As a result, residential fixed investment went from being a significant contributor to growth to a major drag on the economy."[7]

In attempting to find some way to benefit from the downturn, home-owners took advantage of low interest rates to refinance in 2005 and 2006. In all, 85 percent of people who refinanced did so to draw cash out of their homes, the highest level witnessed since the 1991 reces-sion. Between 2001 and 2005, home equity money grew by 31 percent, reaching $10.9 trillion. In the same period, investment and improvement figures jumped 23.6 percent to $228.2 billion. These numbers indicate that although people realized that the housing meltdown prevented them from selling their homes, those with steady, secure incomes could use low interest rates to either remodel or refinance. If housing contin-ues to depreciate, however, these options will not be factors for many households.[8]

REBUILDING AT THE WORLD TRADE CENTER

The terrorist attacks on September 11 took away one of the world's most recognizable buildings. The battle over what would replace it captured imaginations, eventually turning into the biggest prize on a grand scale in the industry. The decision regarding what to build on the World Trade Center site, however, also turned into a focal point of criticism and contempt. Acrimonious negotiations between local and regional authorities further delayed building. Over time, however, the controversy diminished and construction began in late 2006 on the $2.4 billion, 1,776 foot "Freedom Tower" structure, scheduled for completion in 2012. The rest of the World Trade Center site includes four additional skyscrapers (Towers 2, 3, 4, and 5), the National September 11 Memorial & Museum, the World Trade Center Transportation Hub, a retail hub, and a performing arts center.

Designed by David M. Childs of famed architectural firm Skidmore, Owings & Merrill, Freedom Tower will be a 2.6 million square foot building that replaces the double towers of the original World Trade Center with a single spire. The new building will feature a 50-foot high public lobby rising up from the plaza level, followed by 69 office floors that lift the elevation to 1,120 feet. There will be a symbolic metal-and-glass parapet at the 1,362 feet and 1,368 feet levels, the heights of the original twin towers. "The tower is an open, welcoming building that both radiates light and is filled with light. Our design team has achieved our goal of creating a great urban place—a building that serves the people who work in it, welcomes those who visit it, and plays an integral and vibrant role in the city that surrounds it," says Childs.[9]

World Trade Center developer Larry A. Silverstein assembled a world-renowned team of architects to design the buildings and grounds of the site. Lord Norman Foster is designing Tower 2, and Lord Richard Rogers (Tower 3) and Fumihiko Maki (Tower 4) lead the efforts on the other primary skyscrapers. Michael Arad is designing the World Trade Center Memorial, and Frank Gehry is heading work on the World Trade Center Performing Arts Center.

Emotions still run high concerning the design and construction on the site of the terrorist attacks. The *New Yorker*'s Paul Goldberger calls the World Trade Center redesign at Ground Zero, "a sad story." Rather than appeal to the sanctity of the area, he explains, "In many ways, it merely reflects where we are today. It's a commercial development, not a civic place. And it isn't effective urban design." Goldberger sees the challenges with Ground Zero as emblematic of larger problems faced in the architectural profession today. He calls it, "withdrawal, even abandonment, of large-scale planning by the public sector." Corporate partners quickly step into the void and, in many cases, enable the private sector to overtake projects, ultimately deciding what gets built. "At the end of the day, it's not real planning," Goldberger says. "What we're seeing is the development of parallel infrastructures—one built by the private sector and one by the public. I can imagine a time in the future when some people might have little interaction with the public infrastructure."[10]

One of the most critical challenges for the new World Trade Center is safety, the same issue that confronts architects and designers worldwide in the post-9/11 era. Skyscrapers and other significant buildings serve as primary targets for terror. According to journalist Nicolai Ouroussoff, the new Freedom Tower represents the need for safety in a world filled with possible horrors, explaining that it "rests on a 20-story, windowless fortified concrete base decorated in prismatic glass panels in a grotesque attempt to disguise its underlying paranoia. And the brooding, obelisk-like form above is more of an expression of American hubris than of freedom."[11]

THE AMERICAN HOME

Owning a home remains a fundamental tenet of the American Dream. Historically low interest rates and creative adjustable-rate mortgage loans in the early part of the decade gave Americans the opportunity to purchase homes at record rates. As more financiers artificially pumped money into the real estate market, the value of homes jumped, enabling even more refinancing and "cashing out" to occur. People often used the money to finance improvements or as down payment on a second home or larger house in a better neighborhood. Either way, the run up in values, combined with low interest rates and creative financing served as the tinder for the real estate fire sale taking place in the latter years of the decade. Despite the challenges people faced, homes still serve as an aspiration or statement of one's standing. Moreover, housing remains a critical component of the popular culture landscape.

In the early 2000s, people did not have to surf Internet realty sites or wait for the homes section of the Sunday paper to imagine living this fantasy. Instead, they could flip to any number of television programs and channels, such as *Trading Spaces* and HGTV, which featured young hip designers, planners, builders, and architects ready to help them vicariously realize their homeowner dreams. For those who preferred glossy magazines, they could visit the newsstand and pick up trendy remodeling and building magazines, like *Cachet, Real Simple,* and *Dwell.* Hundreds of other regional and city-specific home and luxury magazines gave everyone access to the notion that a home can be a piece of art, while still functional and fun.

TV shows and magazines brought the notion of upgrading and remodeling to the masses. Also contributing to the craze, big box remodeling stores such as Lowe's and Home Depot became destination spots for weekend handymen and women, running seminars on topics from installing granite kitchen counters to upgrading bathroom fixtures.

Host Paige Davis of the popular Trading Spaces *(TLC). TLC/Photofest. © TLC. Courtesy of Photofest.*

The focus on remodeling served as a cornerstone of the housing craze leading up to the subprime mortgage meltdown later in the decade. The value of homes rose sharply as demand outstripped supply. Many millions of homeowners refinanced to take advantage of the low rates and used the cash from the transaction on their homes. This translated into room add-ons, upgrades across the board, and other attempts at adding to one's home.

While all these large forces swirled through the minds of homeowners and those attempting to buy into the American Dream, the idea of what a home meant changed after the 9/11 terrorist attacks. Suddenly, the magical feeling of safety sleeping in one's own bed took on new urgency. According to journalist Bill Saporito, "The national tragedy of 9/11 reinforced a trend that was already under way: the home is not just everyone's castle, it's becoming a resort, an island of comfort in an ocean of insecurity. It's command central for the modern family in all its configurations, the place to huddle, socialize and strategize in an increasingly complex world."[12]

The renewed desire for safety and tranquility away from the chaotic nature of daily life increased the popularity of communal spaces where families could congregate. Floor plans for both pricey homes and those more modest in scale included "great rooms," large, high-ceilinged rooms that were centrally located and viewable from several other parts of the house, and, most important, the kitchen. Also, more builders included office spaces in new homes, providing residents with the option to work from home.

With families thinking about safety and togetherness, the kitchen served as the hub of activities, after decades of secondary status in most housing designs. Kacey Fitzpatrick, a home designer and consultant based in California, called the kitchen: "The meeting place, the eating place, the social gathering place, the communications exchange," adding that, "The new layouts reflect the inherent need of family members to be near the headquarters."[13]

In previous decades, great bathrooms or additional square footage topped the homeowner wish lists. In the 2000s, however, gleaming, full of ego kitchens replaced those desires. Normal people who rarely cooked compared to their parents' generation suddenly had to have a Sub-Zero refrigerator and a Viking range. Designers knocked out walls to open the newly luxurious kitchens up to the living or great room, usually adding a breakfast nook that enabled additional gathering opportunities.

The other great trend in the American home during the decade transformed the master bedroom into a dazzling "suite," with adjoining exercise rooms, sitting areas, computer areas, and multiple walk-in closets. Showers in the master bathroom also benefited from the opulence, with state-of-the-art showerheads and other gadgetry that changed the way people bathed.

DESIGN

Economic prosperity and design walk hand-in-hand. The financial boom that occurred during the early years of the new millennium not only pumped money into the coffers of people in the upper income brackets but also provided more disposable income in general. Suddenly, wealth meant more than being rich—"wealthy" became an aim. People across economic groups wanted to seem well-to-do, whether that meant buying fashions that were similar to what they saw on television or owning the same kind of Sub-Zero refrigerator as a celebrity.

Corporations recognized the public's fascination with wealth and eagerly stepped in to provide both real luxury items and faux knockoffs, depending on what individuals could spend. In one sense, "wealth" underwent democratization—giving more people access to items they deemed important. The fixation, however, also turned the nation away from more fundamental ideas of what constitutes a good life and replaced them with an obsession with money and fame.

In 2000, *Time* magazine dubbed America's obsession with faux wealthy style the "design economy." Explaining the term, it stated, "[Design] is the crossroads where prosperity and technology meet culture and marketing. These days efficient manufacturing and intense competition have made 'commodity chic' not just affordable but also mandatory. Americans are likely to appreciate style when they see it and demand it when they don't, whether in boutique hotels or kitchen scrub brushes." According to Dziersk, president of the Industrial Designers Society of America, "This is the new Golden Age of design." Approximately 20 percent of the $6 trillion Americans spent on consumer goods in 1999–2000 went into purchases for their homes.[14]

An interesting aspect of the democratization of design is that people with money to burn did not necessarily buy designer name products in droves like they did in the Wall Street-fueled 1980s. Instead, they attempted to fill their super-sized homes with kitschy items that expressed some level of individuality. As a result, designers and manufacturers designed items that represented certain ideas that people then bought to say something specific about themselves. For example, Apple introduced personal computers with splashes of color, replacing the staid beige traditionally used for monitors. Stores like Ikea and Pottery Barn mass produced home décor options but offered enough varieties so that shoppers felt some degree of personalization and customization, yet at a more modest price. "Manufacturers recognize that consumers are looking for more than functional benefits," said Barry Shepard, co-founder of SHR Perceptual Management, the design consultancy that helped conceive the Volkswagen Beetle. "A product that matters needs to say something about the person who owns it."[15]

After decades of losing out in discount pricing wars with Wal-Mart, Target changed course and became the "it" store of the 2000s based on the seemingly simple notion that offering less expensive designer knock-offs would attract consumers. The company launched product lines with famous designers such as Michael Graves, Isaac Mizrahi, and Mossimo Giannulli, which overhauled Target's reputation almost overnight.

Larger, Eco-Friendly, and Bold

Interior design in the late 2000s takes its cue from the larger culture, particularly the green movement and a desire for eco-friendly products. Popular trends include expanding the boundaries of the home outside the traditional interior space, filling homes with earth-friendly products, and using colors and patterns that represent a Californian or Southwestern flair.

Nationwide—even in cold climate regions—people are dressing up outside areas and essentially turning them into extra rooms. The focal point for many of these, just like the traditional home, is the kitchen. As a result, people are installing large, high-powered stainless steel grills that dwarf the kitchen stove, as well as outdoor fireplaces that are used for both atmosphere and cooking. Others purchase outdoor stoves and actually use it to replace their one inside. Cathy Whitlock, an interior designer in Nashville, says, "This trend to indoor-outdoor living seems to be going strong. I notice more and more homeowners wanting screened-in porches, particularly with outdoor fireplaces."[16]

The furniture used to decorate newly minted outdoor living rooms is considerably upscale compared with the weaved plastic and aluminum chairs and billowy lounges most people grew up with. Designers recognized the need for more luxurious outdoor furniture and responded with bright colors, use of tiled tabletops, and soft fabrics and cushions. In terms of the color palette of outdoor furniture, varieties of green (celadon to avocado) are popular. Many consumers are also turning to more natural kinds of shading, which combines one's desire to live a green lifestyle with the necessity for shielding outdoor sitting areas.

The move toward eco-friendly consciousness is one of the central themes in popular culture in the new millennium. The totality of the movement ranges from using natural fibers in pillows to adding recycled materials to concrete and drywall. Consumers' demand for attractiveness along with green living led to many producers reinventing their products for the new century. For example, GE and Sharp created new solar panels that do not detract from the picturesque nature of a home. Rather than sit on top of shingles, technological advances and a better understanding of today's customers enabled builders to streamline them seamlessly into the roofing system.[17]

Remodeling Meltdown

The remodeling boom that took place in the years leading up to the real estate meltdown seems like a distant memory in 2008. Across most of the nation, even those at the top of the economic ladder are growing more cautious about big expenditures. Wealthy homeowners are usually the last to halt remodeling projects, as they have more disposable income and can weather financial instability better than those squeaking by basically living month-to-month. As a result, some areas are bucking the trend and still have big-ticket remodels on the books. The Tampa-St. Petersburg area is one example of a region getting hit hard by the real estate crash, but yet plowing money back into high-end homes.

According to Kermit Baker, director of the Remodeling Futures Program at Harvard University, people usually begin remodeling as soon as they buy a new home. Therefore with fewer houses being sold, remodeling is taking a hit. Another critical factor is home value, which also drops during a period when inventory exceeds demand. Homeowners face little incentive to pump money back into their places when they do not foresee getting a substantial return on investment. Finally, the fact that home equity lines of credit and other loans traditionally used for remodeling are harder to get is swaying people away from such projects.[18]

In 2006, the residential remodeling industry hit $228 billion, a figure that doubled the total from the mid-1990s. In the South, the average remodeling project jumped from $1,131 in 1996 to $1,566 in 2006, a 44 percent increase. Baker's research, however, predicts that the remodeling industry will continue to drop at an annual rate of 2.6 percent through 2008. A more concrete example of the drop off in residential remodeling projects comes from Home Depot. The giant hardware chain reported its first annual revenue decline, dropping from $79 billion in 2006 to $77.4 billion in 2007. Daniel E. Ashline, who owns a remodeling company in St. Petersburg, Florida, explains: "Things are not as robust as they were 18 months ago. It's not like it was . . . 2005 was still good, and 2006 was better, but last year was just even. This year we'll do 70 percent of what we normally do." Other Florida remodeling firms report sales declines 50 percent and being forced to lay off workers as a result.[19]

OFFICE SPACE(S) AND SKYSCRAPERS

Whether people love or hate corporations, they are fascinated with the majestic buildings and skyscrapers business leaders build in homage to their companies (and often themselves). Complicit in these striking structures are the superstar architects that turned into celebrities in their own right over the last several decades. Leading the pack is Frank Gehry, who rose to international prominence with the design of buildings worldwide, including the Solomon R. Guggenheim Museum in Bilbao, Spain. As a matter of fact, Gehry is arguably the most famous living architect in the world.

The famed designer's influence is seen nationwide in buildings that highlight curved features, warped steel, and extensive use of glass. The focal points of Gehry's buildings, such as the Peter B. Lewis Building (2002), at Case Western Reserve University in Cleveland, Ohio, showcase intricate ribbon patterns that some observers liken to an exploding wrapped present. The beauty of a Gehry design is its ability to make brick, concrete, and glass come alive with a lightness that seems impossible. The sloped exteriors and bold uses of curves are Gehry's signature designs, so now clients who hire him expect that they will get the full Gehry treatment. On the flipside, however, the trademark style has led some critics to say that he just repeats his design of the Guggenheim over and over.

In the new millennium, Gehry's international acclaim led to projects across the globe. In the United States, he began the decade with the Experience Music Project in Seattle. Gehry designed another high profile venue in his home area, the Walt Disney Concert Hall (2003) in Los Angeles. On December 6, 2006, California Governor Arnold Schwarzenegger inducted Gehry into the California Hall of Fame.

In 2007, the IAC Building, Gehry's first building in the Big Apple opened along the West Side Highway in New York City. The corporate

The Walt Disney Concert Hall in Los Angeles, designed by famed architect Frank Gehry. Sony Pictures Classics/Photofest. © Fernando Gomez. Courtesy of Photofest.

headquarters for IAC, the e-commerce conglomerate run by media mogul Barry Diller, reflects the cutting-edge nature of the Web giant, which includes Expedia.com, Ask.com, LendingTree, and the Home Shopping Network (HSN). The corporate interior of the building provides a view of the Hudson River, accentuating the waterfront appeal so desired by corporate bigwigs.[20]

From a distance, the IAC Building looks as if it is shimmering up out of the ground like sheer curtains blowing in the wind, but at the same time it features a solid rectangular foundation that exudes strength. On closer inspection, the initial understanding of the building's compact power is underscored by its sloped and angled framework, so bent and at odds with the eye that one can hardly imagine that its underbelly is concrete.

FABRICATING "URBAN" CENTERS

Nostalgia for an imagined past drives so much current architecture, particularly when it involves public spaces. One trend playing out across the nation is the movement to build urban-looking downtowns in suburban settings to mimic the appearance of an urban setting. These faux urban environments (often called "town centers") are designed to provide consumers and/or residents with a feeling of a downtown center, but within the safety net of the suburbs.

In Tampa, for example, many of these fake towns are actually disguised shopping malls, built to resemble quaint downtown areas. Typically, these centers are created near large (often gated) housing developments in the well-to-do suburbs, thus providing easy access to shopping, dining, and entertainment for the residents of the subdivision. Some have a small-town feel, and others are clearly derivative of Bourbon Street in New Orleans. Actually, many resemble a scene from Universal Studios or Disneyland.

In Lakewood, Colorado, the shopping center is dubbed a "lifestyle center," what journalist Jamie Reno calls, "an idealized vision of an urban streetscape, with 22 open-air blocks of cafes, performance spaces, offices, housing, parks, and, of course, chain stores familiar to anyone who's spent time in the Galleria (can you say Sharper Image and Victoria's Secret?)."[21] Lakewood happened to be just one of several hundred such lifestyle centers going up around the nation, stretching from Washington, D.C., to Phoenix. The trend is pushed by large shopping mall developers to appeal to baby boomers, who are nostalgic for urban life, as long as it's in the safe confines of suburbia.

Otay Ranch Town Center opened near San Diego in Chula Vista, California, in late 2007 and drew a crowd of 80,000. The lifestyle center featured an outdoor fireplace, child play areas, and a doggie park, along with a slew of shopping outlets. Built by mall developer General Growth Properties, Otay Ranch also has a code of conduct that prohibits skateboarding, swearing, spitting, and congregating in large groups, in other words, restrictions designed to eliminate behaviors people do not like about city life. A man who bought a condo at the California site explained, "It gives you the feeling that you're in a city, but you don't worry about the drunks on the streets."[22]

The town center movement in the Pittsburgh region takes nostalgia one step further—building small town feel within already preexisting small towns. In the suburbs east of the city, developers are building new communities that offer people an escape from modern life's hustle and bustle. Audrey Guskey, a professor at Duquesne University in Pittsburgh, explains: "Everyone is so busy in life—there's so many things to do—that people just want to have that community, that place to go, somewhere like *Cheers*, where everyone knows your name." Guskey views the town center movement in a positive light, saying, "A trend like this is perfect for Pittsburgh. Pittsburgh's like a small town, and people in this area like the feeling of being a part of a community. It's a fun trend . . . a great trend."[23]

In Irwin, a Pittsburgh suburb, the town center work focuses on revitalizing the business district using grant money that city planners hope will enhance the area and attract new businesses. Some of the decisions involved are aesthetic, such as installing all underground wires, thus eliminating potentially unsightly overhead lines. Others require more effort, like devising strategic plans that will attract younger residents. In Plum, a suburb spread out over 29 square miles, a town center built from scratch would draw the community together in ways never before possible. "I really think people are looking for that," says Rich Hrivnak, Mayor of Plum. "They want that sense of community. They want that one place they can go and come together as a community. I think of like Mayberry, with a town hall, an area with a quaint feel to it."[24]

5

Fashion

> Everyone knows the business is sluggish. Somehow they have to keep
> the excitement level up. It's hard for designers to do that . . . But it's
> hard to imagine changing back to a time when the same clothes are in
> stores for four months or more.
>
> —Hope Greenberg (2008)

In the new millennium, fashion is not just stereotypical, waif-thin runway
models flaunting the latest Parisian styles. The idea of fashion goes well
beyond these traditional limitations, although runways and haute couture
are certainly a large part of the industry. Fashion in this decade may better
be defined as a person possessing a sense of style, which is tied directly to
the wider pop culture influences on one's daily life. As a result, fashion is
currently a more important part of everyday life for most Americans than
in the past.

Access to mass media certainly affects style choices, from television
shows, films, and commercials to what one sees on the Web. Drop into
any upscale department store. The endless choices will either dazzle or
depress the innocent shopper just looking for something to wear to work
next Tuesday or for a night out on the town. Journalist Sharon Fink calls
this phenomenon "fashion overload." She breaks the average woman's
fashion needs down to its essentials: "We want basics, kept stylish and
up-to-date; a few well-chosen trends; and a couple of splurges. And we
want it all to fit well."[1]

Perhaps the virtually unlimited access to fashion and trends via movies,
television, and the Internet made designers think that they needed to expand the types of clothes available. They may have hoped to throw many
styles into the system and then waited to see what consumers picked,

rather than offer a limited range of choices. Fink believes the fickle nature and quick boredom of shoppers are at the heart of the challenge. "We love to buy. We get bored easily. And once we got hooked on the fast turnover of styles at chains like Express and Target, everyone from top designers down were forced to crank out as much variety as possible to keep us interested and spending," she said.[2]

DISCOUNT SHOPPING

Novato, California, is located 30 miles north of San Francisco, straight up Highway 101 after crossing over the Golden Gate Bridge. The town's nearly 50,000 inhabitants occupy the northernmost section of well-heeled Marin County, one of the richest areas in the United States. Despite the countless million-dollar homes that dot its hillsides, Novato is actually a blue-collar oasis in the heart of this affluent madness. Nestled between the city and Napa Valley wine country to the north, the town is certainly the closest thing to "normal" in Marin, if not the entire San Francisco Bay area.

Just about any day of the week, the most hopping spot in Novato is Vintage Oaks Shopping Center, a couple miles south of the city, and a convenient exit just off busy 101. By mid-morning on any given weekend a sea of bright, shiny SUVs pushes latecomers to the farthest nether regions of the parking lot, forcing them to sadly wade through a multitude of orphaned shopping carts and dodge other dawdlers on the way to the door.

What's all the fuss at Vintage Oaks? Among its 50 stores, the colossal plaza is home to the two-headed discount shopping monster of Target and Costco. These stores have come to define Novato. Target and Costco give the town an identity distinct from its wealthy neighbors in the southern portion of the county, not only openly inviting a different economic class of shopper to the area, but also a melting pot of workers to staff the stores.

The Target experience is all about brand and image. Drop a shopper in front of any Target across the nation and that person should have a similar experience and feeling as he/she walks through the shiny red doors. The famous Target bull's eye is about more than the merchandise within the store; it is about branding the franchise itself, thus giving shoppers a uniquely Target experience on every visit.

Earlier in its history, Target attracted shoppers searching for bargain merchandise, such as the special on the 300-ounce Tide laundry detergent for $16.88. Over the last decade, however, Target's unique ability to redefine itself as a central point for hip culture enabled it to become a destination for consumers searching for the latest fashion styles and trends.

The Novato Target is a jumble of scurrying workers, shoppers streaming by with red-orange carts, kids crammed into the snack bar, and packed checkout lanes. Target has spent billions of dollars branding its bull's eye logo and unique apple red tint. The result is a constant sea of red everywhere you turn.

A quarter mile down the strip, past the Old Navy, various small beauty shops, and the sporting goods store sits Costco, the king of discount warehouses. The Novato store, like others across the nation, is a cultural wonderland.

There are few assurances in life and most of them are bad, like DMV lines always being long and the mechanic's bill totaling at least $500. In Novato, like places around the nation that have a Costco, there is another certainty—the Costco lot is always full. Nothing slows down Costco shoppers, not a freak blizzard, torrential downpour, or beautiful summer day in which they should be out enjoying the sunshine.

The scene at Costco is utter chaos. Here comes a middle-age woman who must be 5'4" and not much more than 100 pounds pushing an oversize cart filled with giant jugs of olive oil, cases of wine and Diet Coke, various hardcover books, large stacks of boxed food, and just like 90 percent of the people exiting Costco, the ever-present, mammoth package of toilet paper precariously balancing on top. The cart must weigh in at about 200 pounds, easily doubling her weight. She's not only struggling against the weight of the cart on its little frail wheels, but she can't see over the mountain of merchandise. This is a lawsuit waiting to happen—perhaps the smartest thing to do is to park far, far away.

Inside, Costco is a Spartan warehouse. Unlike Target, which sells its own corporate brand as diligently as the wares it carries, the emphasis at Costco is on products and prices. Every nook and cranny is filled with something to buy, whether stacked from cement floor to ceiling on simple metal shelves or on barebones tables that look like they survived your Aunt Elma's last trip to the flea market.

At the end of each row, shoppers may find jars of peanut butter as big as buckets or cases of off-brand shampoo amassed on wooden skids. The Costco experience is shopping stripped to its essence. The message is direct, screaming, "bargain" to the masses picking over its wares. No wonder more than 25 percent of American households are card-carrying Costco members.

Costco doesn't make its customers work to find a deal, but they do have to pile up the mileage as they wander through the isles thick with merchandise. Each twist and turn not only provides a new opportunity for finding a treasure, but also for saving money. This combination is a powerful incentive for middle class shoppers, despite the bare surroundings and long checkout lines that fly in the face of usual demands for high standards of customer care and pampering.

The magic in the Costco experience—making it worthwhile to put up with the crowds and cramped parking—is that it provides grownups with the feeling of a genuine treasure hunt. The "wow" factor, like finding the latest James Patterson novel for less than half price or saving hundreds of dollars on the family's grocery bill through bulk purchases, makes Costco an exciting place to shop. Perhaps some members get slightly woozy when their bill is totaled, but even the shock of plopping down $300 or $400 is softened by the cherished perception that the word "bargain" can be slapped on every item. Costco makes people feel like they got their money's worth.

And what becomes of our friend from the parking lot, the woman valiantly struggling against the weight of her purchases? After loading up her sleek, black Chevy Tahoe, she eventually makes her way back to her subdivision, listening to a message on her cell phone from her daughter Taylor about ballet practice. Arriving home, she finds her son, Jordan playing basketball with his friends in the driveway. As she pulls into the garage, the middle school boys flip open the hatch and take turns carrying boxes and other loose items into the kitchen.

Once Mom gets the haul corralled, the boys go back to their game, each with a can of pop and a handful of cookies from the trip. Letting her mind wander as she fills the pantry and cupboards, she begins to tick off about how much she saved on each item. A little smile forms as she realizes that the total surpasses $250. She can't wait to tell her husband once he gets home from the office.

Not only did Mom save money, she feels great about her Costco trip. She bought the staples essential to running her household, planned family meals, and even picked up a few small gifts for the holiday season. Most important, however, she uncovered bargains. The extra money can be put toward the family's next vacation or into the costs of raising kids quickly approaching their teenage years.

The scenario just described isn't unique—it reveals a trend being played out in homes from coast to coast. Over the years, our thought process as consumers has changed. The shopping ritual has developed into more than merely acquiring life's essentials. Quite the contrary, shopping gives people hope and a sense of control over their lives. They choose items that reflect their own self-image and call out to one's dreams and aspirations.

According to shopping guru Paco Underhill, "If we went into stores only when we needed to buy something, and if once there we bought only what we needed, the economy would collapse, boom." Instead, a shopping revolution took place, fueled by the nation's increased wealth since World War II. "The economic party," Underhill explains, "has fostered more shopping than anyone would have predicted, more shopping than has ever taken place anywhere at any time."[3]

Discount shopping, whether it takes place at Wal-Mart, Costco, or The Dollar Store, takes the experience one step further. A person ventures into Wal-Mart for several reasons, but the primary draws are widespread selection and "everyday low prices." The variety of items fulfills the aesthetic craving, and the lower cost appeals to the feelings of vindication consumers attain when they've saved a buck.

Discount shopping triggers some inherently American values—the availability of an endless assortment of goods and the notion of tracking down the best bargain available, thus saving money and outsmarting the other guy. For many consumers, this notion turns shopping into a new competitive sport, neatly falling into the habit we Americans have of treating most aspects of life as a contest or battle.

Want a perfect example of shopping as a competition? Drive to the local mall on the day after Thanksgiving for the early bird sales, which usually begin before the sun rises. The lot will be packed and impatient, sleepy people will be waiting for the doors to open—all this effort to get wrapping paper for half price or to save 10 bucks on a sweater.

Rescuing the Economy

Conditions were ripe for an economic "Perfect Storm." The collective weight of the dot-com implosion that began in early 2001, the September 11 terrorist attacks, and successive wars in Afghanistan and Iraq resulted in a faltering economy, millions of people losing their jobs, and widespread insecurity.

Stories of retirees losing their life's savings as the stock market tanked and millions of high tech jobs disappearing as companies went belly-up turned the economic boom of the late 1990s into ancient history. Pundits filled the airwaves with chatter about a possible global depression. Republicans and Democrats took turns blasting each other for the dire conditions, bemoaning the lack of leadership necessary to get the economy back on track. All the while, consumers ignored the calamity and went right on shopping.

In a time when common sense dictated that people should save every spare penny and carefully plan for the (gloomy) future, shoppers barely flinched. Unlike other recessions, they continued to spend, despite the economic doldrums. Without consumer willingness to keep on shopping in the face of a troublesome economic situation, the country could have tumbled deeper into an economic quagmire.

On the surface, it seemed as if shoppers had lost their minds. A closer look, however, reveals that consumers did not go crazy during the recession that followed the dot-com bust in the early years of the twenty-first century. Spending habits were not based on a hope and a prayer. The federal government, under the leadership of Federal Reserve Chairman Alan Greenspan, took steps to put money back into people's hands by dropping interest rates to historic lows. More than a dozen cuts have been made since January 2001. For people who had taken out double-digit mortgages in earlier decades, the new rates enabled them to consolidate debt under one low interest umbrella or roll the money they saved into other areas.

The combination of the low interest rates low and increased consumer spending propped up the economy, even as corporations dramatically cut spending and began downsizing millions of workers (estimated at 2.6 million in a two-year span beginning in March 2001). For the first time since 1948–1949, however, consumer spending rose throughout the recession, buoyed by low rates and favorable finance terms, such as zero percent financing on new cars and big-ticket items like washing machines and big-screen televisions. Many people still felt pinched by the 2001 recession, but it "officially" ended after a mere eight months due to these factors.

Household spending now accounts for about 70 percent of the economy. Therefore tracking consumer spending is increasingly important. Every fluctuation has become a defining moment, worthy of front-page news. Policymakers keep an eye on consumer confidence polls on the lookout for trends that prove the economy is improving. Monthly sales figures from Wal-Mart and Target provide a glimpse into American households, revealing the state of the economy on a personal level.

The downside, however, is that all the rampant consuming pushed household debt to record numbers in the early 2000s, estimated at a then-staggering $8.9 trillion. Mortgage debt alone jumped to more than $6 trillion in 2001, a 60 percent jump over the previous five years. In addition, overall family net worth fell considerably as the stock market plunged from dot-com boom highs.

Home equity lines of credit and refinancing enabled many people to transfer high-interest credit card and automobile debt to their mortgage, thus paying down debt in one hand but increasing it in another. In essence, these maneuvers put cash in people's pockets and provided the disposable income that ultimately ends up in the coffers of Wal-Mart, Target, and their discount brethren. The Bush Administration used the same tactic several times during its reign, basically giving people a check from the federal government in hopes that they would spend it on big ticket goods. The 2008 relief efforts, for example, were meant to offset the real estate woes and credit crunch many people experienced.

Consumers saw a significant bump in their paychecks from the Bush Administration's tax cuts and from their employers as bigger raises started to be doled out as the nation began its rocky road to recovery. In September 2003, nationwide retail sales rose 5.9 percent, representing the largest jump since March 2002. Individually among the discount retailers, Wal-Mart's sales rose 6 percent, Kohl's 5.5 percent, and Target saw a whopping 14.8 percent gain. This trend indicated that continued growth was on the horizon. A robust holiday shopping season awaited retailers—good news for the companies and the nation as a whole.

The Wal-Mart Effect

Given that household spending represents 70 percent of the economy, Wal-Mart's enduring strength comes as no surprise. With billions of dollars being pumped into retail coffers, Wal-Mart continued to grow despite the widespread economic woes, not only propping up the limping economy, but also putting it in a strong position to capitalize on the inevitable rebound.

Wal-Mart's command is simply staggering, ranging from 2002 revenues of $245 billion to the mind-boggling reality that 82 percent of American households made at least one purchase there last year. Each week, 138 million shoppers visit one of Wal-Mart's 4,750 stores, almost half of the country's population. Today, net sales for the fiscal year ending on January 31, 2008 reached $374.5 billion, an increase of 8.6 percent over fiscal year 2007. Income from continuing operations for the fiscal year ended January 31, 2008 increased 5.8 percent to $12.9 billion, up from $12.2 billion in the prior year.[4]

As a matter of fact, Wal-Mart is so pervasive that economists and business analysts coined the term "the Wal-Mart effect" on the global economy. On one hand, the company's growth through the recession played a role in suppressing inflation. On the other hand, however, each productivity gain it squeezes out of a vendor or distributor ripples across the global economy. To do business with Wal-Mart, vendors must transform the way they operate to conform to the giant's processes.

On a global scale, Wal-Mart's policies affect the economies in many of the world's developing nations. Several countries in Central America and South Asia are dependent on the company, which in turn, relies on cheap manufacturing to produce low-priced goods. Wal-Mart and its vendors are forced to continually search for ways to cut costs out of production, which means heavy use of workers in developing nations who will work much cheaper than their American counterparts.

Because of its sales prowess, Wal-Mart controls large shares of business done by its vendors, including some of America's largest corporations. In the early part of the decade, Wal-Mart accounted for 28 percent of Dial's total sales, 24 percent of Del Monte Foods, 23 percent of Clorox, and 23 percent of Revlon. Wal-Mart has been almost single-handedly responsible for saving Levi's by signing a deal to sell blue jeans at discount prices. As a matter of fact, Wal-Mart is so powerful that it is considering offering banking services at the same time it is beginning the largest global expansion in company history.

In the early 2000s, Wal-Mart operated 1,309 stores in 10 nations. By 2008, those figures grew to 3,125 stores in 13 markets. It is already the largest single retailer in both Canada and Mexico. In 2003 alone, Wal-Mart added another 130 new stores in foreign markets. In comparison, Target spent

$3.5 billion in 2003 to expand in the United States. Many of its new outlets will be SuperTargets, melding the grocery store with the discount store, just like Wal-Mart's highly successful Supercenters.

If Wal-Mart maintains its current growth rate of 15 percent, the company will record sales of $600 billion by 2011. The retailer is also on pace to top 2 million employees, up from its current 1.4 million. Keep in mind, the record expansion and growth are taking place while the national economy is stumbling along as a result of unemployment concerns and fears regarding the global geopolitical situation, including further fighting in Iraq and future acts of terrorism.

The challenge in a world so thoroughly dominated by Wal-Mart, according to labor rights experts, is that its workers simply cannot fulfill the American Dream (and in many cases, feed their families) on the salaries it pays. Furthermore, as the company puts the screws to its vendors and distributors, these companies are forced to lower their costs, which most often involves outsourcing work overseas and shedding American workers.

There is a catch-22 that may ultimately play out—someday workers and those who have lost their jobs because of Wal-Mart's tactics will no longer be able to afford to shop there. When sales get sluggish at Wal-Mart, the slowdown will have a ripple effect across the global economy, with the potential for cataclysmic consequences. The international economy will not be able to absorb Wal-Mart's stumble—as it did with the fall of Woolworth and, more recently, Kmart—because there has never been a company as pervasive and as powerful as Wal-Mart.

The Bentonville behemoth and its discount brethren are not the only companies that expanded during the recession that gripped the economy in the early 2000s. Some would argue that the truest heirs to the legacy of Woolworth's and other long lost five-and-dimes are the deep discount or closeout retailers such as Save-A-Lot, Big Lots, and Dollar General. This slice of the discount shopping pie has grown into a $20 billion market and has experienced tremendous growth over the last several years.

These stores sell a limited selection of groceries and general merchandise aimed at lower-income shoppers. Their prices are 20 to 40 percent below those of Wal-Mart and remain competitive because they limit operating costs. Hard discounters try to siphon off the bottom third of Wal-Mart shoppers, typically those who earn $30,000 or less annually.

Big Lots, the largest of the closeout retailers, alone had sales eclipsing $3.8 billion in its 1,400 stores in 45 states in the early years of the decade. The company's stores are smaller than the average Wal-Mart or Target, but are located in more diverse areas, often closer to city centers and in strip malls that low-income shoppers patronize. Each location, however, averages $2.85 million in annual sales.

The combination of high interest retail charge cards and less stringent requirements for bankcards sent consumer debt through the roof in low-income households. Predatory credit card companies target these families and studies reveal that lower-income households have seen their revolving debt skyrocket 184 percent in recent years. Expanding the credit pool by blanketing this segment of consumers with high interest cards has pushed the average credit card debt in the United States to $12,000 per household, according to Federal Reserve estimates.

Purchasing goods by credit card—even if charged a prohibitive interest rate—has enabled lower-income families to mimic their middle class neighbors. Closeout stores carry brand name merchandise, although a toy may be last year's craze or a blouse may be slightly irregular. Regardless, these goods cater to our sense of style.

On the psychological front, dollar stores offer the same wonder as other discounters, but at considerably reduced prices. Shoppers still get the same treasure hunt feeling, never quite sure of the bounty they may uncover, but knowing that it will be inexpensive.

Economic Rocket

In the summer of 2003, while the news headlines focused on wildfires ravaging California, which destroyed hundreds of thousands of acres around Los Angeles and San Diego and taking nearly two dozen lives, the nation's gross domestic product soared to 7.2 percent growth, a 19-year high.

Given the increasing criticism over its handling of the situation in Iraq, the Bush Administration immediately pointed to its tax cut program as the driver. Good economic news and positive signs of a full recovery from the latest recession would help the president counter his critics. Tax rebates—whether or not they are good for the nation's long-term economic health—put about $100 billion back into the hands of consumers just before the school shopping season began. In addition, the record number of individuals who refinanced their mortgages in the spring spent the money over the summer.

Once again, the willingness of millions of people to hit the shopping centers fueled this dramatic growth. The sequence of events is almost predictable—any time consumers are given an extra fistful of dollars, they dash off to Wal-Mart to spend the bounty. What George Bush Sr. called "voodoo economics" has been reborn during his son's reign, essentially a trickle-down effect that works because people are not afraid to spend.

Clearly, the seemingly illogical notion that increased consumer spending could dig an entire nation out of economic turmoil has sustained the United States over the last several years. Without the combination of low interest rates and increased consumer spending, there is no doubt that the recession would have lasted much longer, and the residual effects would have devastated countless families and communities.

The prominent role consumers have played in keeping the economy afloat reveals the importance of America's discount retailers. While department stores and upscale merchandisers struggled, the discounters grew more powerful and more central to the economic health of the nation.

Wal-Mart's sprint to become the largest company in the world proves how critical cheap shopping is in today's society. The company's growth also points to America's transition from a manufacturing power to a service economy, a profound transformation for a country historically dominant in heavy industry. Philosophically, Americans view themselves as builders, not as staff wearing cute little nametags and bright blue vests in retail stores.

Wal-Mart plays such a critical role in the nation's economy that the company has moved beyond mere economic importance (particularly for a company that has no direct military or intelligence ties, like a Northrop Grumman or Boeing). Retail analyst Tom Rubel surmised that if Wal-Mart, "ever stumbles, we've got a potential national security problem on our hands." Imagine. The downfall of Wal-Mart could potentially destroy the American economy, then triggering chaos worldwide. "They touch almost everything," he explained. "If they ever really went into a tailspin, the dislocation would be significant and traumatic."[5]

Wal-Mart, that corporate giant, the one that people either love or hate, is now America's bellwether. No barometer of leading economic indicators is complete without taking into account the Wal-Mart effect.

DAILY FASHION

Daily fashion in the new millennium is as jumbled and chaotic as the rest of popular culture. What people wear around the country is based on a complex web of local customs, climate, proximity to New York and Los Angeles, and the hottest television shows, rock bands, and movies. Fashion is a melting pot, just like the nation itself. If there is any unifying theme when examining a national fashion, it is that the industry is driven by celebrities (including celebrity name brand designers themselves) and young people.

Early in the decade, fashion shook off the baggy, grunge days of the 1990s, as well as the hipster cool of northern Californian dot-coms, reveling in more revealing styles. Women ditched their traditional Levis blue jeans for a new style, cut low at the waist, dubbed "low-rise," and tight everywhere else. Other female styles were punctuated with strategically placed tattoos, piercings, and undergarments worn outside clothing. Midriff-bearing tops got hot, almost always accompanied by a pierced bellybutton.

The most influential and enduring fashion statement to emerge from the early decade vaulted into the national conscious piggybacking off the pop hit "Thong Song" by Sisqó. The catchy tune became the virtual national anthem of college students venturing to the beach on spring break and received heavy airplay on MTV. "Thong Song" did more than elevate a

Dance scene from Britney Spears: In "The Zone"
(ABC-TV special, Nov. 17, 2003). ABC/Photofest.
© ABC. Courtesy of Photofest.

piece of women's underwear to the national spotlight; the hit reinvigorated the idea that undergarments could be the most important visible piece of clothing. In its new public role, the underwear industry introduced a variety of new styles that drew inspiration from the thong. The women's underwear industry achieved sales of about $2.4 billion, and the thong garnered a quarter of that market. Writing in 2004, journalist Alex Kuczynski explained, "The thong underpant became a cultural touchstone, the very symbol of the tease. It caught on at a time when lad magazines like *Maxim* and *FHM*, with their photographs of panty-clad but never entirely nude women, took over . . . [and Britney] Spears, the celebrity perhaps most associated with the thong, embraced the virgin/temptress paradox with cutting accuracy. Audiences could look, but they could never touch. The thong is an invitation, not a promise."[6]

For men in that period, hip-hop influenced daily wear, from the urban cool of Sean "Diddy" Combs to the urban aggressive oversized pants, white tee shirts, and backwards baseball cap with a bandana underneath look sported by Eminem. Business casual remained a part of the workplace. Button-downed, short-sleeved shirts cut square across the bottom and worn not tucked in (a modified version of the traditional Hawaiian shirt, minus the gaudy prints) became a foundation in the evolving business wear market.

By mid-decade and later, the fashion world grew more muddled as a variety of new styles grew out of the influences of the previous years, with inevitable backlashes. Many women, for example, resorted to the cleaner, more professional look of 1950s and 1960s fashion after growing weary of the always more skin showing styles dominating the industry. Also jumbling the fashion marketplace are the traditional style categories that remain consistently popular, such as preppy clothes, 1980s styles, and the hippie 1960s look. Perhaps the best aspect of American fashion, at least as it is worn by the hundreds of millions of regular people in the country, is that it is so fluid that one does not often have to make wholesale modifications of a personal style, if at all.

Celebrity Fashion

For celebrities, having one's own clothing line now seems to be part of the "platform" used to build the iconic brand that stars desire. What seemed like a crazy idea decades ago, for example, when actress Jaclyn Smith launched a clothing line with K-mart, appears like a natural part of the fashion world. In the 2000s, there are actually so many celebrities that have their own lines that one would need many pages to fill the list.

In early 2007, for example, Madonna launched a clothing and accessory line, dubbed "M by Madonna," with Swedish retailer H&M, while Jennifer Lopez followed up her hit fragrance and Sweetface line with clothes aimed at juniors, called "justsweet." Other celebrities to launch clothing lines include Sarah Jessica Parker, Venus Williams, Mary-Kate and Ashley Olsen, Ashley Judd, and Victoria Beckham. David Wolfe, a creative director at the Doneger Group, explains, "The consumer is desperate for some guidance to sort out the crowded retail landscape. Because the media tell us so much about celebrities, people have an idea of what their image means in terms of fashion, and if they can connect a name to an image and merchandise, it makes shopping so much easier."[7]

An important question as the decade draws to a close is whether or not the fashion industry can constantly sustain itself with new celebrities entering the fray. Some celebrities have track records to show the power of their brands, such as Combs, whose Sean John line made $450 million in 2002. Some experts estimate that the celebrity-licensed products market accounted for $3 billion in sales that year. Brian Dubin, head of WMA's East Coast commercial division, says: "Your client, whether they are an athlete or an actor or an actress, has intangible assets: a name, a reputation, a credibility and an image. All of those attributes may be combined into

Ashley Olsen, left, and Mary-Kate Olsen show their contrasting fashion styles in the film New York Minute *(2004). Warner Bros./Photofest. © Warner Bros. Courtesy of Photofest.*

something that could be made into a brand. When they are turned into a product or a service, then they become tangible assets."[8]

A NIP HERE . . . A TUCK THERE

In today's "expose all" society, America's obsession with youthful vigor transformed plastic surgery from a behind closed doors topic to one discussed on the front pages of celebrity tabloids and at family dinner tables. Not only were the uses and misuses of augmentation by celebrities from Michael Jackson and Cher to Meg Ryan and Ashley Simpson aired for public consumption, but a whole industry of reality television "makeover" shows attempted to change the way people looked (and viewed themselves) through extreme surgical measures.

In 2004, doctors performed approximately 9 million plastic surgery operations, up 25 percent from 7.4 million in 2000. Three years later, in 2007, the number nearly doubled to 16 million. While the vast majority of these surgeries take place under the care of trained professionals, a growing number are performed quickly, cheaply, and at great risk of complications. In 2004, for example, more than 4,000 teenagers under 18 years old had breast implants, even though the Food and Drug Administration

(FDA) approved the surgery only for those over 18. Another 6,000 teens underwent liposuction, a dangerous and painful procedure for eliminating body fat.[9]

As the number of augmentation surgeries increased, two related results also skyrocketed—either those unhappy with the results and/or people enduring botched procedures. So many people fell into one or both of these categories that it spawned an entirely new segment of the industry—surgeons specializing in fixing errors or mistakes—called "undo-plasties" in common lingo.

The challenge for professionally trained plastic surgeons is that the business is largely unregulated. In many instances, any licensed physician can perform plastic surgery. In some states, dermatologists and even dentists can do nose jobs and other procedures. They may or may not have had much exposure to the field during their internships. Adding to the challenge is that many surgeries are taking place in a physician's office to cut down on costs that would incur for a hospital stay. Because most procedures are paid for upfront, there is little a patient can do in the event of a bad outcome.

Debra Dunn, a New York woman in her forties, grew despondent after two nose jobs left her feeling like she did not resemble herself and wrecked her self image. She avoided going out in public and had several additional procedures done in an attempt to regain her former nose. The additional work cost more than three times the initial amount. Dunn, however, is not alone in feeling regret over her plastic surgery. Celebrities from Courtney Love to Julio Iglesias publicly lamented their procedures. "Such dramatic surgeries can make people feel as though their permanent self is not their genuine self—at least on the outside," explained Kathy Kater, a St. Paul, Minnesota-based psychotherapist. "That can lead to a real feeling of internal discontent or even a very deep grief for a self who now seems to have disappeared."[10]

Fueled by Television

Like so much of popular culture in the 2000s, reality television contributed to the burgeoning popularity of cosmetic surgery, resulting in the mass marketing of the specialty. Soon, just like with fast food joints and drugstores, it seemed as if plastic surgeons stood at every street corner hawking their services. Television shows, such as *Dr. 90210*, *Extreme Makeover*, and *The Swan* demystified augmentation, as well as the pain, suffering, and postsurgery swelling that goes hand-in-hand with such work.

As a result, the potential growth of the industry reduced the cost so that anyone who grew up dreaming of having a nose just like their favorite movie star or celebrity could go under the knife in search of their idealized

The contestants after receiving makeovers on The Swan *(Fox), season 1, May 24, 2004. Shown clockwise from right: Sarina V., Cristina T., Merline N., Cindi I., Kelly A., Marnie R., Belinda B., Beth L., winner Rachel L. 20th Century Fox/Photofest. © Robert Voets. Courtesy of Photofest.*

perfection. In 2004, the average cost of the 10 most popular cosmetic surgery procedures (from liposuction to lip augmentation) cost about $4,000, making it affordable for just about anyone.

In 2003, ABC launched *Extreme Makeover,* a show that gave everyday people the opportunity to undergo a series of procedures to basically become a new person. The program offered a variety of services, including counseling, personal trainers, and dietitians, but the focus revolved around the "reveal" when the contestant debuted his or her new look to the gasps and cheers of family and friends. By 2005, the show averaged approximately 7 million viewers each week. The success launched two high-profile knockoffs: Fox's *The Swan* and MTV's *I Want a Famous Face.* Each show revolved around participants undergoing a variety of cosmetic procedures.

Critics of this programming pointed to the consequences such an emphasis on appearance would have on young females and others who may strive for perfect looks. Lou Gorfain, executive producer of *Extreme Makeover,* countered that his show gave people a new lease on life. "It's therapeutic. The lesson is empowerment," he said. "People have the power to change their appearance." The emphasis on altering one's life by changing looks debate continues, although by the late 2000s, the emphasis on changing one's appearance through safer means does seem to be taking hold. ABC cancelled *Extreme Makeover* in May 2007.[11]

Botox—The Fountain of Youth?

Created in 1989 and approved by the Food and Drug Administration in 2002, Botox is a liquid made from purified botulism toxin that is injected into facial wrinkles. The toxin paralyzes the muscles, thus "smoothing out" wrinkles, and lasts approximately 120 days. After that, additional injections on a regular basis are necessary to keep up the illusion of wrinkle-free skin.

Even before FDA approval, doctors used Botox in cosmetic procedures. The American Society of Plastic Surgeons estimated that 800,000 injections were given in 2000; the FDA believes that the number doubled by the next year. By 2004, about 3 million Botox procedures were given in the United States.[12] Two years later, Botox became the most popular cosmetic drug in the world.

Despite the number of references to Botox in popular culture, the typical customer is a man or woman 50 to 65 years old, although the trend is picking up in younger age groups. The availability of the drug helps its popularity. Botox can be injected by nurse practitioners at a doctor's office, clinic, or spa.

Some cities are even holding Botox parties, such as the one held in Boise, Idaho. In late 2007, a spa threw the party at a local nightclub, handing out cosmetic products and the chance to buy the drug for use when visiting the facility, although no one underwent an actual injection at the bash. Boise cosmetic surgeon Michael R. Bailey sees the use of Botox spreading like wildfire. "Are we seeing more of the common American person having cosmetic surgery? Yes, I've done people who drive vans for a living, are housekeepers," he says. "Cosmetic surgery improves your quality of life. Nothing more, nothing less. It's not going to get anyone a new girlfriend or boyfriend. But it makes people feel better about themselves."[13]

Across the country in Manhattan, Smoothmed opened in early 2007, a Botox-on-the-go store offering injections to busy New Yorkers. Drs. Andrew I. Elkwood and Michael I. Rose teamed to launch the store near Bloomingdale's. Despite concerns from critics that offering Botox in the model of a convenience store or Starbucks is potentially dangerous, Rose and Elkwood see competitive pricing and location as a means to broaden the market. "Botox is the female yuppie heroin," explained Rose. "It's like electricity: If you want to keep it on, you have to keep paying." The pair developed a computerized system for mapping each patient's face, thus ensuring that the exact procedure is duplicated on subsequent trips.[14]

6

Food

Am I trying to be Martha Stewart? I think I'm the exact opposite. She's
made a wonderful living being fabulous at everything. I'm making
mine being very mediocre at everything . . . Yeah, some people find
me annoying. I'm perky. I smile a lot . . . I speak in abbreviations. But
if you had to stand there and talk to yourself for five years, you'd
shorten some words, too. Yum-O? It just came out of my mouth one
day, 'yum' and 'Oh my God' smushed together. Whatever. We sold a
lot of T-shirts with that one.

—Rachael Ray (2006)

Food plays an interesting and important role in popular culture. In the
new millennium, the meaning of food shifts depending on one's perspective. Sometimes food revolves on the chef's preparations; at other times it
is about which foods to eat and which to avoid. The focus also turns to the
presentation of food, whether it is handed to you through your car window
or served on fancy, hand-painted dinnerware at a five-star restaurant. We
are highly critical of some food and food producers and marketers, but to
others we pay homage to the artistry and usefulness of food.

We give our foods many labels, which also reflects our feelings about
eating and weight in general. The hottest moniker in the late 2000s is
"organic," although certainly few people could provide an exact definition. Aisles upon aisles at grocery stores across the nation feature organic
sections, from nonbleached, whole wheat flour to free-trade coffee beans.
Even our restaurant choices have specific names, from the "fast-casual"
experience at Chipotle or Panera Bread to the "sit-down" chains of Chili's,
Applebee's, and TGI Fridays.

On an even more personal level, Americans are counting carbohydrates,
good fats, bad fats, sugars, sugar substitutes, and a myriad of other factors

that may or may not explain the healthiness of a particular food. We know to look on the list of ingredients and nutritional information chart, but the scientific terminology used to mask good things from bad makes it a guessing game at best.

One of the central roles of food in the 2000s is actually about eliminating bad foods and replacing them with healthier choices. The decade could be labeled "the diet decade," actually eclipsing the fitness-crazed 1980s as the real "me" era. Our popular culture reflects this dieting fascination. One needs to look no further than Jared the Subway Diet Guy or the multitude of low-carbohydrate diet books that litter the *New York Times* bestseller list. The NBC series *Biggest Loser* pits average people in a race to lose weight, coached by a variety of fitness experts and dietitians. VH1 is preparing for its sixth season of *Celebrity Fit Club,* which follows the weight loss regiments of eight celebrities divided into two teams. Past participants include film actor Gary Busey, rapper BoneCrusher, 1980s pop singer Tiffany, and television actress Maureen McCormick. The 2008 version of Celebrity Fit Club will feature "alumni" of previous seasons and some newcomers, including *Saved by the Bell* actor Dustin Diamond, *Joanie Loves Chachi* and *Happy Days* actress Erin Moran, and *Family Ties* actress Tina Yothers.

The good health/healthy eating kick grabs the public's attention, but whether or not these fads actually help people get healthier is up for debate. One thing is for certain, however, in the late 2000s more food producers, manufacturers, and restaurants are adopting healthier menu options. The leading indicator of the magnitude of this change is McDonald's, which began offering health-conscious options after surviving the scathing documentary *Super Size Me,* in which an otherwise healthy man essentially stuffs himself on fast food for 30 days and winds up several steps closer to death's doorstep. On another front in the food wars, entire cities and states outlawed trans-fat in restaurants.

Mass media perform a critical role in the nation's fixation on food. Cooking segments are a staple on local news shows and the big national, morning programs such as NBC's *Today Show.* Food aficionados and chefs are a staple on cable television. Some celebrity cooks, such as Rachael Ray, transformed from minor figures in the celebrity world to megastars based on cooking-themed programs. Then, they build early successes into media empires that span across multiple channels, all based on using themselves and their image as a brand name. The modern model for this kind of meteoric rise is Martha Stewart, who overcame many obstacles, including her much-publicized jail sentence for insider trading, to regain her position atop the heap of lifestyle mavens.

Newspapers devote a great deal of space to health issues, more or less covering every report and study that presents some bit of new information about well-being. Without a doubt, the Internet's role in pushing health news, misinformation, gossip, and facts keeps the subject in front of interested viewers. Reality television provides consumers with even more food-related programming. The perfect example of this is the Food Network, owned and operated by E. W. Scripps Company, which also owns HGTV, DIY Network, and Great American Country. The Food Network reaches more than 90 million American households through cable and satellite television subscription packages.

"MCSHAKES" AND "MCGURGLES"

In early 2003, a healthy (6 feet, 2 inches tall, about 185 pounds), young documentary filmmaker named Morgan Spurlock began a journey that revolutionized the way the world viewed fast food. Over a 30-day period, he lived (and gorged) only on McDonald's food, living by the motto that if a restaurant employee offered to "super size" his meal he would. Using the visual power of film, Spurlock, who directed, wrote, and starred in the documentary, revealed the total devastation that McDonald's could have on an otherwise fit person. The film naturally leads to questions regarding the restaurant chain's understanding of the health consequences of its menu, as well as the impact of placing profits above nutrition.

Super Size Me (tagline: "A Film of Epic Proportions") catalogs Spurlock's physical and mental transformation, which left him 24.5 pounds heavier

Morgan Spurlock changed the way people viewed fast food industry in his documentary Super Size Me *(2004). Roadside Attractions/Photofest. © Avi Gerver. Courtesy of Photofest.*

and decidedly less healthy. He suffered from mood swings, liver damage, and sexual dysfunction during the month devoted to eating McDonald's meals. The film features lengthy interviews with his personal physician, who tells him that if he doesn't stop the fatty diet he might die, and his girlfriend, who elaborates on his sexual failings. Spurlock's hair even starts to fall out.[1]

The visceral images alerted the audience to the considerable health risks associated with consuming fast food. Viewers not only saw Spurlock's body mass gain but also watched him throw up out the window of his vehicle after eating a Double Quarter Pounder with Cheese after complaining about the "McGurgles" and "McShakes" the food produced. At one point late in the experiment Spurlock even experienced heart palpitations.

The movie opened at Robert Redford's Sundance Film Festival to widespread acclaim in May 2004 and eventually grossed more than $28 million, making it one of the top-selling documentaries of all time. Spurlock received an Academy Award nomination for Best Documentary, but did not win.

Journalist Richard Schickel finds the true power of *Super Size Me* in its uncovering of the hypocrisies of the fast food industry. Spurlock discusses the mass seduction of children, lured into fast food chains by happy meals and playground equipment. But the deceit runs deeper. "Government at every level is complicit," Schickel explains. "The feds ship sloppy joe makings to grateful school-lunch programs—it's the cheapest grub available. Other schools contract for pizza and sodas from corporate purveyors while cutting back on phys-ed classes. And everyone starts getting fatter younger."[2]

The Fast Food Response

McDonald's openly criticized Spurlock and *Super Size Me*. The company complained that anyone eating a 5,000-calorie-a-day diet without exercise would gain weight. The restaurant also claimed that its typical customer did not eat there as frequently or gorge themselves when they did. As the film's popularity increased, McDonald's did remove the "super size" option from the menu; however, the company claimed that it did so independent of the documentary.

In 2006, McDonald's introduced wrap sandwiches, featuring chicken wrapped in tortillas, and other healthier food options. Although most criticism the company receives is for its red meat, McDonald's currently sells as much chicken as beef, which is 150 percent more than in 2002.[3]

Notwithstanding *Super Size Me*, McDonald's global sales increased 6.7 percent in 2007 (3.3% in the United States) and 6.3 percent in 2006. Revenues also reached a record high of $22.8 billion. In all, 56 million customers visit the fast food restaurant each day.[4] Political commentator George Will calls McDonald's new menu items part of the "Snack Wrap Era," where fast food restaurants responded to "consumer appetites for something to eat between meals and with one hand on the steering wheel."[5]

OBESITY

In the United States, two-thirds of American adults are considered overweight, and one-third fall into the obese category. In addition to the psychological and self-image challenges overweight and obesity magnifies, the condition carries serious health risks such as an elevated risk of heart disease, diabetes, and even an increase in some types of cancer. Some experts have labeled the nation's obesity challenge an epidemic, particularly when one considers the public and private health costs associated with treating people overweight and obese and the overwhelming majority of people who fall into one of the categories.

Obesity and overweight are not new problems, but they are becoming more problematic. Since 1988, the number of overweight individuals has significantly increased. In 2003–2004, 67 percent of adults ages 20 to 74 fell into the category. The obesity rate, however, has remained relatively consistent since the early 1960s, accounting for about 32 percent to 34 percent of the adult population (30% of men and 34% of women). These figures alone prove that the multitudes of diet fads simply have not made a real impact on the overweight and obese.

The number of children who fall into these categories is more shocking and frightening. In 2003–2004, about 17 to 19 percent of children (ages 6 to 11 years old) and adolescents (12 to 19 years old) fell into the overweight category. Most disheartening, the number of overweight children two to five years old doubled from 7 to 14 percent between 1988 and 2004.[6]

Food Portions, Cravings, and Bingeing

One of the primary culprits in America's losing battle with the bulge is the sheer size of foods today. Visit a grocery checkout lane and face the wall of "king size" candy bars or go to Sam's Club or Costco and every food item available is its own monster portion. All the fast food chains have some version of a larger portion menu, with Wendy's even naming its foods "Biggie." Lisa Young, a New York University nutrition researcher, dubs this phenomenon "portion creep," and it leads to overweight and obesity. As Young explains, people eat whatever is in front of them. The more a person gets his hands on, the more he will stuff it down. So what if it's the restaurant size tortilla chips accompanied by a vat of salsa. One can see the wheels turning, "We're Americans, we eat everything on our plates." This is the land of the endless all-you-can-eat buffet from coast-to-coast. "Americans have grown proportionally to increased portion sizes," Young says.[7]

Young researched how portion sizes increased over time and found that many food items doubled or tripled, leading to an exorbitant caloric intake. For example, in 1955 McDonald's sold one size of fries, which weighed 2.4 ounces. Today's large fry order is 6 ounces. The first Hershey's milk chocolate candy bar offered a mere 0.6 ounce in 1908 and 1 ounce in 1960. Today, a person can buy an entire bag or individual bars ranging from 2.6 ounces to 8 ounces.

Restaurants are central to the portion challenge as well. The public assumes that the portions they get at Applebee's or the Macaroni Grill are healthy, but restaurants actually want to please customers and larger sizes give people a better feeling about the establishment. Young explains that consumers should not automatically think that the restaurants are watching their portion sizes for them. The slab of meat that arrives at one's table may represent three or more proper size portions all in one.

When it comes to drinking soda, portion control is out of control. In 1973, 7-Eleven convenience stores introduced 12-ounce and 20-ounce soda drinks. By 1978, it added the 32-ounce Big Gulp, and 10 years later, the 64-ounce Double Gulp (equivalent to a half-gallon). In 2003, 7-Eleven eliminated its 16-ounce size and offered soda ranging from 20 ounces to 64 ounces. The chilling fact is that all these calories add up. Although people may not worry as much about what they drink, because they don't feel it the same way they do a greasy burger or fries, the calories, sugar, and caffeine in soda, energy drinks, fancy coffee drinks, and sweetened teas are costing them their health. University of North Carolina researcher Barry Popkin found that soda, milk, juice, beer, and other beverages accounted for 21 percent of the calories people consumed, up from 16 percent in the 1970s. And Popkin's study took place before the real explosion of energy drinks, which often contain twice the caffeine and calories of other drinks.[8]

Both men and women are affected by food cravings and binge eating. A groundbreaking 2007 study by the McLean Psychiatric Hospital, an affiliate of Harvard, disclosed that binge eating disorder (BED) is America's most common eating disorder, more common than the more publicized disorders of bulimia and anorexia combined. The study defined bingeing as uncontrolled eating at least twice a week for at least six months. The primary feeling one gets during a bingeing spree is the total loss of control over eating. Some scientists go as far as labeling the craving/bingeing issue an epidemic. According to Roger Gould, MD, a professor at the University of California, Los Angeles, 5 million women (the majority are women) suffer from clinical bingeing disorder, and another 15 million experience moderate bingeing levels.[9]

Health.com conducted a survey of 1,000 women to learn more about the reasons for bingeing. Twenty-six percent of them claimed that boredom and loneliness were the triggers; 20 percent felt overwhelmed; 17 percent cited depression, anger, or anxiety; 15 percent were tempted by a favorite food; and stress caused 10 percent to binge. Experts say that at the heart of bingeing is emotion, whether it is insecurity, self-doubt, or anger. "Food helps change our conscious experience. We go into a bubble. Everything feels alright, and nothing can get to us," Gould explains. In many cases, however, food becomes like a medication, but soon wears off or another part of the emotion picks up, forcing the person to start the cycle all over again. Under these conditions, bingeing is more like a food addiction. One 36-year-old Health.com reader said, "I eat when I'm bored or lonely as a way to 'make up' for what I'm missing. Then, I get mad at myself for doing so, which causes me to eat more, which causes me to get mad again."[10]

A challenge for binge eaters is that temptation and fulfillment are all around. America caters to those who eat too much for whatever reason by providing oversized portions, easily accessible junk foods, and no real rationale for not living a sedentary lifestyle. Even people who are actively dieting find reasons to binge. Experts say that this deprivation can actually led to cravings and binge episodes that sabotage the diet altogether. When Health.com asked its readers what foods they craved during a binge, 36 percent said anything they could get their hands on, 24 percent said sweets, 11 percent said chips, and 9 percent said fast food and chocolate.[11]

DIET AMERICA: HIGH PROTEIN, LOW CARBS, LITTLE COMMITMENT

Americans are addicted the idea of dieting, but are fat and getting bigger each year. Bestseller lists overflow with diet- or psychological/self image-related books that focus on getting people to lose weight, but few actually work. Even if a person experiences some short-term weight loss, none of the diet fads really helps keep the weight off for the long term. Until a pill is invented that magically turns obese people into waifs and flab into washboard abs, dieting will remain a central focus in the home and for American popular culture.

The American Institute for Cancer Research reports that about 25 percent of men and 40 percent of women are actively dieting. Jana Klauer, MD, a weight-reduction specialist in New York City, acknowledges that some diets are necessary and potentially life-saving. Diets help in this regard. "There's a psychological benefit as well as a physical one to losing weight in the early stages. People are encouraged because they see improvements in their appearances, or because they feel lighter and maybe are more comfortable exercising," she says. The downside is that dieting is just the first step. She explains, "To keep the weight off, you need a healthy eating style."[12]

The perennial favorite diets of most Americans are both low-carb life-styles: Dr. Atkins and the South Beach Diet. Robert Atkins introduced his high-protein, low-carb in 1972. The reintroduction of his findings, *Dr. Atkins' New Diet Revolution*, topped the bestseller lists and set off a nationwide dieting craze. Observers estimate that at one point, about 17 percent of the total American population followed Atkins's weight loss prescription. The controversial plan includes eliminating vegetables and fruit from one's diet and replacing them with high-protein substitutes.[13] Arthur Agatston, MD, introduced the South Beach Diet, another low-carbohydrate plan, but one that allows for certain fruits and vegetables, sustained over three phases. The South Beach Diet mainly advises dieters to eliminate processed carbs, saturated fats, hydrogenated oils, and trans fats.[14]

The fat epidemic stretches far and wide, cutting across age groups, de-mographics, and ethnicity. About the only dieting "facts" that experts agree on is that obesity and overweight are costing the nation dearly and the culprit is "bad" fats, such as trans fats that make up the bulk of pro-cessed foods. In 2002, after issuing a report estimating that obesity costs the United States $117 billion annually and is linked to 67 percent of deaths, President Bush launched a national dieting initiative with the simple mes-sage: eat right and exercise daily.[15]

The enemy in the war on fats is trans fat, sometimes called "Franken-fats," because they are laboratory created. In most foods, trans fats appear on the ingredients label as hydrogenated or partially hydrogenated oils. These oils are everywhere and almost impossible to avoid. Trans fats, ac-cording to journalist Gail Gorman, "are created artificially by heating liq-uid vegetable oil in the presence of metal catalysts and hydrogen." Trans fats are popular among food manufacturers because they "extend the shelf life of most of the processed foods we consume . . . not only in almost all commercial products that contain fats but also in almost all fast foods, which are usually cooked in partially hydrogenated oil."[16]

Companies solve many challenges with trans fats, such as providing a longer shelf life, reducing transportation costs, and eliminating waste by-products. Despite the scientific studies that show the general harm of all these trans fats in today's foods, the government has not intervened in a dramatic way to eliminate them. Some observers would blame this on the food industry lobbyists and lawyers who help elect politicians with large campaign contributions.

DRINK NATION

At any point before the mid-1990s, coffee served as a setting, usually an awkward way to ask someone out on an informal date ("Would you like to get a cup of coffee?"). Since then, however, coffee has taken center stage, a point of cultural reference, in addition to its brazen, more aggressive tone ("Let's go get coffee."). Consumer goods take on this kind of iconic quality whenever they become a kind of cultural wallpaper—such a part of everyday life that they are no longer really discernible unless one really takes a deep look. Over the last couple of decades, coffee has assumed this role in American society. No one blinks twice at coffee or the daily trips to refill or fill up, whether it is at a local diner, national chain, convenience store, or communal workplace pot.

Coffee, however, is just the chief beverage in America's national obsession with drinks. Even humble water grew in pop culture prestige, as bottled water became a must-have accessory, first for movie stars and celebrities, before then moving on to soccer moms and just about everyone else. In the ongoing soft drink wars, Coke and Pepsi continue to battle, but their lineups have added virtually every other kind of drink one can imagine, hedging that if one brand falters, then another will rise up to take its place. On college campuses, a plethora of high caffeine, additive-laden energy drinks, such as Red Bull and Vault, are highly popular, despite health warnings about excessive caffeine intake.

Coffee Culture

Only in America could a consumer's decision regarding where to buy a cup of coffee be turned into a discussion of political beliefs, yet that distinction serves as a marker in the new millennium. According to writer Conor Clarke, a 2005 poll found that those who leaned left were "twice as likely to go to the world music-playing, fair trade-embracing, Seattle-based coffee chain [Starbucks] as they were to patronize Dunkin' Donuts—a well-known peddler of red-state values."[17] For example, Clarke points to Fox political television show host Bill O'Reilly, who told *Newsweek* that he will not go in a Starbucks, preferring to purchase his cup of joe in mom-and-pop coffee shops.

Regardless of politics, the argument that one's choice for a caffeine fix matters in defining identity indicates the importance people place on coffee in our collective consciousness. The simple fact is that coffee matters in America, not only what kind a person prefers, but where it is bought and how the bean is grown and imported. Coffee and coffeehouses play a central role in mass media, from the multi-Emmy winning show *Frasier* (1993–2004) set in the coffee-rich confines of Seattle to Bob Dylan selling CDs on the Starbucks music label, which the chain decided to dump in early 2008.

Starbucks is the coffeehouse most people imagine when they think about coffee. The coffee industry itself, however, is so large that many others have entered into the high-end market, from McDonald's (dubbed McCafés) to

Dunkin' Donuts. Examining the shelves of the local grocery store, one finds that Folgers, Maxwell House, and the in-store labels have upgraded the flavors they offer, adding more bold and exotic blends.

The combination of increased competition and the idea that the company moved too far away from its core business of selling coffee has hurt Starbucks at the end of the decade. In 2007, company stock dropped 42.8 percent and another 14.7 percent through the beginning of 2008. The dramatic fall, both financially and in reputation, forced founder Howard Schultz to return to Starbucks as CEO. Since returning to the job he left eight years ago, Schultz is focusing on returning the company to its roots—selling coffee that tastes good and being more customer-friendly. The challenge is getting consumers interested in high-priced coffee when they face a disastrous economy, including massive real estate foreclosures and potential job loss. Suddenly, a $4 cup of coffee seems a bit excessive, no matter how fancy the name.

Schultz explains, "I think when you get large and very successful, you have to balance creativity and entrepreneurship with process and strategy. We got a little out of balance, and we weren't as creative and entrepreneurial as we were when we were smaller. And what I'm trying to do is infuse the company with the kind of spirit and innovation [we had] when we were younger."[18] Company research, according to Schultz, reveals that people are simply not going to Starbucks (or a competitor) as frequently as they did before the economic turmoil the nation faces. To counter this challenge, Schultz says, Starbucks must show consumers that it is an "affordable luxury" through "surprise and delight."[19] Whether the public buys into this philosophy will define how the corporation fares into the next decade.

Liquid Energy

PepsiCo made headlines when it purchased the rights for its Amp energy drink to become one of the main sponsors of Dale Earnhardt Jr. Nascar's most popular driver, Earnhardt made a high-profile move to a new team owned by Rick Hendrick for the 2008 season and switched to number 88. Amp, the fifth-leading drink in the $10 billion energy drink market, launched a national marketing campaign starring the driver, which included a slew of new products and collector items. Amp and the National Guard (the other co-sponsor) were rumored to have spent $95 million a year to sign Earnhardt. Included in the deal were the naming rights for the fall race (the Amp Energy 500) at Talladega, a legendary track where Earnhardt has won multiple times.[20]

When initially introduced to the marketplace, energy drinks were targeted at college students and teens. There were some concerns about the consequences of high caffeine intake, but that seems to have leveled off over time. As the industry matures and become more competitive, efforts are underway to link them to a much-needed power boost for busy people. The larger impact is that the formerly fringe status of these drinks has disappeared and, at the same time, has reordered the carbonated-beverage industry. "In convenience stores, the only people going to the fountain and pulling a Coke are old people," explains Mark Hall, creator of Monster Energy and president of Hansen Beverage Co. "If we've been able to do anything, it's to make soft drinks cool for young people."[21]

Monster leads the energy drink market with a 27 percent market share. Red Bull stands second, Rock Star is third, and Full Throttle (owned by Coca-Cola) is fourth.[22] Created by Hall, Monster launched in spite of Red Bull's then-dominant lead in the market. The upstart overtook the giant through successful marketing and branding tactics, including the name of the product itself, placing it in 16-ounce cans, versus Red Bull's 8.3 ounces, with the aggressive claw marks on the label. Next, going after the young male demographic, Hall sponsored extreme athletes from the X Games, mostly in motorized sports. A $25,000 initial investment has grown into a $15 million athlete payroll.[23]

FAST-CASUAL DINING

With budgets tightening in the early years of the new millennium, busy Americans turned away from traditional fast food items (burger, fries, and shake) to embrace a new way of combining quickness with value—fast-casual chains. In the late 2000s, with budgets once again shrinking and in a post-*Super Size Me* world, restaurants such as Panera Bread, Chipotle Mexican Grill, and Quizno's are once again offering an alternative to McDonald's, Wendy's, and Burger King. Less money to spend on dining excursions also means trouble for sit-down restaurants, such as Chili's, Applebee's, and Outback Steakhouse. The fast-casual establishments capitalized on a family-friendly environment (many offering "kids eat free" nights), health consciousness, and price to gain an even stronger foothold in an ever-tightening economy.

According to Darren Tristano, executive vice president of Technomic Information Services, a food industry consulting firm, the immediate drop is seen at major chain restaurants, who face slowing sales growth, down to 4.2 percent in 2007, after hitting 6 percent a year earlier. As a result, chains across the industry are rethinking their menus and attempting to drive home the value-at-a-low-cost message. One option is for restaurants to introduce dollar and/or value menus. "This is something all chains should consider if they want to stay competitive. Price is king right now," Tristano says.[24]

Another aspect of the fast-casual experience customers demand is dubbed "food with integrity," by Janelle Barlow, coauthor of *Branded*

Customer Service. She says, "food with integrity speaks to the trust that a customer places in the consistency of the food" and offers consumers a snack or meal that looks, tastes, smells, feels, and delivers the same experience again and again. Mimicking Bill Clinton's "It's the economy, stupid" phrase, Barlow claims, "It's the food, stupid." She explains, "When most urban dwellers have hundreds of fast-casual restaurants within a five-mile radius of them, standing out from the crowd is the first imperative not only for success, but for survival."[25]

Named the top fast-casual dining establishment in 2007 by *Fast Casual* magazine, Denver-based Chipotle exemplifies the qualities that consumers want from this kind of dining service: better ingredients and affordable food. Since opening in 1993, Chipotle now operates 670 stores all owned and operated by its corporation, unlike the franchisee-based management of most fast food chains. Chief executive officer Steve Ells credits the company's growth and success to focusing on high quality food, healthful ingredients, and consistent, same-store growth, including technology and equipment upgrades.[26]

In 2007, for example, Chipotle stopped serving cheese linked to cows treated with recombinant bovine growth hormone (rBGH) and became the top U.S. restaurant seller of naturally raised meats. In addition, the company opened 88 new locations, while recording a 10.9 percent same-store sales increase through third quarter 2007. "We believe that these results are evidence that people appreciate our continued focus on improving the customer experience in our restaurants," Ells noted. "We believe we are the only restaurant committed to making better tasting, socially responsible gourmet food available and affordable so that everybody can eat better . . . this sets us apart."[27]

IS OUR FOOD SAFE?

In February 2008, the U.S. Department of Agriculture (USDA) initiated the largest meat recall in its history, demanding that 143 million pounds of beef from Chino, California, meatpacking company Hallmark Meat Packing and distributor Westland Meat be pulled from the shelves. The total represented two years worth of production.

Ironically, the governmental agency demanded that the meat be recalled even though officials believed that the product posed little threat to consumers and had been eaten by countless people. The USDA deemed the move necessary after a videotape of employees at Hallmark revealed that they allowed sick and improperly inspected animals to be slaughtered.[28]

As in a good corporate espionage movie, an operative for the Humane Society of America posed as a slaughterhouse worker to shoot the video, which showed sick cows (referred to as "downer cows") being prodded with electric shocks and lifted via forklift to be taken off to slaughter. He then turned the tape over to the Humane Society on January 30, 2008.

The danger with meat recalls is that some of the product may have already made its way into people's bellies by the time the action is taken. For example, about 37 million pounds of meat went to school lunch and public nutrition plans. Ron Vogel, a USDA official, explained, "Almost all of this product is likely to have been consumed."[29] Subsequently, 150 school districts and a couple of fast-food restaurant chains banned Westland beef from their kitchens.

The consequences of tainted food may seem remote, but historically many outbreaks have led to illness and death. In September 2007, the USDA recalled 21.7 million pounds of Topps Meat ground beef after about 30 people got sick from *E. coli* bacteria in the meat. Another threat on the minds of consumers is mad cow disease (bovine spongiform encephalopathy, BSE), which can lead to fatalities.

FOOD AFICIONADOS

The explosion of cable television channels devoted to cooking and food intensified the already growing cooking addiction taking place on local, regional, and national daytime talk shows for decades. Julia Child may have brought cooking to the masses, but today's crop of celebrity chefs expands the notion to an entirely new plane. Much of this expansion is based on the advent of technology such as new cable channels, the Internet, and greater multimedia opportunities.

In today's media-saturated world, a celebrity chef such as Emeril Lagasse not only has his own shows on the Food Network but has coined catchphrases ("BAM!" and "kick it up a notch") that extend him as a brand name. He appears as himself in Crest toothpaste commercials, so excited by the product's minty-fresh flavor that he exclaims, "BAM!" Lagasse also has a string of 11 Emeril restaurants, does other celebrity appearances, and a slew of books, cookware products, and food products.

In early 2008, Martha Stewart Living Omnimedia purchased much of the Lagasse empire for $45 million in cash and $5 million in stock. The merger eliminated one of Stewart's primary competitors, acquiring the rights to Lagasse's TV shows, Web site, licensed products, and cookbooks. In return, Lagasse benefits from Stewart's deep ties to Kmart, Costco, and Macy's. Stewart explained, "His tastes are very different from mine, as is his food, and I think that's good. Being complementary and different is better than being competitive."[30]

Rachael Ray

Rachael Ray's rise from Macy's candy counter help to international celebrity is the stuff of legend and a virtual embodiment of the American Dream. She grew up in upstate New York in a family with vast cooking experience, exposing her to the industry in a variety of food service roles.

Perky food show host turned domestic diva Rachael Ray,
host of 30 Minute Meals *(2002). Food Network/Photofest.*
© *Food Network. Courtesy of Photofest.*

After moving to New York City, she launched a successful career as a gourmet food manager and buyer. Returning to upstate New York, Ray taught
cooking classes, hoping that they would lead to increased sales at the gourmet market where she worked as chef. The popularity of the classes led
to weekly appearances on a CBS station in the Albany, New York, area.
The success of the segments featuring 30-minute meals and a subsequent
cookbook launched her next endeavor—the Food Network.[31]

Ray hosted several shows on the Food Network, including her signature
programs: *30 Minute Meals* and *$40 A Day*. With the success of her cooking
show, which led to a 2005 Daytime Emmy Award for Outstanding Service
Show and a nomination for Outstanding Service Show Host, she launched
a series of cookbooks that filled the bestseller lists, all built around the 30-
minute theme.[32]

One of Ray's greatest successes occurred when she launched the magazine *Every Day with Rachael Ray* in October 2005. In short order, the magazine sold out a total print run in excess of 1 million copies, including 20,000
at Barnes & Noble, which set a record for the chain. Ray possesses what
one publishing insider calls "consumer connectivity," and it is this ability

to understand what people want from her that drives the cooking guru's accomplishments. Explaining her vision of the magazine, Ray says, "The title, to me, means getting more out of every day. Even though you have to work, even though we're all busy, even though we don't have a ton of time, we're not sacrificing the time we do have. That time we're going to have fun with, we're going to make these wonderful meals, we're going to take fun little weekend jaunts."[33]

On September 18, 2006, Ray debuted an hour-long syndicated show *Rachael Ray*, produced by CBS and Oprah Winfrey's Harpo Productions. Combining elements of a talk show with her typical everyday cook mentality, the show garnered seven daytime Emmy nominations in its first year on the air.

The Internet is credited with helping many celebrities gain an audience, but the medium also provides an avenue for criticism that did not exist before the mid-1990s. Like Martha Stewart before her, Ray is roundly denounced—and in some cases, even hated—by a legion of critics who have taken to the Web with sites such as the "I Hate Rachael Ray" blog and the "Rachael Ray Sucks Community," which garnered mentions in *The New York Times, USA Today, The Boston Globe,* and *Slate.* Even a 2005 *Newsweek* article about her couldn't help but stir up the anti-Rachael soup.

Many critics find fault with Ray's general overexposed celebrity, pitching everything from Ritz crackers to GE appliances. She even posed for centerfold-like pinups for the notorious FHM magazine, much criticized for its objectification of women. Ray's reply, "I think it is kinda cool for someone who is goofy, and a cook, just a normal person to be thought of in that way."[34]

Ray also gets denounced for adopting such an obviously fake "aw schucks" persona to explain her rise from local cooking workshop leader to international celebrity. Journalist Florence King writes that Ray's "Recent consecration by Pope Oprah has resulted in so much overnight world-class fame that her face is on everything but the cover of *Tool & Die Quarterly.* TV is now all Rachael, all the time. There's her cooking show, her eating show where she samples restaurants, her own talk show, guest appearances on other people's talk shows, books, book tours, and so many tie-ins and endorsements that she's all over the commercials too." She describes the anti-Ray foes on the Internet as "ready to do battle against the cult of mediocre celebrity."[35] The tie to Oprah Winfrey launched Ray's solo career in ways that accentuated what she achieved on the Food Network, but the push to the next level of stardom required Oprah's anointed touch.

Martha Stewart

Already in her late sixties, Martha Stewart shows few signs of slowing down. By the dawn of the new millennium, she already had numerous bestselling books, a television show, and many endorsement and design

Martha Stewart, popular culture's reigning domestic doyenne. NBC/Photofest. © NBC. Courtesy of Photofest.

deals, in addition to a publicly traded company that bore her name. At the time, it truly seemed like Martha's world. In 2004, however, Stewart's world took a nasty turn when she was convicted of insider trading and sentenced to a five-month jail term and five months of home confinement, what one journalist called "a spectacular public disgrace."[36]

Her status as a public figure brought out pundits for and against her. Some argued that the Securities and Exchange Commission made Stewart a scapegoat for the corporate wrongdoing going on at the time. Others believed she should pay the price for her criminal activity, just like anyone else who would have done the same. Regardless of one's stand on Stewart's conviction and imprisonment, almost nobody thought she would be able to regain her status upon release. For her part, Stewart had no doubts, announcing from the courthouse steps after being sentenced, "I will be back."[37]

After being released from the federal prison in West Virginia and serving her house arrest at her 153-acre home in Bedford, New York, Stewart immediately plotted her comeback. Her return to Martha Stewart Living Omnimedia helped the stock price level off after years of falling in her absence. Stewart's main priority, though, was regaining her place on television. She launched a new daily program, *The Martha Stewart Show*, which earned five Emmy nominations in its first year on the air, and hosted a Martha version of Donald Trump's *The Apprentice* on NBC. The show failed to capture the public's imagination, but it did place Stewart back in the limelight. Next, she worked to jumpstart *Martha Stewart Living* magazine and began a radio channel on Sirius satellite radio.[38]

In a career that spans decades and includes everything from designing homes to pillow sets and bath towels, Stewart is not cowering from the competition from the likes of Ray and others grasping for her throne. In 2006, she summed up Ray's daily talk show for *BusinessWeek,* stating, "Her daily show is much less appealing than her Food Network show. It's very disjointed and loud, and I don't learn anything." This comment was made at a time when Ray's show averaged 2.3 million viewers, or about 46 percent more than Stewart's, according to Nielsen Media Research.[39]

By all accounts, Stewart has been on a tear since leaving prison. Her renewed vigor cuts across media platforms to include a Martha version of the Web, several magazines, and many merchandising projects. Among the many endorsement deals are a line of 1,400 branded plates, linens, and home accessories for Macy's; a 350-color paint line at Lowe's; and the continued association with Kmart. Although the retailer is struggling, Stewart is guaranteed $60 million in the deal, regardless of the amount of product she pushes.[40]

7

Leisure Activities

You have these players who train from a young age and want to be the best, but they know their dreams of winning hang on beating this guy? This guy who's been so incredibly dominant. It certainly has an effect. If a player has perspective, he'll focus on his own game and improvement. Hopefully, you become a champion.
                    —David Leadbetter, famed golf coach, on Tiger Woods (2008)

American popular culture is tied closely to the way people play, whether that is attending a Pittsburgh Steelers football game or watching the X Games on a 46-inch, high-definition, flat-screen television. Leisure time encompasses a broad sweep of sporting events and other fun activities designed to take us outside the drudgery represented by the work world and often harsh realities of everyday life. But leisure activity also includes staying at home and watching a sporting event or movie on one's home theater system.

In the new millennium, social media composes a new leisure activity that has exploded in popularity. Social media Web sites give users a way to broadcast news and information about themselves that appeals to the general narcissism of young people (although surprisingly large numbers of adults over the age of 30 participate as well).

From a popular culture perspective, many of the traditional sports have been eclipsed by activities scoffed at in earlier times. If measured by spectators and television ratings, Nascar, for example, is certainly more popular than any other pro sport except for football. Professional wrestling remains highly popular. More and more viewers are interested in the no-holds-barred world of ultimate fighting, surpassing boxing on most people's radars.

The rising popularity of video games, bolstered by the confluence of technology and culture, has significant consequences. Many young people would much rather spend their days playing games online or via the hottest video console in front of the television or computer screen then go outside to play or engage in a sport. Although critics bemoan video games for contributing to childhood obesity and diverting young people's attention away from schoolwork, the gaming industry is big business. Journalist Laura M. Holson reported on the growth of video games versus movies based on 2004 revenue totals, stating, "Video games are among the fastest-growing, most profitable businesses in the entertainment world. In the United States, domestic sales of video games and consoles generated $10 billion in revenue, compared with movie ticket sales of $9.4 billion."[1]

Cultural transformations are also changing the way people look at the sports they play. Golf, for instance, is losing players at an alarming rate, considering that Tiger Woods is the dominant professional athlete in the world, both on the course and as a celebrity spokesperson. Many younger, married men will not spend four to six hours away from their families on a weekend morning like their fathers did. For younger, single men, there are more entertainment options available today than ever before, from online video games to an endless array of cable television options. As a result, despite Woods's incredible fame, he is not attracting new players to the sport.

Actual physical activity during leisure time is declining and being replaced by time spent in front of the computer, video game, or television. A poll conducted in early 2008, for example, revealed that watching television was the favorite leisure activity for women, with 23 percent identifying it as such, followed by 16 percent who said using the Internet, then 10 percent saying that they liked to play free Web-based games. Only 4 percent claimed that playing sports or exercising was their favorite leisure activity. No other individual physical activity made the top 10 list.[2]

When examining the 11- to 17-year-old demographic, one sees that only 10 percent claim playing sports or exercising. They preferred either using the Web or talking on the cell phone, both at 19 percent. In contrast, women ages 55 to 64 most enjoy watching television (22%) or playing free Web-based games (18%). According to one observer, "More women than men say TV is their favorite leisure activity—almost one-third more. And TV scores as the favorite activity for women, while with men the internet edged it out for first place."[3]

The declining amount of physical activity (and the many health challenges that come with overweight and obesity) may come back to harm the nation, but forcing people up off the couch is not realistic, even if it makes sense. One thing is for sure. The Web-based technology that people love to use has a downside. Pandora's box is opened and the Internet is unleashed.

TECHNOLOGY

Social Media

The rebirth of the Internet after the spectacle flameout early in the decade came at the hands of Web users themselves who started to explore the Internet's capacity for linking people in a personal way, yet with the distance that online communications provides. Upstarts such as Friendster, Classmates, MySpace, and Facebook gave users the freedom to build profiles, a kind of online billboard that provided a public face for anyone who wanted to participate. Observers labeled these outlets "social networking" sites.

Web sites enabling regular users to build their own free homepages and share content, pictures, and other information without first learning intricate programming skills developed relatively early in Internet history. AOL, Geocities, and others served as early pioneers in the effort to get users their own tiny space on the Web. None of these sites, however, caught the user's imagination like MySpace and Facebook. Within a year of their launching in 2003 and 2004, respectively, each social media site changed the way people talk about the Internet. People nationwide could be heard saying, "Do you have a Facebook?" or "Check out my MySpace."

Founded in 2003 by Tom Anderson and Chris DeWolfe, MySpace grew quickly into the leading social network site. Launched as an online hub to showcase upcoming bands and musicians, MySpace rapidly evolved into a phenomenon, acquiring more than 106 million profiles by 2006. The ability to list and link to MySpace "friends" provided the gimmick that caught people's attention. In addition, users could manipulate their profiles to reflect their personalities, or at least the persona that they wanted other MySpace users to see.

MySpace's centrality in the Web 2.0 universe attracted Rupert Murdoch, the magnate who owns the media conglomerate News Corporation. In 2005, Murdoch purchased MySpace's parent company (Intermix Media) for $580 million. Although many users and critics railed against the new corporate owner, MySpace continued to grow and expand, moving into 24 countries by 2007. Under the guidance of its corporate parent, MySpace also charged into new content areas, forming its own record label and producing online video series. With its vast and deep user base, MySpace also developed into an advertiser's dream. Corporations flocked to the site to hawk their wares to the predominantly young demographic. Industry observers estimate that MySpace will draw about $800 million in revenue in fiscal 2008, primarily from advertising.[4]

The success or failure of MySpace's transformation from an independent site to more of a mainstream media outlet may be an indicator of how the Web will evolve in the future. Will independent-minded users keep coming back to the site as it becomes more of a media portal than a place, according to its slogan, "a place for friends." DeWolfe, the founder who runs the business aspect of MySpace, explains, "Some people still perceive MySpace like it was in early 2004, as a niche place for scenesters in New York and Los Angeles. That's how it started, but it's become very mainstream. It's about consuming content and discovering pop culture."[5]

Founded in 2004 by Harvard undergraduate Mark Zuckerberg, Facebook is MySpace's primary competitor in the social networking arena. Originally a tool to link college students at elite universities, Zuckerberg later expanded the site to other colleges and high schools, and then eventually opened to those outside universities. Facebook's strengths are its clean layout style and the ability to track one's friends' actions on the site, whether it is adding a gadget that ranks favorite movies or merely updating an online photo album.

Journalist Michael Hirschorn sees the site's ability to thwart spammers and porn site offers as a key to its popularity and continued expansion. In addition, Zuckerberg opened the site to outside developers, which enabled them to embed widgets that increase the user's experience. For example, members can send each other virtual gifts and challenge one another to music or film trivia contests. The key is that this interaction is contained among one's Facebook friends, which is more selective than the MySpace version. The exclusivity is an attractive quality for today's more discerning Web users. "If the overall trend on the Internet is the individual's loss of control as corporations make money off information you unwittingly provide, Facebook is offering a way to get some of that control back," explains Hirschorn. "In Facebook's version of the Web, you, the user, are in control of your persona."[6]

MySpace and Facebook continue to battle for supremacy among social media sites in the United States. In December 2007, for instance, MySpace logged 69 million unique visitors, compared with 35 million for Facebook. The numbers jump geometrically when examined by page views, with MySpace totaling 38 billion and Facebook 13 billion.[7] Looked at from a global perspective, however, Facebook is actually much closer to MySpace. In November 2007, MySpace had 105 million unique visitors worldwide; Facebook reported 93 million. Examining the total minutes users spent on the site, Facebook actually surpassed its rival: 21 billion minutes versus 17 billion minutes.[8]

Online Videos

The Web fulfilled its destiny in the mid- to late 2000s, finally becoming a kind of on-the-go television or theater. Spurred by technology, such as wider access to broadband Internet connections, and the popularity of social media networks, the Web moved from a primarily text-based mass media channel into one dominated by video. If a single entity can be credited for this shift, it is YouTube, owned by parent company Google.

The pervasiveness of online video is demonstrated by its astronomical growth. In November 2007, for example, more than 75 percent of Web users in the United States watched a video online, averaging 3.25 hours per person during the month. Powered by YouTube, Google is the dominant force in the video market. The company increased its market share in this category to 31 percent. In total, U.S. Internet users viewed approximately 9.5 billion videos in November; 2.9 billion of these were seen at YouTube.[9]

When examined individually, these statistics reveal that YouTube's 74.5 million users averaged 39 videos per person over the course of the month. In contrast, social media site MySpace tallied 389 million videos watched by 43.2 million people, or nine videos per user. The 3.25 hours per viewer is a 29 percent increase from January 2007.

Examined from a demographic viewpoint, the "typical" online video consumer is a male (53% versus 43% female), ages 18 to 29 (70%), with at least some college education (54%). In all, 60 percent of online video watchers claim household income exceeding $75,000. Investigating race/ethnicity, users break down as follows: English-speaking Latino (55%), African-American (46%), and white (45%).[10]

The results of the survey, conducted by the Pew Internet & American Life Project, confirm one's preconceived notions of who uses the Web most often and frequently visits sites such as YouTube. Other interesting aspects of the survey, however, show the true pervasiveness of online video. In all, 30 percent of those 50 to 64 years old said they visited video sites and 16 percent of those older than 65 reported the same. The findings regarding household income show that either viewers themselves are well off, or that the children of upper middle class families are the most likely to go to these sites. The large number of English-speaking Latinos who visit YouTube and other video pages confirms recent research that reveals astronomical Internet usage growth in the Hispanic community.[11]

In December 2007, with the writer's strike crippling television, statistics show that Americans turned to the Web to fulfill their viewing needs, with 141 million people watching more than 10 billion videos that month alone. This served as the heaviest month of online video consumption since comScore Video Metrix began tracking video hits. Market leader Google accounted for 3.3 billion videos, or nearly 33 percent of the total. The time spent watching videos also increased in December, reaching 3.4 hours (203 minutes) per person over the course of the month. That trend shows no sign of slowing, with the figure jumping 34 percent over the course of 2007.[12]

Video Games

Some critics shrug off the video game industry as if it were merely pimply faced kids sitting in a basement playing pong. The reality is that gaming is big business and a major player in the worlds of technology, consumer goods, and entertainment. The industry has morphed from a niche category into an $18 billion enterprise. The names that dominate the field include a who's who of global corporations, including Microsoft and Sony, as well as divisions of all the major film studios.

The biggest transformation in video games in the new millennium centers on making games more accessible to a wider audience. Teenage boys, although still important to the overall picture, are no longer the only market in town. Games like Guitar Hero and Dance Dance Revolution prove that video game companies are designing games that appeal to people of both sexes and all ages. According to journalist Seth Shiesel, "Companies that are making games more accessible are growing like gangbusters, while traditional powerhouses with a traditionally limited strategy of building around the same old (if you will) young male audience have stagnated, both creatively and on the bottom line."[13] The move is toward social gaming, where people interact with each other in front of the television. Then gaming develops into a party atmosphere, a big hit with college students and players in their twenties, who want the social along with the online experience. Nintendo's Wii console is a prime example of this trend, as is Guitar Hero. Nintendo cannot keep up with Wii demand, shipping 1.8 million units a month globally.

Clearly, social gaming is driven by technological innovations and a more robust broadband network, which reveals the tight relationship between culture and technology. Online PC games, for example, allow people to interact on the screen, eliminating physical distances, but necessitate high-speed Internet connections and souped up computer graphics and processors. Although these systems still appeal primarily to lone gamers, the numbers of subscribers are in the tens of millions.[14]

Concurrently, an even faster segment of the market is enabling interaction in front of the screen and bringing in families, older users, and females. Wii symbolizes this revolution, outselling more advanced systems, such as Microsoft's Xbox 360 and Sony's PlayStation 3. Wii Play ranked number two on 2007's bestselling video games. The game enabled interactive, yet simple, play among people using the system, which appealed to those not interested in learning codes or pressing multiple buttons in some arcane sequential order to win. "If new acceptance by the masses is one pillar of gaming's future, gaming's emergence as a social phenomenon is the other," explains Schiesel. "Hard-core gamers are still willing to spend 30 hours playing along through a single-player story line, but most people want more human contact in their entertainment."[15]

Online Shopping

The most pervasive consequence of the Internet is arguably its function as yet another outlet for Americans to shop. Given overcrowded malls and outrageous gas prices, many people choose to shop online, particularly during the Christmas holiday shopping season. Further enticing reticent mall-goers, many Web-based companies dropped shipping prices or eliminated them altogether. Others guaranteed pre-Christmas delivery for orders placed by a given date.

From November 1 to December 27, 2007, consumers spent about $29.2 billion online, a 19 percent jump over the 2006 total. Many shoppers purchased hot video games and consoles via the Web, with Sony PlayStation and Nintendo Wii driving sales.

Citing convenience as the primary reason for purchasing products online, two-thirds of American consumers who use the Internet told the Pew Internet & American Life Project team that they have bought an item online. This equates to about 49 percent of all Americans, up from 22 percent in June 2000. Although people enjoy the time-saving and ease of purchasing online, the Pew study found that people are concerned with the safety of their financial and personal data. A total of 75 percent of Internet users do not like giving this information online. Another sticking point is that nearly 60 percent of Web shoppers have felt frustrated, confused, or overwhelmed by the online experience.[16]

Although these worries are a natural outgrowth of the online experience, the tremendous pace of Web-based shopping grew quickly over the decade. In comparison, 22 percent of Americans said they had bought a product online in 2000, and 35 percent claimed to have used the Web for product-related research. The latter figure jumped to 60 percent in September 2007. Furthermore, although Web users conduct transactions in increasing numbers, the amount of money spent is growing even faster. The Census Bureau estimates that online revenues have skyrocketed up nearly 500 percent, from $7.4 billion in 2000 to $34.7 billion in the third quarter of 2007.[17]

CELEBRITY OBSESSION

Americans are not only obsessed with celebrities, but many actually act like minicelebrities in their own daily lives. This fascination with following celebrities and mimicking their moves is a constant reminder of Andy Warhol's prediction that someday everyone will be famous for 15 minutes.

Across the nation, people are imitating celebrities when choosing their clothing, hairstyles, sunglasses, accessories, and (most important) attitude. One merely needs to walk through a crowded mall to see the consequences of this fixation. For faux-celebs, life is a barrage of people bringing their formerly private lives into public view, just as tabloid journalism has done to celebrities on television shows like *Access Hollywood* and in magazines ranging from *US Weekly* to *People.*

In the 2000s, self-promotion is essential. In many respects, Web sites such as Facebook and MySpace and the never-ending stream of reality television shows actually teach people to expose themselves at every turn. On the social networking sites, for example, a user can describe a current mood, and then have it blasted out to all one's "friends," thus making a broadcast statement about oneself and forcing others into the emotion in at least some small way. Then when one's mood changes, that new information is sent again, just as the changes a user makes to the profile and group membership are posted for all to see. Users can even list their top friends and compare where they are in top friends' lists of their friends—a vicious cycle of self-absorption.

As it now stands, the United States is a country full of average people loudly carrying on via cell phone, bottled water in hand, wearing a tee shirt emblazoned with the message: "It's Always About Me." We do not look away in horror or subject these kinds of people to ridicule, as past generations might have done to those who tried a bit too hard to be the center of attention. We're all trying to be the center of attention. These displays of nihilism are commonplace occurrences; new millennium America is self-fascination at its zenith. Millions of people go through life with the feeling that they are one coincidental event from being discovered and becoming the celebrity they all dream of becoming. Ironically, many of Hollywood celebrities are fighting just as hard to remove themselves from the public eye, at least until their next picture is released.

Britney Spears

The headlines scream: "Last Day with Mommy," "Brit's Fight to Get Well," and "Inside Her Ordeal." The subject is Britney Spears, pop singer, celebrity, and popular culture icon. Americans cannot get enough Spears news, particularly when it focuses on her meltdowns, brushes with the law, hospitalizations, or battles with the paparazzi. She graces the covers of "celebtainment" magazines such as *People, InTouch,* and *US Weekly* with alarming frequency. Her every move seems to be captured on film nightly on *Entertainment Tonight, E! News,* and *The Insider.* Spears always ranks among the top-searched names on various Internet sites and a recent Google search returned 80.2 million hits.

Britney-mania even found its way into the venerable *Atlantic Monthly* in early 2008. Reporter David Samuels spent time with the paparazzi as they stalked Spears in and around Hollywood (ironically, as the wildfire threatened to burn down large chunks of L.A. and Hollywood). Samuels explained Spears's importance, saying: "History's best-publicized celebrity meltdown has helped fuel dozens of television shows, magazines, and Internet sites, the combined value of whose Britney-related product easily exceeds $100 million a year." Part of the Britney-economy is driven by an underground network of spies, tipsters, and photographers, who all pocket "stipends" for their work charting her every move, including "500 or 600 parking-lot attendants, club kids, and shop girls in and around L.A."[18]

In late February 2008, *The New York Times* chimed in, speculating about the status of Spears's net worth, estimated at anywhere from $50 million to $125 million. The article came on the heels of a series of involuntary treatments at the UCLA Medical Center. Jamie Spears, her estranged father, became co-conservator, or de facto control over her daily life. A team of lawyers set out to protect her financial interests, along with several family members, including her brother.[19]

As events in her life spiraled out of control, from allegations of heavy drinking to her failed marriage to former backup dancer Kevin Federline, Spears squandered a myriad of endorsement deals, said to earn her $12 million, from the likes of Toyota, Nabisco, Clairol, Sketchers, McDonald's, and Pepsi. She has an ongoing relationship with Elizabeth Arden for Britney perfume. Despite the steady stream of chaos and uproar that surrounds Spears, she is already mounting a comeback with a recurring role on the hit CBS comedy *How I Met Your Mother*. One insider explained her continued star power, saying, "Because we're so incredibly fickle as a society, the perfect entertainment is someone who's in the bottomless pit and rising again. If she's together, fit, beautiful and on her game, it'll be just printing money."[20]

Paris, Lindsay, and Anna Nicole

Since the birth of mass media, people have longed for news of celebrities, particularly those who shine bright, while at the same time appear somewhat dangerous. Paris Hilton, Lindsay Lohan, and Anna Nicole Smith each symbolize the celebrity obsession of the new millennium. Hilton is famous for being a mega-rich heiress and Los Angeles party girl; Lohan parlayed an early acting career into teen stardom; and Smith embodied the rags-to-riches story of a poor girl who transforms into a star.

Unfortunately in the world of celebrity, death actually propels a star's legend. In the case of Smith, she rocketed to success in the 1990s after appearing in Playboy and in several high-profile advertisements. She could not sustain the success and by the beginning of the new decade, her star power fizzled. But Americans love it when a celebrity makes a comeback. The E! cable network provided Smith with such a vehicle in 2002, *The Anna Nicole Show*, which centered on her bizarre behavior and interactions with an entourage of hangers-on. The show ran for two years and put Smith back in the spotlight.

Smith appeared in several films after her celebrity rebirth, but her fame grew exponentially when she became a spokesperson for the diet company TrimSpa. On the diet plan, she dropped about 70 pounds. Her outlandish behavior continued in late 2004 when she appeared at the American Music Awards, slurring her words and speaking incoherently. The next three years of Smith's life turned out to be a whirlwind of triumphs and tragedies, including the death of her son by an accidental overdose, marriage to longtime attorney Howard K. Stern, and the birth of a baby girl.

On February 8, 2007, a friend found Smith passed out in her hotel room in Hollywood, Florida, where she later died. Officials determined that she died from an overdose of a combination of medications. Smith lived in a media circus for most of her life, but after she died, the frenzy intensified significantly.

Cameramen and reporters fought for space outside her hospital after news of her death hit the airwaves. Enterprising journalists filed stories from Mexia, Texas, her tiny hometown. Smith news then hit the accelerator when the dispute over her daughter's biological father got played out in the national media. Soon, questions about her state of mind, battle with drugs and alcohol, and the multimillion dollar fortune she left behind were topics for discussion on celebrity news shows, Web sites, and magazines.[21]

In the 24-hour-a-day world of modern popular culture, it is difficult to determine whether the antics of celebrities such as Lohan and Hilton are the mindless deeds of young women who symbolize their generation, or the carefully plotted actions of media-smart celebrities who understand the goal is to stay in the news at all cost. Hilton, for one, hardly warrants the title of celebrity, her early fame derived from being rich and possessing a famous name. Since getting in front of the paparazzi, however, she has

Paris Hilton, left, co-star with Nicole Richie of The Simple Life Goes to Camp *(Fox) Season 5, Spring 2007. Fox/Photofest. © Fox. Courtesy of Photofest.*

built herself into a one-woman brand empire, from a singing career and reality television show to illicit video propelled by the Web and a short stay in jail.

Lohan is more difficult to understand, although her repeated stints in and out of rehab clinics makes one less certain that these are planned publicity stunts, resulting in a sinking film career and detrimental party girl image. If she meant to stay in people's minds this way, the effort certainly backfired. Lohan launched another offensive in March 2008, appearing on *New York* magazine as Marilyn Monroe and on the cover of *Bazaar*, looking innocent and clean, not at all like she just stepped out of a detox clinic. Such appearances sell magazines and provide celebrities with the chance to redeem themselves. "Scandal-craving readers snap up the issues, which often promise a star's first on-the-record account of her troubles," explains journalist Ruth La Ferla. "Ms. Lohan's Marilyn Monroe-inspired striptease for *New York* was the magazine's biggest selling issue of the past four years."[22]

SPORTS

In the summer of 2007, with ESPN cameras rolling, 32-year-old professional skateboarder Jake Brown fell 45 feet while performing at the X Games in Los Angeles. In the famous "Big Air" competition, competitors took turns dazzling the crowd and television viewers with aerial stunts on the 62-foot high, 293-foot long Mega Ramp. After the fall, spectators and other skateboarders in the games thought Brown died in the fall, although he walked off the ramp with assistance several minutes after the disaster. He wound up in an L.A. hospital with a liver injury, two sprained wrists, a bruised lung, whiplash, and a concussion. Luckily, Brown survived his brush with death. In fact, he became more famous after the fall, particularly as the video spread via the Web.[23]

This kind of willingness to push boundaries is a central tenet of the way people approach leisure time in the new millennium—at least among those who perform their leisure activities by getting up off the couch. What one might have assumed to be the limits are now just another goal for fitness-crazed people, whether that means doing yoga in a studio with the heat cranked up to 110 degrees or 40-year-olds running 5K races at less than six minutes a mile. In the United States, however, the fitness buffs are a vocal minority among an otherwise sedentary population.

Between 1999 and 2004, a study concluded that summer leisure time in the United States increased from five hours a day to six-and-a-half hours daily. This extra time, however, is being eaten up primarily by computers, television, and video games. Also taking up a great deal of leisure time is food (eating out, cooking/baking) and "me time" (reading, religion, pets). Gardening, for example, jumped 60 percent from 2000 to 2004. The greatest growth over that span, however, was watching a movie at home.[24]

Since the late 1990s, 20 million people stopped being active, many of them aging baby boomers. Of those over 45 who keep up fitness programs, they are more likely to be women than men (81% versus 66%). Baby boomers often turn to swimming as a primary form of exercise; people under 45 prefer running and jogging. About 80 percent of those considered active live in the western United States, where a healthy lifestyle is a given more than a task.[25]

Nascar Speeds to the Top

Everything about Nascar is larger than life. The drivers buzz along the super speedways at speeds eclipsing 200 miles per hour with just inches between them. The stands at the massive racetracks shoot up several hundred feet, seemingly straight up in the air. And, just for good measure, nearly every inch of the cars, drivers, and fan areas are covered with corporate logos from the most important brand names in the world. Of course, when racing at high speeds, what seems like a simple fender bender can turn into a multicar pileup with billowing smoke, fire, and near fistfights among drivers and fans alike. That is the beauty of Nascar—its fans are as passionate about the sport and the teams they root for as the teams are themselves.

The overwhelming fan support pays dividends for Nascar. In terms of dedicated spectators and corporate sponsorships, no other sports come

Nascar race day at Martinsville Speedway. Warner Bros./Photofest. © Warner Bros. Courtesy of Photofest.

close to professional football and stock car racing. The NFL and Nascar have a stranglehold on American culture, grabbing headlines whether in season or out. Racecar drivers such as Dale Earnhardt Jr., Jeff Gordon, Tony Stewart, and Jimmie Johnson are celebrities, growing in popularity more than the sport itself.

Gordon, for example, made headlines nearly as often during the 2007 for the birth of his daughter as for his racing. In the past, the popular four-time champion also appeared on both the *Regis and Kelly* morning show and *Saturday Night Live*. On November 29, 2007, more than 100,000 fans watched two-time Nextel Cup champion Johnson take his car on a victory lap around Times Square in New York City. The driver then made appearances on several national morning news programs.

If there is a chink in racing's armor, it is that the sport's tremendous growth over the last decade makes it difficult to keep up the pace. Regardless of its popularity, at some point the numbers will start to level out, particularly with every other sport in the world gunning for its audience. Television ratings, historically one of stock car racing's tried and true strengths, are leveling off, dropping 12 percent from 2005 to 2007. This figure is in line with other major professional sports, but still a sign of potential pitfalls ahead.

Another challenge Nascar faces is the rising cost of participation. Top organizations like Hendrick Motorsports or Joe Gibbs Racing have large facilities filled with engineers, software specialists, and technicians that cut into operating margins. Estimates show that the cost of fielding a team can eclipse $20 million. Granted, corporate money offsets team cost, but given the dicey national economy, some companies are cutting back.

Primary team sponsorship by Office Depot, Mountain Dew, or DuPont, for example, costs about $15 to $20 million. A secondary sponsorship, which may mean a small decal on a top driver's car, is $2 to $4 million. Teams, however, are not the only ones to gain in the relationship. A marketing firm estimated that each sponsor received $5.2 billion in television exposure during the 2007 season. Larry DeGaris, president of Sponsorship Research & Strategy, explained: "There's a lot of competition for sponsors right now. Teams are going to be selling against each other."[26]

Nascar's coffers certainly are not empty, even though some aspects of the business have stagnated. Nextel signed a $700 million, 10-year deal in 2004 for the primary naming rights and Nascar-licensed merchandise sales topped $2 billion each year from 2004–2006.

A survey of stockcar fans revealed that 71 percent "almost always" or "frequently" choose products or services because of their Nascar affiliation. So a Jimmie Johnson fan chooses Lowe's over Home Depot, and a Jeff Gordon supporter will drink Pepsi rather than Coke. More than any other professional sport, Nascar fans buy the products endorsed by their favorite teams.[27]

Table 7.1
Cost to Run a Nascar Nextel Cup Team

Feature	Cost (millions)
Engine Program	$3.5–$4
Cars (15–18 per team)	$2–$3 ($150,000 per car)
Tires	$1
Travel	$1.5
Team Salaries	$3–$4
Driver Compensation (salary, winnings, bonuses)	$2–$12
Total	$13–$23

Football

Football's inherent violence carries weight on and off the field. Between end zones, the game is full of career-threatening traumas, from multiple concussions to ruptured tendons and knee ligaments. After the game has ended, the violent nature of the game presents itself in the situations some players find themselves, from college stars getting into fights outside bars to professionals encountering gunplay. These kinds of stories dominate the news headlines and serve as fodder for radio and television talk shows. When a big name star is confronted with such challenges, the question becomes whether the game can survive, or will fans in some way turn their backs after reaching a breaking point.

In 2007, the NFL came under fire for the dog-fighting allegations and indictment of Michael Vick, the star quarterback of the Atlanta Falcons. A search of the three-time Pro Bowl player's property in rural Virginia uncovered more than 50 pit bulls and graves of dogs killed in an extensive dog-fighting ring sponsored by Vick. After a lengthy trial and protests by animal rights organizations nationwide, the judge sentenced Vick to 23 months in prison. Although he could be released early, the former star also faces state dog-fighting charges that could result in additional jail time.[28]

Pundits wondered whether the NFL could withstand having one of its highest-paid and most prolific players jailed for such cruel charges. After the verdict and authorities carted Vick off to jail, however, the media machine turned to other stories. Vick became old news, as stale as a week-old donut. The 2007 and 2008 football seasons went off without a hitch, although when Atlanta Falcons games were televised nationally, one could see many "7" jerseys in honor of Vick. Commentators made the obligatory remark or two, but they basically avoided the topic and the game continued. Despite the Vick verdict, football remains the most popular American sport. By the time the 2007 season ended, there were fewer and fewer mentions of Vick.

Football, however, continues to thrive. Millions of people participate in fantasy football leagues across the nation, and betting action in Las Vegas picks up dramatically during the season, culminating in the college bowl games and Super Bowl. When the Pittsburgh Steelers beat the Seattle Seahawks in the 2006 Super Bowl, people bet $94.5 million in Vegas, a then-record. Experts estimated that the latest game between the New York Giants and New England Patriots topped $100 million. Although it is impossible to prove, pro football is thought to generate about $10 billion in gambling, both legally and illegally. In contrast, the NFL makes about $7 billion in revenues each year.[29]

Basketball

A handful of years ago, on the playgrounds in and around Cleveland, whispers circulated about a young kid in nearby Akron who might be the next Michael Jordan. He possessed otherworldly athletic ability with attributes that cannot be taught: size, speed, vision, and a natural feel for the game. The budding superstar's name was LeBron James. When sketchy rumors turned into hard facts, the story seemed too typically rags-to-riches to even be true, like the creation of the perfect athlete by some shoe company for marketing purposes. He helped lead his team to the state championship—despite a tumultuous home life and being raised by a single mother in Akron's toughest ghetto.

Two events changed James's young life forever: appearing on the cover of *Sports Illustrated* in early 2002 (when only a junior in high school) and christened "The Chosen One," and then seven months later playing a game against perennial high school champions Oak Hill Academy nationally televised on ESPN2. The *Sports Illustrated* article and flurry of copycat stories that followed put him on the national radar screen. The hype machine included another cover story, this time for *ESPN The Magazine,* revealing a much different James dealing with his newfound fame and the subsequent avalanche of publicity. As the region's largest newspaper, The *Cleveland Plain Dealer* took over the James watch, virtually covering his every move, including "The James Journal," a compendium of all things LeBron.

The attention of the print media placed James on a pedestal. Before the rise of the Internet and countless new media outlets (from talk radio shows to cable television programming), this degree of buildup would have been reserved for a mere handful of proven superstars. In the twenty-first century, however, when many celebrities are famous for little more than being famous, a high school superstar can grab the interest of the world. And yet, despite all the hype, a relatively few people had actually seen James play basketball.

That all changed, however, in late 2002 when ESPN2 televised the Saint Vincent-Saint Mary (SVSM) match-up with Oak Hill Academy. The network then followed the first broadcast with an early 2003 game against Mater Dei High School at the famed Pauley Pavilion on UCLA's campus, a basketball temple in the heart of La-La land. Befitting a legend in the making, James responded to the limelight in both games, thus cementing his position as the next big thing in the sports world.

A crowd of more than 11,500 spectators packed Cleveland State University's Convocation Center to see the game against Oak Hill, some paying more than $100 for courtside seats. Also in the mix were dozens of NBA scouts and officials and even a couple of players from the Cleveland Browns, all out to judge the skills of the 17-year-old high school phenomenon. More important, for the television network, the game drew a 1.97 rating, which equates to 1.67 million homes tuning into the high school basketball contest. James's star power made the telecast ESPN2's highest rated program in the two years since its coverage of the death of NASCAR legend Dale Earnhardt.

The final box score revealed SVSM's utter dominance over the former number one high school basketball team in America, 65–45. James lit it up for 31 points, 13 rebounds, and 6 assists in his television debut. After the Oak Hill game, LeBron James would no longer be an urban legend, like playground heroes from yesteryear. His national debut and astounding success against one of the country's best high school teams turned skeptics into believers. The James hype machine went into overdrive.

Many of today's sports and entertainment heroes have an edge. They appear a little dangerous, often just half a step away from a good brawl or jail cell. This hardcore image appeals to the MTV generation. Teenagers always seem to fall for the kind of corporate-sponsored rebellion MTV peddles, whether it is the latest rap single providing a glimpse of street life, the "bling-bling" lifestyle, or violence-filled videogames and movies. As a matter of fact, many young people would rather sit around playing videogames than actually play a particular game itself, so the videogame companies fill their wares with action and graphics that are cartoon-like. Basketball games feature crazy dunks, high-flying acrobatics, and little, if any, fundamentals. Why shoot a 15-foot jump shot when a dunk could be had?

What may make LeBron James the perfect NBA idol for the twenty-first century is that he combines the style and grace of Michael Jordan with a healthy dose of urban culture, personified by young rappers and sports stars, such as Nelly, Jay-Z, Ludacris, Allen Iverson, and the late Tupac Shakur. James has that big smile and natural good looks, which appeals to consumer product marketers, while at the same time possessing the skills and toughness that attracts the free-spending teenage demographic.

Although a combination of talent and personality fueled Jordan's rise to icon status, James differs in that he is from the ghetto, thus naturally possessing more "street cred." James also more readily identifies with black urban culture. Unlike Jordan, who lived a middle class lifestyle growing up in Wilmington, North Carolina, James has risen from the ghettoes of Akron, a rough town in the aging Rustbelt, struggling to stay vibrant as the manufacturing-based economy vanished, leaving high unemployment rates and many people struggling to survive.

James and his mother (who gave birth to him when only 16 years old) jumped from apartment to apartment when he was little, always searching for a little better way of life, but unable to escape the vicious cycle of poverty. Like many young black men across the nation, James has never met his biological father.

Unlike some athletes who embellish the tough times of their youths to gain respect among their peers, James does not have to exaggerate his experiences in the roughest sections of town. He told *Sports Illustrated*, "I saw drugs, guns, killings; it was crazy. But my mom kept food in my mouth and clothes on my back."[30]

On the court, James personifies the popular cultural influences that shape today's teenagers. He wears it on his skin, in the form of multiple tattoos (which he had to cover with white athletic tape while in high school according to SVSM school rules) to the dress code teens follow—the ever-present headband, armband, droopy shorts, and oversized jersey. In the videogame and cable show world of spectacular dunks and highlight reel plays, James excels at symbolizing his generation, even though his individual game is about so much more than freewheeling acrobatics. For corporations looking for a fresh face, the youngster will appeal with his good looks and bright smile.

On the streets, and particularly in the African America community, respect is a key tenet of an individual's social mindset. The idea of respect among young black males has been portrayed in numerous popular culture vehicles, from a slew of television shows and movies to the lyrics of slain rapper Biggie "Notorious B.I.G." Smalls and other hip hop stars. James shows his respect for those who have given him guidance and support by publicly thanking God and showing his reverence for his mother. In return, James asks for the community to respect him for turning raw ability into brilliance.

James is not immune to the chest pounding, trash-talking style that pervades basketball, whether on the blacktop behind the local high school or in NBA arenas around the country. After dunking on an opposing player, James ferociously yells, "King James," or "You sorry," reports a writer who has covered James.[31] At one time this kind of behavior would have been punished or scorned, but now popular culture glorifies displays of individual self-importance that give athletes a kind of signature gesture that kids can then mimic. Showing up an opponent not only ensures that an athlete "gets his," but can make him more famous (or infamous).

There are many similarities between James and Michael Jordan (circa the early 1980s) in addition to the familiar number 23 they each wear. On the court, both have tremendous quickness and jumping ability. When the game ends, they each flash a similar multimillion-dollar smile and display an innate, natural charisma. Like the youthful Jordan before him, James is even criticized for having a weak jump shot—about the only Achilles's heel in his game.

Because he is routinely compared with Jordan and seemingly destined for NBA superstardom, James faces incredible pressure every single day of his life. These demands intensified when he became the first pick in the 2003 NBA draft. Observers expect James to single-handedly resurrect the hometown Cleveland Cavaliers, despite the franchise's history of under-performance and disappointment.

In fact, this level of anticipation and expectation separates Jordan and James. Over the last several years, James has already experienced Michael Jordan-level attention. Every move he makes on and off the court is up for public consumption and scrutiny. Jordan, on the other hand, did not face this pressure as a rookie because the NBA was a different place then. Jordan certainly did not have much of a grace period, but there was a time when he still had some measure of privacy. Of course, as the team's number one draft pick, Jordan was expected to help the club right away. No one, however, expected the scrawny kid out of the University of North Carolina to become the Michael Jordan that he developed into.

In contrast to the way James's star has risen, there is almost an innocence to Jordan's ascent to global icon status, even though he became a star in his freshman year at the University of North Carolina after hitting the game-winning jump shot against Georgetown in the NCAA Championship game. Observers who watched Jordan realized that he had the potential to be a special player, but no one thought he would develop into the greatest player to ever live. The general public gradually recognized Jordan's immense talent, hand-in-hand with seeing his face on television in Nike ads.

One NBA Western Conference scouting director explained how James would have to push himself to achieve the level of Kobe Bryant, Tracy McGrady, and the handful of top pro stars. "He's able to get by on his physical ability right now," the scout told sports writer Marc Stein. "The question is, what happens when he can't just get by on physical ability alone? The mental side, the emotional side, those are unknowns. In high school, the only thing we're seeing is the physical ability."[32]

James is already considered the game's next great marketing hope. Experts estimate that his first shoe contract—signed with Nike after a years long battle with Adidas—approached or exceeded $90 million over five years. Although he waited until after the draft to sign the Nike deal, college was never really an option for the youngster. He had been marketed too long to be put on the shelf while competing for any major college program.

Jordan took a liking to James, inviting him to Chicago to play together and giving the youngster his top secret cell phone number. It is a role Jordan has taken with other young, African American superstars, such as his close friendship with golf sensation Tiger Woods. Critics, however, view the James-Jordan relationship with a grain of skepticism, thinking that the move was intended to get James on the Nike payroll, like his basketball idol.

As James's on-the-court exploits continue to electrify and his jumper has started dropping on a regular basis for the Cavs, thus muting the one criticism of his game, the only issue that concerns basketball experts is how the young man will deal with the fanfare. An NBA Eastern Conference scout explained the way a high school player affects a team, stating: "The problem with taking on a high school player is that, for the coach, you're dealing with a lot of things you don't normally deal with. And it takes up a lot of time." Summing up the challenge of easing a teenager into the game, the scout explained, "These kids don't even know how to keep a checkbook when they get to the NBA."[33]

In the years since joining the NBA, James developed into one of the league's most popular players and one of its fiercest competitors. He won Rookie of the Year after the 2003–2004 season, in which the Cavs tallied 18 more victories than the preceding year. The next year, James averaged more than 27 points per game, then surpassed that figure at 31.4 points per game in 2005–2006. That season the team made its first playoff appearance since 1998 and James won the All-Star MVP.

In 2006–2007, James led the Cavs to the NBA Finals for the first time in team history, although they were swept in the best of seven series by the San Antonio Spurs, the closest thing the NBA has had to a dynasty in the last decade. The ability to lead his somewhat undermanned team to the championship round evoked comparisons to Michael Jordan, the same comparison James faced since bursting on the national scene as a teenager. According to Howard Beck, "What James does best, other than win, is make the game look simple. He can fill a box score and dominate on the court without ever looking as if he is trying to do either. The greatest measure of an N.B.A. star is how much he lifts up his teammates, and James excels in this category."[34]

Golf

There is a serious conflict in the world of golf today. On one hand, Tiger Woods is possibly the greatest golfer who ever lived and draws the sport huge television ratings, in addition to his global fame. Woods's wins and winning personality, however, have done little to popularize golf or draw more people into the game. One could argue, however, that the true measure of Woods's work in this regard will not be reflected for another decade, but the numbers as they currently exist reveal that playing golf is dropping in popularity.

Tiger Woods in the made-for-TV golf match Lincoln Financial Group "Battle at Bighorn,"
ABC Sports, July 29, 2001. © 2001 ABC, Inc. Courtesy of Photofest.

Woods is not only the best golfer in the world, but he is the king of endorsements. His phenomenal popularity led to a wide range of gigs as celebrity spokesperson, from Gillette razors and Nike to management consulting firm Accenture and Buick. In early 2008, *Chicago Sun-Times* columnist Jay Mariotti went as far as to declare that measured by "his impact on sport and fashion and popular culture and the American condition" that Woods has now surpassed the legendary Michael Jordan. When combining the level of excellence on the playing field with the carefully managed aura in the celebrity world, it does seem that Mariotti's statement rings true.[35]

In pro golf, the ultimate measure of success is the number of major tournaments won. Woods stands in second place on the all-time list with 13 majors, behind Jack Nicklaus who owns 18. Eleven of Woods's major wins took place in the new millennium, as well as many of his other notable achievements, including winning 11 tournaments in 2000 and possessing all four major trophies at one time by winning over the 2000–2001 timeframe. Through 2007, Wood earned $76.6 million on the PGA Tour and $94 million overall.[36]

While Woods won tournaments, drove revenues for corporate partners and the PGA Tour, and brought in countless millions for charity, the number of people who play golf in America either stayed flat or has declined since 2000. The National Golf Foundation and the Sporting Goods Manufacturers Association estimate that the total number of people who play golf has dropped from 30 million to 26 million since 2000. More troubling than this figure is the significant drop in the number of people who play 25 times a year or more (6.9 million in 2000 and 4.6 million in 2005) and eight times or more (17.7 million in 2000 and 15 million in 2006). "The man in the street will tell you that golf is booming because he sees Tiger Woods on TV," explains Jim Kass, research director of the National Golf Foundation. "But we track the reality. The reality is, while we haven't exactly tanked, the numbers have been disappointing for some time." Kass is optimistic, but the combination of an aging population in the United States and a less active younger generation spells real trouble for golf and many other recreational sports.[37]

Ironically, given golf's link to consumerism and corporate sponsorship, the difficult economy is the primary factor people claim keeps them from playing more often—if at all. According to Kass, the surveys show that people are working more, making less in real wages, and corporations are cutting back golf-related perks, such as the country club membership. In the early years of the 2000s, observers believed that the retiring baby boomers would actually increase the number of golfers. Playing on this hunch, many additional golf courses were built, with more than 3,000 created between 1999 and 2003. The surplus actually resulted in a glut, and many facilities are up for sale or gone bankrupt, mainly in Arizona, Florida, Michigan, and South Carolina.[38]

Mind, Body, and Spirit

Business travelers serve as a wonderful barometer for new pop culture trends. In the 2000s, many hotels catered to these harried consumers by mixing the idea of a traditional hotel with spa-like amenities, such as personal trainers, yoga instructors, and professional masseuses. The dichotomy is typical of life in the new millennium: on one hand, business travelers are contending with the stress of being away from love ones in an often hostile (even scary) environment in today's air travel world, while at the same time, travelers are offered spectacular perks that are a sign of how pampered many people want to be. Consumer desires drive sales and hotels respond to the money-making opportunity. According to Joe McInerney, president of the American Hotel & Lodging Association, hotels are eliminating corporate meeting facilities and replacing them with spa equipment. "Everybody's putting one in," he explains. "If you don't have one, you're not competitive." In the cutthroat fight for revenue, the focus on upscale features wins business.[39]

Many travel experts rank New York's Mandarin Oriental as the nation's top hotel/spa. Though in the heart of the Big Apple, the 14,500-square foot facility boasts a swimming pool that looks out onto the city's skyline. Among the 38 services the Mandarin offers are 110-minute Oriental Harmony massages (featuring two masseuses and a $615 price tag) and 20-minute manicures. Although the hotel spas are geared toward business travelers (primarily men), women make up about 60 percent of the clients. Bob Thompson, an attorney from Washington, D.C., stays at hotel spas to balance out the stress of air travel. Visiting Dallas and Austin, Thompson choose hotel spas "only because they have whirlpools, steam and saunas to rest my feet and weary bones after putting up with airport screeners, late flights and surly flight attendants."[40]

The hotel spa trend is part of a larger movement designed to not only get Americans more active and spiritually fit but to move New Age thinking into the mainstream. Yoga, for example, has become big business in the new millennium. The 2008 "Yoga in America" market study released by *Yoga Journal* magazine indicates that Americans spend $5.7 billion a year on yoga classes and products, including clothing, equipment, vacations, and media (books, magazines, videos, and DVDs). This is an 87 percent increase over the amount spend in 2004. Approximately 15.8 million people practice yoga in the United States, about 7 percent of adults in the country. Another 4.1 percent of survey participants who do not currently practice yoga said that they plan to begin in the next year, which translates to about 9.4 million people. What the numbers reveal is that yoga participation has stabilized somewhat, but yoga-related spending has nearly doubled, which shows how the *sport* has transformed into a *lifestyle*.[41]

The popularity of yoga and other conditioning exercises, such as Pilates, is being driven by adoption in mainstream gyms and fitness centers, a move away from yoga's mystical roots. A nationwide chain with more than 385 locations, 24 Hour Fitness features traditional yoga classes and classes that mix yoga with additional strength exercises. The International Health, Racquet & Sportsclub Assocation (IHRSA) reports that membership in U.S. health clubs remained virtually unchanged between 2004 and 2007 at about 41.5 million members, which it attributes to the economic downturn and belt-tightening consumers are experiencing.[42]

Even video games, such as Nintendo's Wii system, are attempting to get users up off their couches and into shape. For example, the game Wii Fit blends new technology with old fashioned working out. Standard measurements, such as body mass index and balance, are combined to derive the person's "Wii Fit age." The user can then set workout goals specific to their own bodies. Using a balance board that comes with the game, the user is led by a virtual trainer through exercises in yoga, balance, aerobics, and strength building. The balance board provides instant feedback as one completes the tasks and other exercises built into the game, including slalom skiing.[43]

JUICED: BASEBALL'S STEROID CHALLENGE

In February 2008, Roger Clemens—by nearly all accounts the most dominating pitcher in his era and one of the greatest of all time—appeared before a Congressional panel investigating steroid use in baseball. For fans who grew up idolizing Clemens and other big name legends, the day crushed dreams. For cynics already skeptical about the state of the national pastime, Clemens's testimony (shown live on ESPN) sounded phony—another nail in baseball's coffin. A survey conducted shortly after the pitcher's testimony revealed that a majority of baseball fans (57%) did not believe his claim that he never used performance-enhancing drugs.[44]

Clemens is the most recent legend caught up in the steroid scandal that has rocked baseball for years. Standing at home plate is Barry Bonds, baseball's all-time homerun champion, the virtual poster boy for illegal performance-enhancing drugs in the game, allegations that have dogged him for a decade. Sitting on the bench are other superstars (Andy Pettite, Rafael Palmeiro), mid-level players (Brady Anderson, Jason Giambi), and regular players (John Rocker, Brett Boone) who are accused of using steroids to elevate their games in an era when drug use seemingly ran rampant.

Few players have admitted to using steroids or growth hormones, although much of the current debate about drug use can be traced to a tell-all book by former all-star Jose Canseco, *Juiced* (2005). Although widely ridiculed at the time of publication, Canseco's book foreshadowed much of what followed over the next three years. Taking a different approach, Jason Giambi, for instance, publicly apologized to New York Yankee fans without ever specifically stating what he had done to warrant such an apology.

The Clemens accusations came to light in the final report of an investigation commissioned by Major League Baseball and headed by former Senator George Mitchell, dubbed "The Mitchell Report." A media circus erupted after the release of the findings, although a deeper read revealed that much of Mitchell's juiciest information came from disgruntled trainers and other peripheral people loosely affiliated with the game. This information diminished the report somewhat, but did not stop the wall-to-wall coverage of the names involved, including the big fish caught in the expedition, Roger Clemens.

Journalist Tom Verducci calls the reaction to Clemens part of the "perpetual, multimedia cycle in the Britneyfication of events," which included live events and a nationally televised interview on *60 Minutes*. Clemens, however, deserves a special place in the history of steroid investigations, because he chose to publicly defend himself. According to Verducci, "Hundreds of ballplayers have used performance-enhancing drugs. Only a fraction of them have been publicly identified as users. None have gone anywhere near the lengths Clemens has to defend themselves. He even asked to appear before Congress."[45]

The Mitchell Report grew out of a series of events that dominated the headlines in the 2000s, including the 2003 raid of the Bay Area Laboratory Cooperative (BALCO), which revealed that Giambi and Bonds were clients. A series of Congressional hearings in 2005 featured testimony by Mark McGwire and Palmeiro. The former refused to say anything about possible steroid use, but the latter angrily declared his innocence in a video clip that has been played countless times then and since. That Palmeiro tested positive for illegal drugs just months afterwards forced Major League Baseball to act, thus leading to the formation of the Mitchell commission. According to professor Abraham Socher, "The pharmacological genie has long been out of the bottle . . . still, the report is valuable for the wealth and specificity of its detail."[46]

BREAKING INTO THE MAINSTREAM
Mixed Martial Arts

In the early years of the new millennium, Ultimate Fighting Championship (UFC) dominated the then-underground sport of mixed martial arts, a modified street fight that took place in an octagonal ring in which contestants were either knocked unconscious or submitted. The fights, unlike professional wrestling, were real and often bloody. The gritty realism of splattering blood and forced submission or true knockouts gave the sport a brutality that fans desired, even as commentators and legislators questioned the legality of such fights. The payoff for Ultimate Fighting and other sanctioning mixed martial arts organizations was the dream 18- to 34-year-old male demographic that large companies battle to attract.

Before ultimate fighting's recent popularity and legitimacy as a sport, fans who wanted to see UFC were basically limited to pay-per-view events, which some states would not even allow to take place in their jurisdictions. Quickly, however, mixed martial arts moved from the extreme fringes of the sports world to center stage. The spectacle of watching two men basically knock the snot out of each other captured the interest of fight fans growing weary of mismatched boxing matches and the deterioration of the heavyweight division, most notably by the seemingly invincible Mike Tyson and the bland fighters that blundered through the weight class after Lennox Lewis retired.

From these rather auspicious beginnings, mixed martial arts grew into a force in the sports world. By 2007, cable network Showtime aired matches. Then in early 2008, CBS announced that it would become the first major broadcast network to show mixed martial arts fights. The network said that it will place bouts on Sunday nights, which is the least watched night on television. The goal is to draw in young viewers who have traditionally shied away that night. Not incidentally, CBS owns Showtime, which is helping with production.[47]

UFC is the elite organization for mixed martial arts. In the 1990s, the company had been marred in legislative and regulatory battles at the hands of critics who lamented the sport's violence, including Arizona Senator John McCain. The move to the mainstream began in 2001 when Dana White and two old sparring partners bought the company for $2 million. By 2006, UFC had pay-per-view sales of $223 million and sold out arenas across the nation. White bought out Pride, an Asian competitor, for $70 million in 2007. The company also started a reality television show on Spike TV, a Viacom-owned cable network directed at young males. In June 2007, the season finale of The Ultimate Fighter 5 drew 2.6 million viewers.[48]

Some commentators believe that mixed martial arts is the perfect vehicle for attracting young male viewers who have been raised on ultra-violent video games. Others point to the UFC's real fights, a far cry from the scripted world of professional wrestling. At least in part owing to the power of the Web and online videos as a distribution channel, a number of mainstream and underground no-holds-barred sites exist, ranging from the illegal to the outlandish. In early 2008, on YouTube alone, thousands of amateur fight videos are available, from *Fight Club*-style matches to high school females squaring off in suburban locations. And, of course, clips from UFC and other companies are freely available online.[49]

Extreme Sports

For a generation of young people raised on the constant movement and whirl of video games, traditional sports often lack the thrill-a-minute pandemonium they crave. To fill the void, spectators turned to extreme sports, everything from high-flying skateboarding stunts to Ironman triathlons. While a person over the age of 35 who grew up playing baseball or basketball may scratch his or her head in amazement, wondering why many of these events are even labeled sports, the combination of television, corporate sponsorship, and hipster cache have turned extreme sports into an important part of modern popular culture. The International Olympic Committee (IOC) certainly recognizes the attractiveness of extreme sports. The Winter Olympic Games added snowboarding and freestyle skiing to its lineup of events to draw the younger set. The Beijing Summer Olympic Games is following suit, adding BMX bicycle racing.

The attraction of BMX racing for extreme sports fans is the three-story start ramp, which competitors hurtle down, often reaching 40 miles per hour. With eight bikers on the track, the potential for nasty pitfalls increases exponentially. The inherent danger attracts spectators and ratings, which Olympic officials and corporate sponsors long for. Donny Robinson, of three Americans on the U.S. Olympic BMX team, highlights the danger, saying, "It's like doing a rollercoaster on a bike."[50]

A new extreme sports superstar may emerge from the Beijing games, but the Michael Jordan of extreme sports is legendary skateboarder Tony Hawk. Like Jordan, Hawk built on his athletic prowess, becoming a mainstream popular culture icon and transcending his sport. For many people, Hawk is transforming skateboarding, formerly practiced by angry teens and misfits, into a legitimate sport. As a result of Hawk's popularity, countless young people aspire to a career as a professional skateboarder, in addition to the pro circuits in surfing, snowboarding, and others.

If corporate America can be used to measure mainstream success, then Hawk is certainly one of the most popular athletes in America. He has marketing and licensing deals with a whole host of businesses, including Activision, Jeep, Kohl's, and McDonald's. In addition, Hawk's empire expands to clothing, skateboard gear, sports event management, and amusement parks. The "Tony Hawk's Big Spin" rollercoaster ride is opening at Six Flags parks nationwide and a 30-city tour, dubbed "Hawk's Boom Boom HuckJam," appeals to teens by fusing daredevil extreme sports with rock and rap music. Hawk even started a multimedia production company that does projects for ESPN, Fox Sports, and others, while he has his own weekly radio show on Sirius Satellite Radio. Market analyst Marshal Cohen calls the mix of urban, hip-hop, and suburban lifestyles the "skurban market." He explains that "there's tremendous growth opportunity, and Tony Hawk can represent more than just skateboarding. This market has evolved into a worldwide cultural phenomenon."[51]

8
Literature

All my first lines will hopefully suck you in. I have a low attention span, and I think in today's society, I need to grab you on page one and suck you in—and not by cheap tricks, but by making you care.
—Harlan Coben (2008)

In 2000, after a disappointing theatrical run in which it made only $37 million (compared to production costs of $63 million), *Fight Club* came out on DVD. Released in two editions, the set revolutionized the medium, because director David Fincher supervised its production, including now-commonplace "extras," such as commentary tracks, deleted scenes, and other special features. The immediate popularity of the DVD led to the film becoming an instant cult classic. Imagine—all over the nation actual fight clubs sprung up based on the popularity of the movie.

More important, the success of the DVD turned Chuck Palahniuk, author of the *Fight Club* novel, into a cult figure in his own right. Based on word-of-mouth popularity and a crazed fan base tuned into every known detail about him and his work on the Web, Palahniuk transformed from former diesel mechanic to one of the hottest writers in the world. Fast forward to 2007, with the release of *Rant: An Oral Biography of Buster Casey,* and Palahniuk's 10 books have sold more than 3 million copies.[1]

The hub of Chuck-related activity turned out to be "The Cult," his official Web site, created and run by Dennis Widmyer since 1999. Early in its existence, the site featured news and interviews with Palahniuk. "Members" of The Cult, however, soon took on more cultish activities (in some senses peacefully replicating "Project Mayhem" from *Fight Club*), such as guerrilla marketing techniques in major cities around the nation to publicize his books. As a result, the author scored a string of *New York Times* bestsellers.

Palahniuk is one of literature's central figures in the new millennium, not only for his sales and dark subject matter, but also for the way he grew from unknown to global superstar. His upward trajectory is a combination of movie adaptation, quirky subject matter that appeals to readers across the spectrum, Internet mania, and highly effective marketing. Palahniuk, although now going on a decade of unparalleled success, represents the forces that come together in the twenty-first century to propel winning writers into another stratosphere. There must be a mix of word-of-mouth marketing, Internet hype, differentiated content, and some modicum of luck. Palahniuk is a popular culture phenomenon in his own right, perhaps in some circles more famous than any of the celebrities that starred in *Fight Club*—of course, except Brad Pitt, but that is a discussion best saved for another section of the book.

This chapter examines the literature of the new millennium—both epic, bestselling works and the highbrow fiction reserved for English literature grad classes. Included is a discussion of the many forces that turn seemingly ordinary writers (fiction or nonfiction) into pop culture icons.

Actor Daniel Radcliffe portrays boy wizard Harry Potter in Harry *Potter and the Sorcerer's Stone (2001). Warner Bros./Photofest. © Warner Bros. Courtesy of Photofest.*

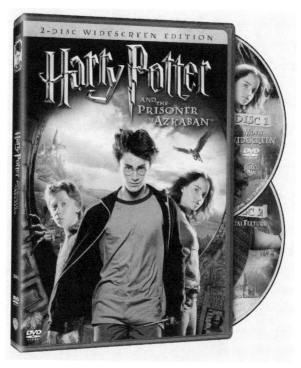

DVD box art for Harry Potter and the Prisoner of Azkaban
*(2004). Warner Bros./Photofest. © Warner Bros. Courtesy of
Photofest.*

FICTION

Harry Potter Mania

No one could have predicted the worldwide phenomenon the Harry Potter
books would set off when virtually unknown British author J. K. Rowling
published the first book in the seven-novel series in 1997. By 2004, *Forbes*
magazine estimated that Rowling parlayed the Potter fame into a billion-
dollar enterprise complete with movies, tie-in products, toys, and a variety of
other related products. During the height of the series and subsequent films,
the release actually led to increased business in affiliated industries. Observers estimated that the Harry Potter brand name is worth $15 billion.[2]

Warner Bros. is an example of Potter's influence in other media; the company benefited from the $2 billion the first two movies grossed worldwide.
The fifth film, *Harry Potter and the Order of the Phoenix*, grossed $44.8 million
on its Wednesday release, then the highest first-day sales figure in history.
The summer blockbuster went on to make a whopping $140 million in its
first five days. The movie company plans to release the final film for the
last book in two parts in the summers of 2010 and 2011.

Online bookseller Amazon.com also benefited both financially and in its branding efforts from the scope of the Potter series. The site allowed consumers to preorder the last book, *Harry Potter and the Deathly Hallows,* in February 2007, and the book shot to the top of its bestselling titles five months before publication. Amazon then partnered with the U.S. Postal Service and UPS to ship 1.3 million copies on its release date under unusually tight security measures. Potter mania grew to white-hot intensity and the bookseller did not want to allow early copies to make their way into the public spotlight.[3]

The Harry Potter phenomenon not only made Rowling rich and increased the profits of many partners tied to the brand, but the wizard also had a broader cultural impact, most notably increasing literacy rates among children. A 2006 report issued by The Kids and Family Reading Report and publisher Scholastic revealed that the series helped get more kids reading for fun and do better in school. In all, 65 percent of respondents claimed that they performed better in school since starting the series, which 76 percent of parents also said. "Only once in a lifetime does a children's literary phenomenon like Harry Potter come along," said Lisa Holton, president of Scholastic Book Fairs and Trade Publishing. "Harry Potter has become part of our culture, and what it has done so magically is to prove that even in the digital age, well-written books are and will remain a great source of enjoyment and enrichment for adult and young readers."[4]

The Da Vinci Code

Although Harry Potter received more media attention over a longer span, Dan Brown's *The Da Vinci Code* (2003) stayed parked atop the bestseller list. In 2004, Brown's publisher, Random House, brought out a "Special Illustrated Edition," of the book, which also saw sales skyrocket. By mid-2006, more than 60.5 million copies were in print.

Few could have predicted such stellar heights for Brown, a moderately successful thriller writer up to that point in his career. *The Da Vinci Code* centers on Harvard professor Robert Langdon's investigation into a murder at the Louvre Museum in Paris. There are several secret societies involved, including the Roman Catholic Opus Dei.

Of course, any book that becomes so intimately ingrained in the popular mindset is also going to be turned into a movie. The big screen adaptation, directed by Ron Howard and starring Academy Award-winner Tom Hanks, debuted in May 2006 to decidedly mixed reviews. Still, the movie grossed $224 million worldwide its opening weekend. Over the next six months, the film grossed $758 million.

Bestsellers

The book section of a Costco store is a sight to behold for booklovers. Seeing a couple hundred copies of a single popular title under one roof is like entering a fantasy world. Then, realizing that there are dozens of titles

Audrey Tautou, left, and Tom Hanks, stars of the film version of Dan Brown's bestseller The Da Vinci Code *(2006). Columbia Pictures/Imagine Entertainment/Photofest. © Columbia Pictures/Imagine Entertainment. Courtesy of Photofest.*

and hundreds of paperbacks available, one simply swoons. The discount price is icing on the cake.

The person responsible for the Costco book section is its book buyer, Clark (Pennie) Ianniciello. According to one publishing insider, Ianniciello "has an uncanny knack for leading customers to buy books, for molding their taste. She seems to know what they'll enjoy discovering." Along with the traditional big name writers, the Costco team picks cookbooks, children's books, coffee-table books, reference works, and others that may appeal to the company's sometimes-quirky clientele.[5]

For admirers, the upside of discount retailers, such as Costco and Sam's Club, is that they make books affordable and available. For many people, the option of going into a bookstore, which houses hundreds of thousands of titles, and browsing around the stacks, simply rings too closely to forced library days at schools. Critics contend that big box bookstores, discounters, and online mega sites have too much control over what America reads. In cahoots with the small handful of publishing conglomerates, the booksellers more or less select which titles to get behind and push hard.

On any given week, the likes of James Patterson, Stephen King, John Grisham, Danielle Steel, Nicholas Sparks, and Harlan Coben battle for the spot on the national bestseller lists. Increasingly, these name brand authors live and die by the blockbuster mentality adopted by the movie and music industries. They release their books in hopes that the first week out scores that number one placement.

Each of Harlan Coben's books fight for the top of the bestseller lists. Once a year, he publishes one thriller. It debuts at number one or somewhere near the top. The process is like clockwork. His novels are plot-driven. "I start with an idea, not a character," he explains. "I write about people who are living right and wrong still finds them." This seemingly simple formula leads the reader on a wild ride, with multiple twists and turns—the book equivalent of riding a great rollercoaster ride.[6]

Book critic Chuck Leddy describes American's literary culture as "schizophrenic," because observers routinely criticize books that sell millions of copies or show up on the bestseller lists for somehow being naturally inferior based on popularity. On the other hand, the title "artist" is reserved for the select few who have been deemed worthy by a select group of prize jury participants or members of university English departments. "Elitist prejudice against genre fiction is undemocratic and unfair—and misses the truth that genre writers have as much artistic aspiration as literary authors," Leddy says. "The schizophrenia that has fostered the false dichotomy between art and commerce should end. Commercial success isn't a curse, nor obscurity a perverse badge of honor."[7]

Literary Fiction

The notion is that literary fiction does not sell, but 2007 saw numerous critically heralded books climb onto *The New York Times* Bestseller List. Some of the notable titles include Michael Chabon's *The Yiddish Policeman's Union;* Ian McEwan's *On Chesil Beach,* Norman Mailer's *The Castle in the Forest;* and Ann Patchett's *Run.* Still, the market for literary fiction is shrinking as the nation continues its digital transformation. The squeeze is felt by publishers, agents, and writers themselves, who increasingly find difficulties getting published or noticed in a world filled with multiple James Patterson novels on the bestseller list.

According to journalist Rachel Donadio, "The pride and joy of publishing literary fiction has always been wonderfully ill suited to the very industry that sustains it. Like an elegant but impoverished aristocrat married to a nouveau riche spouse, it has long been subsidized by mass-market fiction and by nonfiction ripped from the headlines. One supplies the cachet, the other the cash."[8] As a matter of fact, the entire publishing system seems built to keep most novels from selling well, focusing on timing and volume first and foremost. This is strikingly ironic considering that the entire industry is built on sales. Like movies, DVDs, and music CDs, books destined for the bestseller lists are shipped in huge quantities to satisfy the needs of the large retail chains. Grassroots marketing efforts and attempting to build an audience over time are tactics that used to work, but have lost their footing in the 2000s.[9]

In 2005, for example, nearly half of the literary fiction sales came from the top 20 books. This means that fewer literary works sold many copies at all, even from those with faithful fans and a minor following. Some established writers are pulling out all the stops to bolster sales. When promoting *The Plot Against America* in 2004, Philip Roth appeared on the *Today* show and PBS's *Newshour,* his first American TV appearances since 1968. Even with the television tie-in, however, most observers believe that it was Roth's critique of the Bush Administration that propelled the book onto national bestseller lists (the book sold more than 415,000 copies).[10]

Michael Chabon

Michael Chabon has "the look" of a serious writer—tall, with piercing blue eyes, and dark curly hair—although he could probably also pass for a former actor or musician. When he talks about writing, his face gives way to a radiant smile and a kind of deeply intellectual look around his eyes, adding gravitas to his voice. He is the type of person who really *listens* to a question and then answers with wit and thoughtfulness, more interested in the interplay than just using it as a dramatic pause to hear his own voice, like so many successful people today. What is more important (even in our media frenzy world) is that Chabon possesses enormous talent. His accolades grow with each subsequent novel and include a then-record highest advance ever given for a first literary novel ($155,000) and the granddaddy of them all, the Pulitzer Prize in 2001 for his novel *The Amazing Adventures of Kavalier and Clay.*

Chabon's first novel, *The Mysteries of Pittsburgh* (1988), won him widespread acclaim as a kind of late 1980s Fitzgerald, even though he was only several years out of undergraduate work at the University of Pittsburgh and fresh off an MFA at University of California, Irvine. A literary career was born. After a collection of short stories came out, however, Chabon stalled for a handful of years on a novel that he just couldn't finish. His frustration grew into the wonderfully quirky *Wonder Boys* (1995), later adapted into a critically acclaimed movie starring Michael Douglas and Tobey McGuire, released in 2000.

The same year the film came out, Chabon published *The Amazing Adventures of Kavalier and Clay.* Set in the World War II era, the main characters—a Jewish Czech artist named Joe Kavalier and a Jewish American writer named Sam Klayman—create a comic book in the "Golden Age" of the industry, *The Escapist,* which draws on their fascination with real-life escape artist Harry Houdini. Using pieces of the real lives of many of the comic book industry's founders, Chabon tackles ideas about patriotism, Jewish folklore, exploitation, and discrimination. The big themes addressed in the novel, combined with Chabon's lush style, certainly led to the Pulitzer Prize, one of the most prestigious prizes a novelist can earn.[11]

Since winning the Pulitzer, Chabon has published two other adult novels: *The Yiddish Policeman's Union* (2007) and *Gentlemen of the Road* (2007); a novella, *The Final Solution* (2004); and a young adult work, *Summerland* (2002). He also put out a collection of nonfiction essays and pieces in 2008, *Maps and Legends*. Like many fantastic American writers before him, Chabon ventured into the gates of Hollywood, pitching several movie ideas. The comic book aspect of *Kavalier and Clay* earned him greater credibility, as well as his association with director/producer Scott Rudin, who adapted *Wonder Boys* for the silver screen. He wrote for the 2004 sequel *Spider-Man 2*, which grossed more than $783 million worldwide.

Literary Lions

While highbrow critics lament the popularity of lowbrow novels and trashy autobiographies that capitalize on the often-fleeting fame of the latest sensational news story, many of the writers that have dominated the last four or five generations continue to pour out critically acclaimed novels that provide insight into the American soul. John Updike continues his prolific production, averaging a novel every other year, from 2000's *Gertrude and Claudius* to 2008's *The Widows of Eastwick*. In the decade, he also published a book of poetry, several short story collections, and two books of nonfiction. Norman Mailer, who died in late 2007, published *A Castle in the Forest* earlier that year, which reached bestseller lists nationwide.

Mailer's death marked one of many that slowly thinned the ranks of the nation's literary greats: between 2004 and 2007, Kurt Vonnegut, Hunter S. Thompson, Saul Bellow, and Susan Sontag died.

Although the dons of the American writing community keep in the public eye, many have taken on a quieter tone, which is a far cry from the situation at the beginning of the 2000s. The decade began with Tom Wolfe chiding John Irving, John Updike, and Norman Mailer. He labeled them "the Three Stooges" and Mailer and Updike "two piles of bones." Wolfe's attack centered on what he viewed as his fellow writers' unwillingness to address the world around them; he believed they were navel-gazing writers, wrapped up in their own lives instead of addressing the wider world. Wolfe, on the other hand, advocates a new brand of realistic fiction, like the kind written by Sinclair Lewis in the early years of the last century. The feud continues, albeit less dramatically, and with each new publication, the authors take another jab at one another.[12]

Many of the nation's literary lions gained new readers after being named selections of the Oprah Winfrey's Book Club. Toni Morrison had three books highlighted by Oprah, and a select handful of writers had two novels climb the bestseller lists after being spotlighted by the powerful talk show personality. Others who benefited from the Oprah touch include Jane Hamilton, Maya Angelou, Barbara Kingsolver, Joyce Carol Oates, and Cormac McCarthy.

Winfrey's impact on publishing in the late 1990s through the new millennium cannot be overstated. "It's not true that Oprah Winfrey's book club was the most important development in the history of literacy," explained journalist Richard Lacayo with tongue firmly in cheek. "For instance, there was the invention of the written word. Then there was movable type. So Oprah comes in third. But no lower, at least not in the opinion of publishers and booksellers, who binge every month on the demand for whatever title she features on her show." Lacayo believed that Oprah's pick had the power of making serious fiction as popular as professional wrestling.[13]

With more than 25 million viewers who hinge on her every word, Winfrey continues to exert considerable force in publishing. In 2002, for example, when she shuttered the Book Club for a year, claiming that she could not keep up with the demands of a monthly pick, book experts thought it might spell doom for the industry. Upon returning the next year, Winfrey picked classic literature, beginning with John Steinbeck's *East of Eden*. As a result, the book spent weeks atop the *New York Times* paperback bestseller list.

In 2006, after being named an Oprah pick, author James Frey admitted that his book *A Million Little Pieces* contained half-truths and fabrications about his years as a recovering addict. He appeared on the show to apologize and Winfrey, according to one journalist, "turned on him with calculated efficiency, using him to mop up the floor and clean up her reputation at the same time."[14] Many observers were in Winfrey's corner, for the pick helped Frey sell about 3.5 million copies.

In true digital age fashion, investigation Web site the Smoking Gun (www.thesmokinggun.com) exposed Frey's exaggerations, which Winfrey and others initially discounted. As more allegations came to light, however, the insurmountable mountain of evidence against Frey forced Winfrey and others to change their tunes. The Frey controversy followed on the less damaging scandal in 2001 when Winfrey chose *The Corrections* by Jonathan Franzen. He criticized some of her picks and asked that the Book Club stickers be removed from his book. Some observers saw Franzen's postpick criticism as a way to generate further publicity (and sales).

NONFICTION

The combination of the war in the Middle East, an unpopular president, a general celebrity obsession, and the nation's diet and self-help craze propels the nonfiction market. In any given week, the books topping bestseller lists range across these topics, from celebrity memoirs to investigative pieces that promise to go inside the war machine guiding the war in Iraq.

The New York Times even began an "advice" list to shuffle these titles into their own category. The advice list is dominated by authors like Rhonda Byrne (*The Secret*), Joel Osteen (*Your Best Life Now*), and Deepak Chopra (*The Third Jesus*).

War Books

The wars in Iraq and Afghanistan generated enough books to fill a small library. Part of this glut resulted from journalists being embedded with troops in Iraq. The combination of on-the-ground reporting and the fascination with the war propelled many of these books. Another set of books came from Washington insiders, those with access to administration and military sources. The big change in terms of the publishing industry is that the more people who bought war books, the quicker publishers would get them out. Some books presented events that happened six to eight months previously. The hotter the topic, the quicker the book got into print.

The attraction of military books is obvious and continues a trend that takes place after each war, particularly with soldier memoirs. Journalist Chris Ayres, who wrote a book based on his experiences embedded with the Marines, explains, "When you actually stand back a few paces, you see the absurdity of the embedded scheme, the horrible accommodations, the terror of being there, and the strain it puts on your psychology."[15]

Blogs

The intersection of technology and demand for 24-hour-a-day news combined to make blogs an important part of the nonfiction world in the 2000s. Blogs are a type of online diary that enable the writer to post and publish almost instantly. With the advent of easy to use blogging tools, millions of people joined the online community. In recent years, users have added voice-based entries (dubbed podcasts) and video-based ones (vodcasts). In late December 2007, there were about 112 million blogs.

Much of the blogosphere is akin to digital diaries, family albums, and pages dedicated to celebrity or band worship. Others, however, have taken the medium more seriously, elevating it to a new mass media channel. Andrew Sullivan (www.andrewsullivan.theatlantic.com) and Arianna Huffington (www.huffingtonpost.com) are examples of mainstream journalists who used blogging to expand their reach. In addition to the online-only blog groups, newspapers and magazines have a cadre of bloggers who write exclusive or syndicated material for them.

9

Music

I was touring the country at the time, saying America is not just a
country, it's an idea, and that idea is under attack. When you're under
attack, you have to double-lock the doors. You have to rethink things.
You have to make sure of what you believe in.
—Bono, discussing 9/11 (2005)

From Thomas Edison's invention of the wax cylinder phonograph in 1877
to the latest Web-based innovations, technology is at the heart of the music
industry. Technological innovation and change go so completely hand in
hand that one can chart the advance over time from records and phono-
graphs to MP3s. Each subsequent invention builds on its predecessor and
revolutionizes music performance and consumer response. The intersection of performance (the music itself) and consumer response (people listening and/or purchasing) defines the music business.

In the new millennium, divergent forces compete with each album released, new video produced, or ring tone created—media convergence and
the white noise produced in a culture that churns on and on nonstop. The
idea behind convergence is that lines between media channels no longer
exist. For instance, where does viral marketing for a new band begin and
how does that intersect with traditional forms of advertising?

In the music business, convergence provides greater opportunities for
artists and management to compete in the battle for consumers across all
mediums. The sheer volume of messages produced in a converged society,
however, also leads to information overload, or a seemingly endless cloud
of marketing, advertising, sales, and informational touch points demanding something from consumers—their attention, money, memory, or actions. Therefore every artist in a converged culture operates in a setting
that enables constant interaction with consumers across numerous media

outlets, but the idea that everyone is always adding to the system creates a crisis situation in which people cannot decipher or distinguish the messages.

The search for a footing in the slippery, converged world really defines what popular culture is all about in the new millennium. For most artists and the corporate marketing efforts supporting them, convergence leads to a blockbuster mentality or an all-out program designed to create huge release day sales that will then lead to greater exposure, thus greasing the marketing gears that keep the pop culture industry churning.

In 2006, Epic Records built such a program around "A Public Affair," the new single from pop singer and actress Jessica Simpson, who is a virtual case study for how to build a celebrity in the new millennium. Already a well-known singer, Simpson developed into a megastar based on her highly publicized MTV reality television show with then-husband Nick Lachey, which portrayed her as less than intelligent, but somewhat normal. She rode that momentum into starring roles in several films, including the remake of *The Dukes of Hazzard,* playing Daisy Duke. Epic produced two videos for the song, one a big-budget typical video; the second was pieced together from fan clips. The fan angle also led Epic to provide customizable versions of the song on Yahoo! Music, which it then followed with a poster that provided a text message for people to sample the song. Epic marketing executive Lee Stimmel explains the need for such a comprehensive program, saying, "It's hard to break a record these days—it takes a lot more avenues of exposure."[1]

Pulling the fans into the creative process and then giving them a chance to interact with their submissions plays on the general narcissism of Americans today. With outlets like YouTube, people know that they can create their own version of their favorite songs, so record companies and artists attempt to bring them into the process sooner through such contests.

A constant yearning for fame—almost a feeling of being entitled to it—gripped the nation in this decade. As a result, young people would do just about anything to have their moments in the public eye. For a tiny minority, the payoff takes place, but the vast majority either never get their bit of fame or wash up on the wreckage that is a natural by-product of the reality industry. *American Idol* has ruled the television airwaves for most of the decade, despite being little more than a televised talent show. The payoff is that a "normal" person will survive the process and achieve the American Dream.

The fascination with reality television brought the world *American Idol,* one of the biggest influencers on the music world. Even the runaway success of the series, however, cannot overshadow the impact of technology on two primary fronts: the widespread theft of digital music and Apple's iPod.

Another curious phenomenon that points to the intersection of music and technology is the out-of-this-world success of interactive rock video games such as Guitar Hero and Rock Band. Since being released in 2005, Guitar Hero I and II grossed more than $360 million. The video games, perhaps fueled by the idea that the player gets to morph into a celebrity for a few minutes, sparked a renewed interest in classic rock by a younger generation who does not instinctively know The Sex Pistols, ZZ Top, or the Ramones.[2]

APPLE'S iPOD

A Google search for "iPod" in early 2008 returned 319 million hits. A search engine is hardly a scientific indicator, but the figure certainly reveals how deeply the iPod rests in our national psyche. Not only has the term *iPod* become virtually synonymous with *digital music player*, but the device led to an entire industry of other products to support it, from Bose headphones to combination speaker/base systems to turn an iPod into a complete home entertainment unit. The iPod also influenced styles of dress, requiring designers and manufacturers to come up with clothes that enable one to easily carry the device.

In 2006, the iPod celebrated its fifth anniversary and, in many regards, the rebirth of Apple as one of the world's great consumer goods companies. Steve Levy, author of a book about the device, *The Perfect Thing*, practically gushes, "The iPod nano was so beautiful that it seemed to have dropped down from some vastly advanced alien civilization. It had the breathtaking compactness of a lustrous Oriental artifact." In addition to changing the way people interact with their personal music library, the iPod also presented music lovers a way to download music legally, a far cry from the days of Napster.[3]

On October 23, 2001, Apple chief executive Steve Jobs launched the first iPod, saying "With iPod, listening to music will never be the same again." Even Jobs, however, could not have realized the impact the music player would have on Apple. When he made the announcement, shares sold at around $9 per share. In April 2008, the stock stood at $147 a share, an astronomical increase in such a short time. Furthermore, although Microsoft and SanDisk launched their own MP3 players to compete, Apple dominates with more than 70 percent of the market.[4]

DOWNLOADING MUSIC—FREE AND OTHERWISE

The rise of the Web in the mid to late 1990s led to the popularity of the mp3, a new kind of compressed music file condensed enough that it could be swapped online. Although compressing the file reduced the sound quality, manageability trumped aesthetics. For the most part, only true aficionados could tell the difference between an mp3 file and an audio CD track. Depending on a person's computer modem speed, an mp3 could be downloaded in minutes or as quickly as a few seconds.

The ability to trade music over the Internet had a mushrooming effect culturally. First, users essentially violated copyright rules when swapping music online. Then, as is typical of a capitalist system, innovation runs with money-making potential. A number of file-sharing companies formed, the most infamous being Shawn Fanning's Napster, which became synonymous with free downloading. Soon, however, consumers seemed to believe that the ease of downloading music from Internet sites somehow made the music "free."

In the early days of file-sharing, most users stored the music on their computer hard drives, either using their computers as a sound system or burning the files onto CDs to play on the go. Later, with the rise of portable mp3 players, most notably the iPod, people uploaded the files to the device directly.

Despite rampant file-sharing and the music industry's weak initial reaction, the courts eventually caught up with Napster. In 2001, the U.S. Supreme Court ruled against the company, declaring free music swapping illegal and in violation of music copyrights. Although the music industry shut down Napster as an illegal file-sharing site, others such as KaZaA and Limewire used a new innovation, called peer-to-peer (P2P) networking, to continue the practice. P2P is a decentralized file-swapping service that enables users to download from computer to computer without housing music or video centrally.

CD Sales Plummet

Despite the challenges the music industry faced from online piracy, full-length CD/album sales reached 785.1 million units in 2000. Optimists chalked the figure up to listeners basically previewing songs and bands online, and then purchasing CDs afterward. At that time, the music business seemed like it would weather the online theft storm, although sales dropped to 762.8 million in 2001.

Nevertheless, as the decade progressed, industry watchers realized the complete devastation music piracy inflicted on the business. The pessimistic viewpoint—that piracy would kill album sales because consumers would not pay for what they could download for free—came to fruition.

In 2002, total album sales fell to 681.4 million, more than 100 million less than two years earlier. Three years later, the number dropped to 618.7 million. By 2007, CD sales dropped to 500.5 million units, a 36 percent plummet over the course of the decade. The 2007 figure stands as the lowest sales number since Nielsen began estimating the data in 1993.

Although music piracy decimated the CD business, the ubiquitous MP3 player led to burgeoning sales of digital singles. When calculating total music sales, including singles and digital songs, overall sales jumped 14 percent to 1.4 billion units from 2006 to 2007. Although these numbers seem encouraging on the surface, most of the new transactions were digital tracks. In addition, the total sales year-over-year figure was less than the previous year, down from 19 percent. Even digital track sales fell from a 65 percent increase in 2006 to 45 percent in 2007.

The primary challenge for the industry, according to Kenneth Kraus, a music attorney in Nashville, is that "we've lost a whole generation of kids" who grew up illegally downloading music. As a result, CD sales may never regain the losses from earlier in the decade.[5]

Perhaps revealing the depths of the battle the music industry faces regarding online piracy, the top two selling albums in 2007 were not by hip-hop, rock, or rap artists. Instead of rap impresario Kanye West or timeless rocker Bruce Springsteen at the top of the charts, adult contemporary singer Josh Groban charted the best-selling CD in 2007, reaching 3.7 million units. The second-ranked album was the soundtrack to the Disney Channel TV movie *High School Musical 2,* which sold 3 million units. In contrast, Usher's album *Confessions* sold about 8 million copies in 2004.

In 2007, CD sales also fell in every major music genre, from hip-hop (30%) to country (16%). Only three rock groups sold more than half-a-million CDs: Fall Out Boy, the White Stripes, and Paramore. With the music labels in a freefall, retailers who sell CDs turned to alternatives to get into the fan's wallet, including selling more DVDs and computer games, such as the incredibly popular Guitar Hero. Classic rock icons The Eagles

Josh Groban performs at the 2006 American Music Awards. ABC/Photofest. © Craig Sjodin. Courtesy of Photofest.

Table 9.1
Total Album Sales, 2000–2007

Year	Total (millions)
2000	785.1
2001	762.8
2002	681.4
2003	656.3
2004	666.7
2005	618.7
2006	588.1
2007	500.5

Source: Nielsen SoundScan

circumvented the labels altogether, selling their album *Long Road Out of Eden* directly via Wal-Mart. The gamble paid off, with the band charting the third highest selling CD of the year, totaling 2.6 million copies.[6]

AMERICAN IDOL

An argument about whether *American Idol* is more a music or a television topic would be a difficult (if not impossible) debate to win. The show has changed both industries. From a music viewpoint, a slew of new pop singers (and, ironically, not just the winners) have emerged based on the show's popularity. The biggest names include first season victor, Kelly Clarkson, second season runner-up Clay Aiken, and fourth season winner Carrie Underwood. Some performers have launched surprisingly strong careers based on their *Idol* work, but others who were considered sure-fire successes have fizzled after the show's glaring lights went dim.

The successes and failures of *Idol* contestants shows the difficulty of breaking into the music business, even when handed the keys to one of the industry's strongest franchises. For example, Taylor Hicks did not parlay his fifth season victory into a major debut, stalling at the lower rungs of the sales list. His album sold more than 700,000 copies, a respectable figure for a new artist, but not when one considers that the final episode drew more than 33 million viewers. Chris Daughtry, however, used his experience as a springboard to selling more than 3 million records and reaching number one on *Billboard*. As a matter of fact, some of the singers who scored big on their first albums after victory then found rougher roads on their follow-up efforts.

Some Idol singers find themselves on independent labels after the season ends. For some it is a risky move, but has an upside if fans respond. Elliott Yamin, who scored a third-place finish, signed with new label Hickory Records.

His debut has sold more than 300,000 copies. "I don't have any gimmicks. I wanted to be genuine, I wanted to cross over," Yamin explains. "I wanted to make a singer's type of record, and it is selling. People are responding to it."[7]

NEW ORLEANS SURVIVES KATRINA

Hurricane Katrina destroyed much of the Ninth Ward district in New Orleans. Among those losing their homes stood legendary rock-and-roll pioneer Fats Domino, who had lived there for nearly 50 years. The news of his rescue gave music fans something to cheer about, after initial reports indicated that he went missing as the flood ravaged the region.

All over New Orleans, similar rescues took place as other areas slipped deeper and deeper underwater. The levees holding back Lake Pontchartrain gave way, obliterating much of the city's musical heritage. Thousands of little bars, nightclubs, and music venues were devastated in the flood, what some observers believed to be New Orleans's true gift to music history. In addition, countless New Orleans musicians, from band leaders to recording session players, lost their homes and livelihoods in Katrina's wake.

As the musicians of New Orleans regrouped, others put together benefit shows to help the residents of the Big Easy. A giant show put together by MTV, VH1, and CMT featured the Rolling Stones, Paul McCartney, and many others. BET offered its own relief effort, led by Russell Simmons, Jay-Z, Chris Rock, and Stevie Wonder. Master P, a New Orleans resident and founder of No Limit Records, discussed the ruin, saying, "All of the houses are gone—everything people worked for and sacrificed for. Most of the stuff washed away."[8]

RAP AND HIP-HOP

A 2007 survey conducted by the Pew Research Center revealed that a significant number of Americans view rap and hip-hop as a bad influence on society, citing offensive language, violence, and negative portrayals of women. In all, 64 percent of whites and 61 percent of blacks think hip-hop is a bad influence; 74 percent of whites and 71 percent of blacks say the same about rap music. Among Hispanics, 59 percent perceive hip-hop negatively, and 48 percent view rap the same.[9]

When examined by gender, there are significant differences. The report shows that, "Among whites, men are much more likely than women to say hip-hop and rap have a bad influence on society. Among blacks, however, the gender relationship tilts in the opposite direction—women are more likely than men to say these forms of music are having a bad influence."[10]

Blacks (45%) and Hispanics (40%) are far more likely to listen to hip-hop than whites (23%). Those who do listen often or sometimes to hip-hop tend to be younger, 79 percent of blacks ages 18–34 listen to hip-hop, and 64 percent to rap. Young whites, however, also listen to hip-hop (56%) and rap (47%).

In 2007, radio shock personality Don Imus served as an unlikely catalyst for public outrage against rap lyrics by calling the Rutgers women's basketball team a derogatory phrase for prostitutes and linked it to race. The media frenzy against Imus transformed into a more general demand that rap and hip-hop musicians clean up their work. Bill Cosby, Oprah Winfrey, and the Rev. Al Sharpton led the demand for change. The aimed their outrage at the ostentatious displays of wealth in hip-hop videos, the objectification of women in the songs and videos, and the virtual nonstop use of the N-word in their lyrics.[11]

Despite hip-hop's negative image among the general population, young people are avid fans and consumers. Both album and singles charts are constantly filled with the work of rap, hip-hop, and other entertainers that fall somewhere in between. It would not be a great stretch to say that hip-hop and rap have defined the music of the new millennium, so much so, in fact, that many now claim that these music genres are now the mainstream.

Rap artists consistently top the charts. For example, 50 Cent (a.k.a. Curtis Jackson) scored 2005's top-selling CD and had four songs in the top 10 on Billboard's pop chart—the first artist to do so since the Beatles.

Hip-hop's centrality to the nation's popular culture can be seen in an exhibit held at the Smithsonian Institute in 2008, featuring portraits of hip hop stars, such as LL Cool J, as well as music. Artist Kehinde Wiley painted the four original pieces in the exhibit in 2005 as part of a VH1 tribute program. Assistant curator of photographs at the Smithsonian Frank Goodyear says that the mainstream has attempted to push hip hop from the center, however: "There's nothing marginal about hip-hop at all. Hip-hop is at the center of our culture. It's the most influential cultural phenomenon that extends beyond the music."[12]

Yet, although hip-hop maintains its cultural importance, actual album sales have fallen off over the past several years. Rock music continues to lead in market share, with country music placing second. In 2006, rap/hip-hop slipped to third place, accounting for 11.4 percent of the market at about 131 million.[13] Certainly when discussing rap and hip-hop, one must acknowledge that the cultural influence surpasses the actual popularity in terms of sales, indicating that hip-hop is a lifestyle, perhaps to an even greater extent than it is a music genre.

Hip-hop's influence crosses into other areas that show the genre's increasing cultural importance. Sean "P. Diddy" Combs, for example, is an internationally acclaimed fashion designer, with his "Sean John" clothing line that extends him as a brand name. At the same time, Combs continues to produce other young stars and perform. He is also a budding actor, not only starring in the movies *Made* and *Monster's Ball,* but also appearing in the 2004 Broadway version of *A Raisin in the Sun,* which followed with a televised adaptation in 2008. Combs even owns a movie production company and restaurants.

Table 9.2
Top-selling Rap Artists, 2006

Artist	Album
1. T. I.	King
2. Lil Wayne	Tha Carter II
3. Eminem	Curtain Call: The Hits
4. Ludacris	Release Therapy
5. The Notorious B.I.G.	Duets: The Final Chapter
6. Chamillionaire	The Sound of Revenge
7. Yung Joc	New Joc City
8. Rick Ross	Port of Miami
9. Juelz Santana	What the Game's Been Missing!
10. Busta Rhymes	The Big Bang

Source: Billboard

PERFORMERS

Timeless Rockers

Although pop music grabs a great deal of attention, particularly from those under the age of 25, rock and roll remains a lynchpin of American culture. At the same time, however, the music industry is moving toward a blockbuster mentality in which musicians are judged by their hits today, with much less emphasis on their careers. In an era of downloads and ring tones, the traditional idea of a "rock star" may soon disappear. In the future, we may not have rock's elder statesmen, but rather a collection of hyped artists who could not sustain a career of any lasting impact.

The notion that the rock star is at an end really proves the greatness of timeless rockers such as the Rolling Stones, Neil Young, Aerosmith, and Bob Dylan. The subsequent generation has also proved its longevity, with artists like Madonna, Prince, U2, and Bruce Springsteen still making groundbreaking and popular records. For example, Springsteen's 2007 album *Magic* debuted at number one, a great feat for an icon who released his first album before many of today's music listeners were even born. The Rolling Stones's *A Bigger Bang* tour, which lasted from 2005 to 2007, became the biggest tour in music history, grossing $558 million.

Bob Dylan

Bob Dylan remains a prolific singer/songwriter and iconic figure in popular culture. In the new millennium, he has released a series of

Table 9.3
Top Ten Classic Rock Ring Tones, 2006

Artist	Song
1. AC/DC	"Back in Black"
2. Lynyrd Skynyrd	"Sweet Home Alabama"
3. Ozzy Osbourne	"Crazy Train"
4. Pink Floyd	"Wish You Were Here"
5. Journey	"Don't Stop Believin'"
6. Def Leppard	"Pour Some Sugar on Me"
7. Steppenwolf	"Born to Be Wild"
8. AC/DC	"Hell's Bells"
9. Van Morrison	"Brown Eyed Girl"
10. AC/DC	"Thunderstruck"

Source: T-Mobile

Table 9.4
Top Concert Tours in 2007

Year	Total (millions) $
The Police	133.2
Justin Timberlake	70.6
Van Halen	56.7
Rod Stewart	49
Genesis	47.6
Bon Jovi	41.4
Dave Matthews Band	41.1
Billy Joel	39.1
Roger Waters	38.3
Bruce Springsteen and the E Street Band	38.2

Source: Pollstar

groundbreaking CDs, including *Love and Theft* (2001) and *Modern Times* (2006). His reissues have been just as prolific, including *The Essential Bob Dylan* (2000), *Live 1975* (2002), *Live 1964* (2004), *No Direction Home* (2005), *The Best of Bob Dylan* (2005), and *Dylan* (2007). In 2000, he won both a Golden Globe for Best Original Song and an Academy Award for

Bob Dylan continues to redefine himself as a performer in the new millennium. Columbia/Photofest. © Columbia Records. Courtesy of Photofest.

Best Song for "Things Have Changed," which appeared on the *Wonder Boys* soundtrack.

In addition, as he approaches age 70, Dylan has taken a more public role than any time in the recent past, doing advertisements for Cadillac, Victoria's Secret, and Apple. He also hosts a highly acclaimed radio show ("Theme Time Radio Hour") on XM Satellite Radio. Dylan published *Chronicles: Volume One* in late 2004, the first of a rumored three-volume memoir. Dealing with the early years the singer spent in New York City and flashes of later years, he took a nonlinear path through his career that enticed readers. The book spent many weeks atop bestseller lists, both nationally and regionally, and got nominated for a National Book Award.

In 2003, the film *Masked & Anonymous,* which Dylan co-wrote (using a pseudonym) with television writer/producer Larry Charles made its way into theaters, starring Luke Wilson, John Goodman, Mickey Rourke, and a host of well-known actors. Most thrilling for "Dylanologists" was that Dylan himself starred as former rock legend Jack Fate, who is bailed out of jail to perform a one-act benefit concert in a society spiraling out of control. People either loved or hated the film. In typical Dylan fashion, the movie either confounded viewers or just presented another vision of the musician's unique view of a nation at the end of its rope.

Dylan served as the subject of two other projects in the new millennium. Famed director Martin Scorsese released a two-part documentary, *No Direction Home,* in 2005. The film, which featured taped interviews with the singer himself, focused on his early rise to fame through his near-fatal motorcycle accident in 1966. In 2007, the film *I'm Not There,* written and produced by Todd Haynes, used six different actors to represent various parts of Dylan's life, including Marcus Carl, a 13-year-old African American actor and Academy Award-winning actress Cate Blanchett, who won widespread praise for portraying Dylan's mid-1960s "mod" phase. The daring film earned critical acclaim and spots as one of the year's 10 best films at *The Washington Post, Premiere, The Village Voice,* and many others.

U2

Two titans of the music business came together in 2004 when U2 and Apple teamed up to launch an ad campaign for the iPod. That project, which Apple dubbed the fusion of "Art, Technology & Commerce," cemented Apple's place at the center of the digital music revolution and helped keep the Irish rock band in the forefront of consumers' minds. The early iPod U2 Special Edition digital player held up to 5,000 songs and had unique features, such as a red click wheel and signatures of each member of U2 engraved on the device. For Bono, the new player took him back to the early days of listening to music with headphones via a bulky cassette player. "We want our audience to have a more intimate online relationship with the band, and Apple can help us do that," he said. "With iPod and iTunes, Apple has created a crossroads of art, commerce and technology which feels good for both musicians and fans."[14]

In addition to the stylistic innovations, the U2 iPod launched as the band prepared to release its new album *How to Dismantle an Atomic Bomb* and gave fans access to its first single, "Vertigo," through the iTunes Music Store. Even more directly, however, U2 starred in a television commercial for the player and the new song, silhouetting images of band members against a red background.[15]

The ad received heavy rotation on network and cable television, ensuring that the player and the band's new CD would be successful. The partnership between the corporation and U2 may have seemed pretty typical in terms of using celebrity and music to sell goods and services, but the key attribute of the U2-Apple campaign served to further legitimize digital music, downloaded legally, and the iPod's centrality in the music industry. Before long, brokering deals with Apple became more important than virtually every other retail outlet.

U2 appears on The Tonight Show *in 2001 to entertain the armed forces. NBC/Photofest.
© NBC. Courtesy of Photofest.*

Although it is hard to believe given their enduring popularity, U2 formed
in 1976. The four-man group (Bono, the Edge, Larry Mullen Jr., and Adam
Clayton) rose to prominence in the early 1980s as a wave of European
groups broke big in the United States. Back then, U2 played "alternative
rock," emerging as an underground favorite of college students. In 1987,
however, U2 released *The Joshua Tree,* a landmark album that sold millions
of copies, produced number one hit singles, and propelled the band into
the upper echelon of rock stardom. They sold out sports stadiums across
the country and U2 videos played continuously on MTV. In 2007, celebrating the 20-year anniversary of the groundbreaking album, the band re-
released *The Joshua Tree*—digitally remastered—along with a DVD from
the accompanying tour and footage of the recording process.

In 2000, U2 released *All That You Can't Leave Behind,* a monumental CD
that earned the group seven Grammy Awards, including "Record of the
Year." The album reflected the spirit of the early decade, examining ideas
about individual and collective contributions to the greater good and the
enduring love of family. "It's an album about essence, about the casting
away of the nonessential things and realizing what those essential things
are: family, friendship," Bono explained, reflecting on the album in 2005.
"I wanted to make a really raw record about the things you just cannot
live without." Interestingly, Bono had a health scare during the recording

of the album, a possible throat cancer that remained secret at the time. His facing mortality may help explain the lyrical content and force of the family/friendship bonds.[16]

U2 followed up the success early in the decade with *How to Dismantle an Atomic Bomb*. Accolades followed and the band's fame rose on the back of the Apple partnership and Bono's increasingly public work as a peace ambassador, particularly for African nations and AIDS patients in those regions and worldwide. In 2005, the singer raised $15 billion by working with government leaders from around the world, including George W. Bush, who one would assume would have little time for a rock-and-roll star from Ireland. Bono's work in Africa and for eradicating AIDS even began rumors about his possibly winning a Nobel Peace Prize—high praise for a singer who has taken on a much higher calling by using his fame for good in an era where there is little benefit in doing so.

MUSIC BUSINESS GURUS

Rick Rubin

Rarely do music producers become as famous as the stars they help shape. Rick Rubin is an exception. Sporting his distinct shaggy hair and long, unruly beard, Rubin led the "comeback" efforts of Johnny Cash and Neil Diamond, and infused new life into groups such as the Red Hot Chili Peppers and the Dixie Chicks. As a record company executive, Rubin signed Public Enemy and the Black Crowes.[17]

Rubin gained fame initially as a rap and hip-hop producer, working with LL Cool J and Run-DMC. In the late 1980s, he went from underground prodigy to mainstream star after shaping the Beastie Boys's debut *Licensed to Ill*, which sold 9 million copies and virtually launched rap music commercially. He parlayed that success into a series of high-profile ventures with other artists, although it was his work with legendary country star Cash that showed the full power of his artistic vision. "I don't think I have a sound. I think it's more about capturing the most direct sound of the artist—what they're supposed to sound like," Rubin explains. "I would say my production tends to be sparse, and it tends to be minimal."[18]

In 2007, *Time* magazine called Rubin "the most widely accomplished record producer of the past 20 years," which he accomplishes with "teddy-bear sensitivity that defies every stereotype of his profession."[19] That year, he had albums nominated for a Grammy in rock, country, and pop/soul categories. At least part of Rubin's magic with artists is getting them to realize their artistry again, as writers, vocalists, or whatever else he can pull from their souls. "I try to get them in the mid-set that they're not writing music for an album," he explains. "They're writing music because they're writers and that's what they do."[20]

10

Performing Arts

Thirty-two million people watched the Oscar broadcast last week, fewer than tuned in for the debut of *American Idol* in January, which means that a network-confected competition starring people named Ramiele Malubay and Robbie Carrico trumped a show with eight decades of history and stars like George Clooney and Cate Blanchett for the ultimate achievement in entertainment. That's the Hollywood equivalent of an Ultimate Fighting Championship outdrawing the Super Bowl (just wait, that's coming, too).

—David Carr, *The New York Times* (2008)

In 2008, the New England Patriots carried a perfect regular season mark into the Super Bowl, television's biggest annual event, against the underdog New York Giants. The Patriots attempted to become only the second team to finish undefeated. Star quarterback and budding pop culture icon Tom Brady led the Patriots. In the weeks leading up to the game, however, Brady filled more airtime, column inches, and computer screens for dating Brazilian supermodel Gisele Bündchen than his play on the football field.

The media frenzy chronicling what seemed like virtually every moment of the hoopla sparked even greater public interest. Money flowed into the tills of the gambling houses in Las Vegas, while global corporations placed their own bets by snapping up commercial time during the game at a whopping $2.7 million per 30-second spot. The American culture machine and the hypercapitalist system hummed as one.

The Retail Advertising and Marketing Association estimated that Americans spent $10 billion preparing for the big game. That figure includes the 3.9 million people who bought a new television, along with another 1.8 million new pieces of furniture. In response, companies such as Circuit City offered special incentives to pry people's money from their pockets. The retailer, for example, guaranteed delivery and installation for anyone purchasing a 32-inch or larger TV by the Wednesday before the Super Bowl. Anyone suffering from later delivery received a $50 gift card for their troubles.[1]

On the way to the coronation of the Patriots as the greatest team in NFL history, a stumble occurred—an unfathomable hiccup—the Giants scored in the game's closing minutes to upset New England, 17–14. While sportswriters raced to rewrite their columns and come up with hyperbole big enough to capture the enormity of the victory, television aficionados soon learned that 97.5 million viewers in the United States watched the game, making it the second most viewed show in television history, behind only the 1983 *M*A*S*H* series finale. Television retained its hold on the national psyche.[2]

The super performance of the 2008 Super Bowl is not the only example of the way the performing arts steer popular culture, especially television and movies. For example, reality television first transformed its industry, and then swept through American culture as more and more people grew fascinated with the chance of becoming a celebrity. YouTube and MySpace enabled users to upload videos of themselves—a form of instant television—that actually gave them a platform for celebrity. Who could have imagined that a video of someone dancing to 1980s hits or wildly singing off-key could lead to a form of fame and/or infamy?

As the decade progresses, traditional television shows made a comeback, but many rely on increased violence and gruesome scenes to draw viewers. It seems as if the boundaries have been eliminated in the 2000s. Then, just as it seemed a new era had dawned on the small screen, the Writers Guild of America went on strike, which placed the new television season in jeopardy and forced the networks to fill airtime with repeats, mid-season replacements, and reality shows.

In the movie business, studios grew even more reliant on blockbusters to carry the industry. For most big money flicks, opening weekend determines success or failure. In addition, more movies feature computer-generated graphics, revolutionizing the way people see films. At the same time, studios developed new and interesting ways to tie-in films to other products, saturating the market with toys, clothing, video games, and an endless number of trinkets designed to help sell films. From a pop culture standpoint, these attempts are a fascinating aspect of the intersection of technology, media, and culture in the new millennium.

TELEVISION

Simultaneously, technology put televisions on steroids and shrunk them to sizes only considered worthy of science fiction in the not too distant past. In fact, it is difficult to even define what a television is in the new millennium. Is a person's video iPod a TV? What about one's computer screen? Do we need a new name for these devices that reflects their mobility? Regardless, viewers are increasingly turning to places away from home or outside the living room to watch television programming.

What remains constant is that television is a central component of American popular culture. The age-old debate about the merits or lack thereof (education versus entertainment) in watching TV continues in some segments of society. Many people even claim to never watch television, a kind of badge of honor worn by people one might meet in San Francisco or New York. For the rest of us, television serves a variety of purposes, from simple entertainment and news-gathering to education and even mindless background noise.

Since the beginning of the 2000s, the percentage of households with a television has held steady at 98.2 percent, or 100.8 million in 2000 and 112.8 million in 2008. The growth aspect within homes is the length the television stays on, in 2006 topping out at 8 hours, 14 minutes daily. The average man watches about 4 hours, 35 minutes each day; women view 5 hours, 17 minutes on average. Neither teens (3 hours, 22 minutes) nor children (3 hours, 26 minutes) watch as much as the average man or woman.[3]

Advertising on television is another growing aspect. From 2000 to 2006, ad volume jumped from $60.3 billion to $71.9 billion. The latter figure represents more than 25 percent of the total advertising volume in the United States. ($281.7 billion). Of the top 25 advertisers on television in 2006, 9 of the first 10 were automotive companies, including the top 5: General Motors Corporate Dealers Association ($528 million), DaimlerChrysler ($501 million), Ford Dealers Association ($439 million), Toyota Dealers Association ($384 million), and Honda ($377 million). The only non-automobile company to crack the top 10 was AT&T, placing sixth at $293 million.[4]

The Super Bowl remains the most costly advertising venue each year. The average 30-second commercial spot in prime-time on a major network, however, is creeping higher as the decade progresses, from about $82,000 in 2000 and $118,000 in 2007. Survey information confirms that the companies spending on television are benefiting. In all, 81.8 percent of adults ages 18 and older feel that TV advertising is "most influential" versus newspaper (6.6%), radio (4.5%), Internet (3.7%), and magazines (3.5%).[5]

According to Susan Cuccinello, senior vice president of research at the Television Bureau of Advertising, "Television reaches more of an advertiser's prospects each day than any other medium, and adults spend significantly more time with television than with other media, in almost every major demographic segment." Not only is TV where adults say they learn the most about products and brands, but television still ranks as people's "primary news source, and as their primary source for local weather, traffic and sports news."[6]

The Magic of *American Idol*

Although it is difficult to fathom, *American Idol* almost never made it on air. Pitched in the early part of the decade to all the network stations by co-creators Simon Fuller and Simon Cowell, the execs all passed. Even Fox, which eventually picked up the show, gave the idea tepid interest early on. If it weren't for the intervention of Elisabeth Murdoch, daughter of New Corporation founder and CEO Rupert Murdoch, who loved the British version (*Pop Idol*) of the show, *American Idol* may never have existed. She urged her father to buy the rights to the show and the rest is television history.

The real stars of American Idol are its judges: British record executive Simon Cowell, former pop star and choreographer Paula Abdul, and American producer Randy Jackson. Each judge plays an archetypical character. Cowell is the sarcastic, mean judge, Abdul quirkily acts as the nice one, and Jackson is the outgoing, gregarious member. The chemistry between them propels the show, in addition to the showmanship of host Ryan Seacrest.

Although the music takes over as the series progresses, the real star of stars is Cowell. According to journalist Bill Carter, Cowell transformed into a celebrity based on his work on the British version of the show, becoming "one of the most talked-about cultural figures in Britain in the winter of 2002. He was a tabloid newspaper's dream: seen by millions every week on television, saying something outrageously quotable ('You're a disaster'), doing something unconscionably cruel (several young women left the auditions convulsed in tears after hearing his corrosive assessments of their talents) and tirelessly promoting his program (by doing every sort of interview in print and on television and radio)."[7]

In the first season of *Idol*, Cowell let loose, telling one contestant to get a lawyer and sue her vocal coach; others were frankly labeled pathetic, horrible, awful, and pathetic. His acerbic wit, mixed with genuine enthusiasm when they uncovered a talented singer, turned Cowell into an instant hit. Ten million people watched *American Idol* its first night and the second eclipsed 11 million. More important for Fox, the show topped the charts for viewers ages 18 to 34, the prime television demographic. According to journalist Ken Barnes, "It's conceivable that *Idol* may have ended up a middling success without the unprecedented candor and (at times) brutal wit he [Cowell] directs at contestants—no other vaguely similar show had such a consummate dasher of dreams, and none since has been able to duplicate the effect. (And how they have tried!)"[8]

The Unreality of Reality TV

Imagine a 1 in about 20 shot at winning $1 million. The only catch is that you have to live in a desolate location, fend for your own food and water, and compete in physical and mental challenges. Not only does this include building shelter and gathering food (or facing hunger), but it could involve standing in the punishing sun on a small platform for as long as possible, wrestling in a pit of muck, or any variety of trivia challenges. As is now well known, to win *Survivor*, a person must simply "outwit, outplay, and outlast" the other contestants.

When CBS launched *Survivor* in June, 2000, no one predicted that the show would change the face of television for the rest of the decade. *Survivor* was not the first "reality" TV program. That honor is difficult to assess. One could argue that Allen Funt originated the genre with *Candid Camera*; others would claim that it was the series of wacky game shows of the 1950s, such as the decades-long running *Truth or Consequences*. *Survivor*, created by former British Army soldier Mark Burnett, caught the nation's attention and each subsequent week the excitement grew. As more viewers tuned in, the media picked up the trend and fed the hunger with countless articles, updates, and special sections. The Internet added to the anticipation. Web sites devoted to the show sprouted up, and others posted supposed "spoilers," or insider information claiming to know who would win. Certainly the notion that "regular people," not actors would win the $1 million played into the public's curiosity.[9]

Host Ryan Seacrest announces Kelly Clarkson's victory over Justin Guarini on the season 1 American Idol *finale (2002); from left, Ryan Seacrest, Kelly Clarkson, Justin Guarini, Brian Dunkleman. FOX/Photofest. © FOX. Courtesy of Photofest.*

The contestants row ashore on Survivor: Thailand, *Season 5, 2002. CBS/Photofest.*
© *CBS. Courtesy of Photofest.*

A total of 6,000 people filled out applications to appear on *Survivor* before that first season. CBS then added to the marketing effort by holding auditions in cities where it had stations, including Los Angeles and New York. The idea that something potentially dangerous might take place on the tiny island where the contestants were stranded added to the public fascination with the premise. Burnett also picked 16 players that mixed across demographic segments and backgrounds. "The early wave of media attention to the show paid off for CBS," explained journalist Richard M. Huff, "The network sold all of the advertising time on the show to eight companies—before the first episode aired."[10]

It is interesting to note that *Survivor* went head-to-head against ABC's immensely popular game show *Who Wants to Be a Millionaire,* hosted by Regis Philbin. Although *Survivor* lost that night, the hype led to an even larger audience the next week, 18.1 million viewers. Hosted by Jeff Probst, the reality program became a runaway hit and forced people across the nation to make sure they were home in time to watch. Internet sites and Web reports added to the popularity, as well as newspapers covering *Survivor* as if it were a sporting event. The most interesting marketing tactic CBS used shrouded in mystery the outcome and events leading up to it. The network threatened anyone who gave away secrets with a $5 million lawsuit and forced contestants to stay quiet until after the finale by withholding pay until the season ended.[11]

When Richard Hatch, an openly homosexual corporate trainer, emerged from the first season as victor, America had the role model for its first reality show villain. Hatch proved to be a master manipulator, and the audience both loved and hated to watch him pull the strings of other contestants such as Rudy Boesch, a 72-year-old former Navy SEAL. Hatch stood as a fitting winner, as much of *Survivor's* appeal came from the way people related their own lives to the antics players went through during the game. "A show's fundamental meaning must dovetail with the dominant meanings of its audience for it to be compatible with the lives of its viewers," explained media scholar Derek Foster, "As a microcosm of American values . . . *Survivor* . . . reflected and reinforced the Horatio Alger theme of the self-made individual whose hard work and self-reliance will invariably triumph in the face of adversity."[12]

As *Time* magazine noted shortly after the show's debut, *Survivor's* popularity prompted the rise of what it called voyeur television (VTV).

Despite *Survivor's* gross-outs, its dark premise and its wall-to-wall cheesiness—the faux-Lion King sound track, the 'tribal councils' held in what looks like a Holiday Inn Polynesian lounge circa 1963, the somber narration of Jeff Probst, former host of VH1's *Rock 'n' Roll Jeopardy!* and challenger to Regis for luckiest-man-in-America status—despite all this, viewers have embraced the desert-island soap with fascination and bemused contempt.[13]

A Time/CNN poll from mid-2000 revealed that 31 percent of adults would allow a reality television show film them in their pajamas, 29 percent kissing, 26 percent crying, and 25 percent having an argument. Only 8 percent said that they would be taped naked, and just 5 percent said they would be taped having sex. One wonders if the latter figures wouldn't be much higher in 2008.[14]

Cable Television

The economic woes facing consumers in 2007 and 2008 led to the unthinkable—people actually ditched cable television. True, some decided to move to satellite television for premium access, but cable companies across the country reported losing subscribers to the bad economy. Comcast, for example, lost more than 73,000 customers in the first three months of 2008; Time Warner Cable dropped 21,000. In contrast, DirecTV and Dish Network gained a combined 320,000 customers in the same timeframe. Most troubling for the big cable companies is that the difficult financial picture is leading to cutbacks in the ancillary services they offer, such as high-speed Internet and cable-based phone systems.[15]

At the same time, there is little love lost between most consumers and their cable television providers. Most operators have a virtual monopoly over their service area, so people are forced to accept whatever outrageous rate hike the company sends their way. In New York City, for example, Time Warner instituted a 9.6 percent hike, and Cablevision increased 4.7 percent. At the same time that the bills increased, city officials reported that consumer complaints against the two cable companies jumped 41 percent. In most of the cable business, customers expect poor service, delays, incomprehensible bills, and outages. Despite the technological advances made in the industry, many basic challenges remain to be solved.[16]

While consumers balance cable bills with their other monthly expenses, the quality of television programming is getting stronger as the decade advances, particularly when considering the handful of acclaimed series running on the cable networks. Journalist Tim Goodman sees the storytelling element of TV setting it apart from other mediums, explaining: "Television is also different from film in that the storytelling is alive, the series are evolving (or devolving, as the case may be), and opinions can change with the content. A film tells a story in two hours or less most of the time, then history judges it. A television series tells 13 or 22 hours of a story, then comes back to do it again the next year—and if there's a noticeable drop-off in quality, then the critical perception also evolves (or devolves)."[17]

Not so many decades ago, Americans were happy with fewer television channels and whatever the major networks put out each year. Fast forward to the new millennium, however, and those antiquated ideas are out the window. Today's television landscape is crawling with niche channels that specialize in everything from specific college football conferences to an all-day menu of home improvement shows.

In the 2000s, the hottest commodities on cable TV have been the premium series, such as *The Sopranos* (HBO), *Deadwood* (HBO), *Sex and the City* (HBO), *Dexter* (Showtime), and *Weeds* (Showtime). In addition, basic cable stations are making their mark with original series, including *Mad Men* (AMC), *Breaking Bad* (AMC), *Monk* (USA), and *Psych* (USA).

Cable network executives realize that fewer consumers turn to them to see movies, as access to first-run films spans mail-order, the Web, demand television, and DVD rentals. As a result, they turn to original series to attract new viewers, even if such programming can be costly. Tony Vinciquerra, President and CEO of Fox Cable Networks, explains: "Original programming helps build a brand." On Fox's FX channel, this idea worked on the back of critically acclaimed shows, such as *The Shield, Rescue Me,* and *Nip/Tuck.* HBO built the blueprint for these networks by proving that viewers would tune in (and pay for) good shows on a premium channel. The basic cable networks are replicating that strategy and have the added benefit of drawing advertisers through commercials.[18]

Bringing in viewers and advertising dollars is critical, as production costs are increasing by about 10 percent per year. Dramas on basic cable run about $1 million per episode; costs at pay channels can be in the

$3 million range. Marketing budgets are also increasing, as it takes greater (and more costly) effort to reach potential viewers who are spending time online or playing video games.[19]

The Networks

With basic and premium cable networks upping the ante in both quality and quantity of shows, the networks have had to respond with better programming. Like the cable networks, however, they have also relied heavily on reality shows to offset costs. As a result of the necessity for better quality, the networks produced shows such as *CSI* (CBS), *Heroes* (NBC), *24* (Fox), *Desperate Housewives* (ABC), *Grey's Anatomy* (ABC), and *Law & Order: SVU* (NBC). These shows feature strong writing, quality cinematography, and filmic production.

At the same time quality must be increased, the cost of network television is skyrocketing. Jeff Zucker, President and CEO of NBC Universal outlined some of the challenges the networks face in trying to find programs. "Last year, the five broadcast networks spent more than 500 million dollars . . . more than half a billion dollars . . . on development of new series, scripts and pilots," Zucker explains. "Some 80 pilots were made. Next fall, or whenever the next television season begins, at most eight of those series will return. And of those eight, none could be considered a big success." In an era marked by increased competition for advertising dollars and viewer eyeballs, the old models no longer work as well for the major networks, Zucker's call to arms notwithstanding.[20]

Another jolt to the network model is that digital video recorder (DVR) technology enables viewers to bypass commercials, the lifeblood of the television economic model. Many observers see the DVR as just another innovation that provides the consumer with greater power than previous eras. "The amazing variety of choices consumers have today has important implications for consumer behavior. It's a shift from habit to choice . . . to individuals making choices when and how to consume media," Zucker says. "There is less and less habitual plopping down in front of the TV— and more and more media consumption made by conscious choice. This is a new kind of appointment TV, but one where the appointment is made by the viewer, not by the network scheduling department."[21]

Watching Online

Technology plays a critical role for television, not only in its continuing central role as furniture in one's living room, but in expanding the ways people can watch their favorite programs when they are away from home. More frequently, primetime television viewing is occurring via the Web and on smaller screens, such as cell phones and iPods. This move forces the major studios to rethink their use of technology and how to interact with consumers who want more of this programming.

Like other forms of online entertainment, once the brush fire has been lit, a raging inferno is soon to follow. The future of television viewing online already has role models for its growth based on what happened in the music industry. When consumers felt that they could get the content for free, they flocked to legal and illegal sites to access what they wanted.

According to Solutions Research Group, about 80 million Americans watched a TV show online, approximately 43 percent of the total online population. This is a significant increase over the 25 percent that claimed they viewed a show on the Web the year before. Perhaps more telling and pointing to the future of primetime TV, 20 percent of respondents said that they watch television via the Web weekly.[22]

One in five visitors to major network Web sites said that they did so to watch a specific show. The results of the specific shows they tuned into online, however, do not automatically conform to the demographics one would imagine. Some of the top TV shows viewed on the Internet include *Heroes, Grey's Anatomy, Dancing with the Stars, CSI, House,* and *Gossip Girl.*

Many online television viewers turn to the network Web sites to avoid commercials, although more skipping through ads is still done via a DVR. Examining the top 20 prime time shows, the study found that a whopping 55 percent of the shows were time shifted by DVR or by viewing online. A full 65 percent of DVR users say that they always skip commercials, up from 52 percent the previous year.[23]

FILM

In 2008, the Academy Awards turned somber, with dark films, as well as the actors and actresses who starred in them, winning major awards. *No Country for Old Men,* Joel and Ethan Coen's story of a battle resulting from a drug deal gone bad won the Oscar for best picture. Daniel Day-Lewis won best actor for his portrayal of a ruthless oil tycoon in *There Will Be Blood.* In discussing the somber tones of the awards, two journalists noted that the contest turned into "a tug of war over sensibilities: Academy voters were being asked to choose between the nihilism of *No Country for Old Men,* in which the serial killer prevails; the hopeful spunk of *Juno,* in which a pregnant teenager forges her own solutions; or, perhaps, a saga of child-hood betrayal and lives destroyed, in *Atonement,* set against the backdrop of British retreat in the early days of World War II."[24]

In many instances, the tone of Academy Award-winning films either represents the feelings of the nation or counters the prevailing mood. The 2008 batch clearly struck a dark nerve in America's thinking, about itself, the ongoing overseas war, and the impending economic troubles facing the nation. For viewers, the difficulty is tuning into the Oscar telecast when such intense films are honored. In 2006, for example, when *Crash* won the best picture award, less than 39 million people watched. The 2008 version, hosted by "The Daily Show" star Jon Stewart, attracted a mere 32 million, earning the distinction of the least-watched Oscars ever.

Many experts attribute the disconnect to Hollywood snobbery, awarding movies that fewer and fewer people want to see. Journalist David Carr explains, "While there is much to be admired in the five best-picture nominees, all told, they have pulled in around $313 million so far at the box office, a few million less than *Transformers* did alone."[25]

DVD Sales

Innovation enabled DVDs to relegate VHS tapes to history's dustbin. In the new millennium, purchasing a movie on VHS seems archaic and perhaps most often done by those looking through a remainder bin at a big box superstore or on a dusty shelf in a used bookstore. The next iteration, however, is on the launch pad—the high-definition DVD—which may someday destroy the traditional DVD business, which currently accounts for about 60 percent of studio profits. Sony introduced the Blu-ray disc, which has been named the industry standard. But rather than cheer on this new innovation, studio executives worry that the hit the DVD business will take is going to disrupt their profits.

In 2007, for example, DVD sales in the United States fell 3.2 percent to $15.9 billion, the first time in the history of the business that sales dropped year-over-year. Adams Media Research anticipates a further decline in 2008 and 2009. Although the Blu-ray high-def disc is a formidable foe, the real challenge for DVD sales is competition with technology companies. Apple now offers movie downloads on iTunes, while broadband communications companies that pipe entertainment into people's homes are testing movie downloads. The threat is so steep that the movie studios responded by providing consumers with a digital file when they purchase a DVD. The file lets users burn the movie to a computer or transfer it to their iPod.[26]

George Clooney

Tom Hanks, Charlize Theron, and Johnny Depp are a few of the many fine actors and actresses working in the new millennium. Of this illustrious list, however, George Clooney may just be the most important, not only for the kinds of films he has made, but as a throwback to a nostalgic age when those on the stage were charming, yet rugged, and graceful, yet stereotypically manly. In recent years, Clooney used his star power to rally support for the struggling people of Darfur. In December 2007, he won a Summit Peace Award from the Nobel Peace Prize Laureates. In early 2008, officials at the United Nations appointed Clooney a UN peace envoy, recognizing his commitment to the region.

Clooney spent the years just before the new millennium (1994–1999) playing Dr. Doug Ross on ER, the highly acclaimed television series created by bestselling writer Michael Crichton. After leaving the series to pursue movie work full-time, Clooney acted in a series of successful films, from the Coen Brothers' depression-era romp *O Brother, Where Art Thou?* (2000) to a trilogy of Las Vegas Rat Pack movies: *Ocean's Eleven* (2001), *Ocean's Twelve* (2004), and *Ocean's Thirteen* (2007).

Moving back and forth from blockbuster star to more serious roles, Clooney starred as a CIA operative in *Syriana* (2005), which won him an Oscar as best supporting actor. Journalist Caryn James places Clooney's star power at the nexus of his onscreen stardom and activism. She sees his popularity in this ability to "raise a question with an old-fashioned ring—'What's the right thing to do?'—and apply it to issues that are totally of the moment." As a result, she explains, "he avoids preachiness because

Actor George Clooney at the Golden Globe Awards show in 2006. NBC/Photofest. © Chris Haston. Courtesy of Photofest.

his films don't pretend to answer tough moral questions; they simply insist the questions are worth asking."[27]

Clooney possesses the uncanny ability to be one of only three men to ever be named *People Magazine*'s "Sexiest Man Alive" twice (1997 and 2006), while also tackling parts that transform his handsome features into a kind of vulnerability or everyman quality. He is able to come off as overtly modest on one hand, but then own up to his stardom the next, and audiences love him for it even more. In *Michael Clayton* (2007), Clooney plays a faltering lawyer whose world is unraveling. In January 2008, he received a nomination for an Academy Award for Best Actor for *Michael Clayton*.

Brangelina: The World's Hottest Couple

The multimedia revolution sparked by the Internet made celebrity watching a 24-hour-a-day spectacle. Regardless of how much gossip, rumor, and misinformation spooned out to the American people, it seems as if they cannot get enough. Brad Pitt and Angelina Jolie symbolize the transformation in celebrity coverage, from media and photographers following them around when new movies came out to an environment where nothing is off limits. Given the current craving for illicit gossip, however, it seems appropriate that Pitt and Jolie met while shooting the movie *Mr. and Mrs. Smith*, while they were still both the Mr. and Mrs. in another relationship.

Before his relationship with Jolie, Pit and *Friends* sitcom star Jennifer Aniston had a highly-public marriage—seemingly creating America's "perfect couple." The rumors of a tryst between Jolie and Pitt began in late 2004, on the set of the action movie they starred in as a married couple, secretly assassins, who are hired to kill one another. Shortly after the public announcement about Pitt's separation from Aniston, the weekly tabloids and Web sites buzzed with news of Pitt and Jolie. Then the new couple took a very public vacation together in Africa, where photographers caught them frolicking in the surf and Pitt playing with Jolie's adopted son Maddox.[28]

Since then, Pitt and Jolie have continued to dominate the tabloids and entertainment gossip. In what seems like collusion, as all the celebutainment magazines appear to feature the same stories each week, the couple lives in the public eye. In this age of media sensationalism, each photo of one of them alone is interpreted as a soon-to-be breakup or the end of their fairytale life. The headlines predict a marriage one week, a split the next, and constantly ponder the fate of poor Aniston, America's jilted sweetheart.

If there is a hidden benefit to the high-octane merger of two mega brands like Pitt and Jolie, it is that the social justice causes they work for get more attention. Both entertainers have led efforts to gain recognition for conditions in Africa. Closer to home, Pitt started the Make It Right foundation to rebuild homes in New Orleans's ravaged Lower Ninth Ward. The organization teamed with 13 architects to design, then rebuild, 150 houses with state-of-the-art features, such as solar heat and light, 5-foot elevated first floors, while in some designs the homes even float. Pitt and Jolie also moved into a residence in New Orleans to keep the media spotlight on the city as it rebuilds in the deep wake of Hurricane Katrina.[29]

Pitt used his star power to coordinate rebuilding efforts after growing frustrated with the slow response of the national and local government. After contributing $5 million of his own money to the cause, Pitt reached out to foundations, corporations, and other individuals to help. He explained his reasons for getting involved, saying, "I've always had a fondness for this place—it's like no other. Seeing the frustration firsthand made me want to return the kindness this city has shown me."[30]

Failure of Iraq Films

"Failure" is a stark word that boldly defines itself in its brashness. One need not ponder long and hard about what failure is; the word is tied to the American Dream so closely that we all know failure when we see it, touch it, or brush up against it. To say that films playing on the post-9/11 terrorist attacks and subsequent overseas wars have failed is to accuse them of not helping define what life should be like in this new age, rather just merely playing on patriotic stereotypes and racial intolerance.

On the surface, one could reject this notion of failure by pointing out that "United 93" grossed $43 million after being made for just $15 million. This kind of limited viewpoint, however, just says that people are interested in the post-9/11 world, not that it has really transformed their lives. As journalist James Poniewozik explains, "saying that 9/11 has entered pop culture is not the same thing as saying that 9/11 has changed pop culture." He points to the Bush Administration for downplaying the force of the new world order on ordinary people. "The Administration's message to citizens since the attacks has been, Believe that 9/11 changed everything when it comes to foreign and domestic policy and that 9/11 changed nothing when it comes to spending and living," Poniewozik says.[31]

Almost immediately after the September 11 attacks, critics proclaimed the end of irony, a notion that, according to *Time* magazine, "Our metaphors have expired. Pleasure seems mocking and futile . . . language that artists, comedians, storytellers and actors use to explain us to ourselves now seems frivolous, inappropriate or simply outdated."[32] Looking back from the vantage point of early 2008, these messages not only seem outdated, but ineffectual. What America learned in the post 9/11 world is that they should not stop the frantic national buying spree or worry too much about the war—pretty quickly it would become news for the back page, not the headlines. The utter failure of films to reflect the world after 9/11 or add to the national dialogue in a meaningful way proves the point that the talk of a world transformed was nothing more than that day's lead story.

Movie critic Richard Corliss sees the challenges in presenting filmic interpretations of the Iraq war in more artistic terms, saying "this war is tragic but not inherently dramatic." Up to this point, there has not been the kind of stereotypical war movie aspects in the current campaign in the Middle East—clear-cut good guys and bad guys and romance immediately standing out. Corliss also notes that it is difficult to present the United States in its World War II heroic sense when the country has bungled all its wars since then. "We may have to wait for Hollywood's definitive Iraq-war film," he says. "But that's the way the movie industry works. It took years for *The Deer Hunter, Coming Home* and *Platoon* to appear and leave their indelible marks."[33]

THEATER

Broadway is the gold standard of American theater. In late 2007, however, a 19-day stagehand strike crippled the industry. Although pundits worried that the strike would destroy the December holiday season, the Great White Way bounced back from the work stoppage. Sales Christmas week, which are usually good for Broadway in a typical year, went through the roof, topping $30 million. Fourteen shows brought in more than $1 million each, with *Wicked* topping the rush at $1.8 million.[34]

Although the strong holiday season helped Broadway regain its footing, the strike took a toll on grosses for the season (down 5% year-over-year) and attendance (dropping 4.5%). Both figures had been up before the strike: grosses 5.8 percent and attendance 5.5 percent. Producer Stewart Lane provided a personalized look at the strike's financial consequences, saying: "The profits we could have had during the second-most-important week of our business cycle is money we couldn't recapture. I have nightmares about how much we lost that weekend."[35]

Weekly sales figures provide observers with a glimpse of how Broadway is faring. In the week ending March 30, 2008, for example, 26 musicals (attendance: 245,290) grossed $18.4 million or 87 percent of the Broadway total. Seven plays (attendance: 39,418) accounted for $2.7 million. The overall paid admission price stood at $74.31 for all shows.[36]

11

Travel

The Web was made for travel. You're selling a virtual experience—the
customer doesn't need to touch or see the product—they're buying on
faith and look for great brands. Travel is the perfect vehicle to be on
the Web.

—Bruce Rosenberg, Senior Vice President, E-business,
Hilton Hotels (2001)

In 2000, the future looked bright for the travel industry. The Internet enabled airlines, hotels, and car rental agencies to interact and sell to customers in a whole new way. Big name Web-only companies, such as Priceline,
Expedia, and Travelocity, used extensive advertising and branding campaigns to become household names. For consumers, the Internet allowed
people to find less expensive means of travel, virtually eliminating the need
for travel agents. Self-service travel reigned supreme in the industry.

The online sites tackled astronomical growth. For example, in early 1998,
research firm Jupiter Communications predicted that online travel sales
would reach $11.3 billion by 2002. At the time the organization considered
this a gutsy call, considering that online sales accounted for less than a billion dollars the year before. In fact, Jupiter could have been bolder in its
prediction. Forrester Research, another analysis firm, estimated that nearly
19 million households made travel purchases on the Web in 2001 and accounted for $16.7 billion in revenues.

The terrorist attacks on September 11, 2001 initially devastated the airline industry, forcing some carriers (barely holding on before the tragedy)
into bankruptcy. Furthermore, the entire travel and tourism market suffered as the uncertainty following the attacks led people to reexamine their
priorities, including whether business travel could be done safely. Experts
estimate that the travel and tourism industry lost $30 billion after 9/11.

Even a national tragedy could not destroy the travel industry. Travel, particularly air travel, had become a normal part of everyday life for too many people in and out of the corporate world. Low-cost carriers, most notably Southwest Airlines, made air travel seem more convenient than packing up the car and kids for a long road trip. Consequently, passengers did not stay away for long, even as security measures, threat assessment codes, and safety procedures made it more difficult to board planes and wait lines snaked through airports. The travel agency community also rebounded by refocusing on specialized and luxury travel.

By the later years of the 2000s, airlines faced a different set of challenges, including rising fuel costs, which translated into higher fares, and a weakened economy that forced consumers to rethink trips and travel. From an overall perspective, however, the most important change was that people generally saw travel and tourism as a regular aspect of their lives. Thus they were not going to stop, despite rising costs associated with travel, just like their insistence on driving, regardless of gasoline prices. The proof is in the numbers, which reveal that by 2010, online travel is estimated to reach $150 billion.

ONLINE TRAVEL SITES

Way back in the ancient days of 1995—remember, we're talking about the Web here—a *Brandweek* article asked rhetorically: "Are Travel Agents Dinosaurs?" Despite the industry's $93.5 billion in yearly billings at the time, most onlookers assumed that the Internet would make travel agents obsolete.

A half dozen years later, travel agents still roamed the earth. They were a bit disgruntled but also empowered by the demons sent to smite them. As it turns out, travel agents plugged into the latest and greatest technology, which helped them retain a competitive edge, just like savvy headhunters who listed job openings on Monster.com or HotJobs.

One shouldn't judge the success of online travel sites by the continued existence of travel agencies, however. Unquestionably, travel is one of the industries that benefited most from the Web. Analysts estimated that the online travel industry hit $17 billion in 2001 and grew to $68 billion by 2005. Even though most of the big names in the online travel game initially focused on air travel, such as Priceline.com, Travelocity, Expedia, and Orbitz, the public soon learned to shop for travel savings across different kinds of travel-related sites.

In early 2001, the Travel Industry Association of America released two reports detailing America's fascination with online travel. The association concluded that more than 59 million travelers used the Internet to get information or check prices, and 25 million from that group purchased travel products or services on the Web. The kinds of items they purchased varied as well:

- 84 percent bought airline tickets
- 78 percent purchased lodging
- 59 percent rented vehicles
- 51 percent bought tickets for amusement parks, sporting events, and other occasions
- 17 percent purchased travel packages
- 8 percent purchased a cruise

Ben Cutler, senior analyst of the Internet consumer practice at research firm Cyber Dialogue, said online travel "is the first e-retail category to be shopped by a majority of online adults." Cutler estimated that 43 million online adults shopped for travel via the Web in the early years of the new millennium, which represented 51 percent of total Web users. These figures were significantly higher than 1999 numbers, which revealed 17.2 million people shopped for travel online, or 28 percent of the total online population.[1]

Most online companies failed to revolutionize business or live up to a sliver of the incredible hype brought on during the dot.com feeding frenzy. The stories of failure are more abundant than the stories of success; however, several travel sites broke the mold and made money on the Internet, such as Expedia, which morphed into an online travel bazaar, and Hilton Hotels, which married its Web site and back office functions so well that some analysts believed that the company had the best e-commerce organization in the world.

Turbulence at Takeoff

Like so many other businesses in the mid-1990s, travel companies did not know what to make of the Internet. Some early pioneers realized the medium's potential, but back then, the technology had not caught up with the inspiration. No one really knew what a good Web site should and shouldn't do or even how it ought to look. As a result, the first travel sites were bulky and difficult to use. Years of trial and error ensued before really good travel sites developed. By early 1996, most American businesses raced to establish a presence on the Web, but rushed headlong into Internet projects before really understanding how the medium could help them. There were few people who understood how a site should be designed and even fewer who could articulate a Web strategy.

A pioneer in the online travel game was the Raleigh-based PC Travel, which launched in June 1995. Founder and president George Newsom put up the site as an extension of his 25-year-old travel business and estimated that users filled out 1,000 reservation-profile forms a day. PC Travel focused on selling discounted airline tickets, vacations, and cruises. The firm also gave extra discounts and bonus frequent flier miles to travelers who joined its Web-Net Traveler Club, at an additional cost of $49.95.

As soon as online travel started to show promise, like at PC Travel, many critics sprang to action, determined to prove that using travel agents still resulted in better savings. In 1996, magazines from *Popular Science* (concluding that the sites were "long on information, but short on savings") to *Fortune* (warning "don't dump your travel agent just yet") ran stories hopeful about the future of online travel, but cautioning the reader to still keep an agent's number handy. The *Fortune* article also discussed a major problem for all Web users in the mid-1990s: the time it took to get the computer booted, signed on to a service provider, and then navigating to the individual sites. Back then, dealing with a travel agent by phone was probably a much easier task.

The critics made some good points in the short term and only cautiously explored the future implications of online travel. Booking travel via the Web challenged even the most patient early users because many corporate Internet sites had no e-commerce capabilities. For example, the Avis car rental site did not offer online reservations. Instead, if you wanted to use Avis, you sent the company an e-mail and waited for a response.

Although detractors had their knives sharpened, surveys from the mid-1990s showed that 70 percent of Internet users used the medium to get travel information, and 15 percent booked airline tickets via the Web. In 1997, Web users booked $900 million in travel, an impressive figure, but less than 1 percent of the total travel market, so obviously if online travel sites met customer needs at a better price, they could continue to build on these numbers. The proof of online travel's potential clearly existed.

What travel sites like Expedia and Travelocity needed was more people to become Web surfers and the technology to gain wider acceptance with the general public. Once that happened, it would not take a large spark for online travel to ignite. The leading sites took the time to build technology to meet customer expectations, and then waited for enough users to go online to form a critical mass. In a short while, the explosion of venture capital money and publicity hype combined to set off that spark. Before long people could not even remember what it was like before the Internet. As the Web became omnipresent, travel developed into its first killer category.

Erik Blachford, an executive at Expedia, believes travel is the ideal Internet industry and sees the reasons falling into three neat little categories. First, travel-related information is difficult to aggregate offline. Basically, there isn't a traditional way to gather all the disparate content into one location better than the way it can be done online. Next, information is electronic-based, so there is no need for warehousing or a supply chain and other necessities that tripped up so many Web companies. Finally, there are tremendous cost savings because no one is sitting around waiting for customers to walk in the door or call on the phone, as is the case for traditional travel agencies.

Companies have to use technology to deliver information correctly the first time and every time a customer goes to the site. One of the biggest cultural changes brought on by the Web is the expectation of perfection. Zero tolerance is commonplace, especially because the competition is a click or two away. The heavy reliance on technology is the first exposure of Expedia's roots as a Microsoft company. Because the company originated within the Redmond-based software giant, it had top-notch talent working on what was essentially an online startup.

The second instance of Expedia revealing its heritage occurred among senior management. Richard Barton founded the company while working on a travel CD-ROM that Microsoft founder Bill Gates wanted him to develop. Barton realized the CD idea would fail, but an online travel site had a chance for greatness. Like Barton, Expedia's other leaders cut their teeth in Microsoft's highly competitive environment, so they developed a quasi-Microsoft culture.

As a matter of fact, Blachford explains, Expedia leaders also modified the culture to fit their startup mentality. "We kept our discipline and style, but changed what we didn't like about Microsoft. As Expedia developed, it was definitely not Microsoft, but its foundation stones were Microsoft," he says. Blachford views this as a distinct advantage over the willy-nilly startups being led by college students and MBA dropouts. "You can't just invent that culture," Blachford says. "We had skilled product development people, good training, and a commitment to technology."[2]

The success of Expedia in almost immediately carving out a sizable market share poses interesting questions about the role of startups launched by corporate parents. Like Monster.com, backed and financed by the power of TMP Worldwide, Expedia had an almost unfair advantage from the start. "Could we get where we are today without Microsoft?" Blachford asks. "Probably, but that foundation made it much better. Look at Travelocity, it also grew up with Sabre in the background." Microsoft's technical resources also helped Expedia overcome the severe engineer drain that tech companies faced in 1999. Microsoft attracted the talent and could assign people to work on the travel site. "In the long run," Expedia's Blachford points out, "sites differentiate on service, which comes down to technology. The customer doesn't see it, but technology plays into the overall customer experience."[3]

The technology push by Microsoft had a key impact early in Expedia's life. From the start, Expedia planned to become a one-stop travel hub in cyberspace, so it used Microsoft's connections with resorts, hotels, and other travel-related companies to offer discounts that no one else offered. Certainly every advantage Microsoft could deliver was important for Expedia in the dogfight that broke out between the company and archrivals Travelocity and Priceline.com. Launched in April 1996, Priceline had more than 1 million visitors to its site in its first week. The auction mentality, so popular on the Web, helped Priceline become an early leader in the New Economy. Founder Jay Walker was even likened to an electronic age Thomas Edison in a 1999 article in *Forbes* magazine. Priceline went public in March 1999 at $16 a share and rocketed to $88 its first day and then jumping higher to soon trade at $130 a share. Priceline's market cap reached an extraordinary $18.5 billion and Walker's share of the pie equaled a tidy $9 billion. Walker's status as a New Economy paper billionaire was a far cry from Edison, who gained and lost several fortunes over the course of his life.

In March 2000, just before the Internet bubble economy popped, Travelocity went public by merging with Preview Travel, then the distant third company behind Expedia and Travelocity. The combined entity immediately became the ninth largest travel agency in the United States and the leader in market share among online travel agencies. More important, the new Travelocity jumped to number three among online commerce firms, right behind Amazon and eBay.

After the merger, the company's market capitalization reached $2.54 billion, but gradually dropped down to about $700 million—much of the drop resulting from the Nasdaq crash that spring. With Preview Travel's long-term marketing deals with AOL, Excite, Lycos, and Snap (the leading portals in early 2000), the combined entity (with more than 6.2 million monthly visitors) worked to convert visitors into paying customers, a challenge that plagued online travel firms from the start. Less than 10 percent of people who went to the site ended up purchasing anything.

By late 2000, Travelocity extended its lead to account for more than 21 million users. The company's market share hit 35 percent, compared with Expedia's 25 percent. Both companies also turned a profit much quicker than anyone expected. Expedia beat its own predictions for profitability by five quarters, and Travelocity did the same one quarter early.

Orbitz Flies into Battle

In an unprecedented display of solidarity, the five largest U.S. airlines (Delta, United, Northwest, Continental, and American Airlines) came together to form Orbitz, a $145 million online travel site to rival Expedia and Travelocity. Orbitz attracted quite a buzz when it launched in June 2001. Observers noted its potential antitrust implications and the site's chances at knocking off its main competitors. It may be telling that Orbitz began life as a project code-named "T2," supposedly either after the Arnold Schwarzenegger movie of the same name or the more ominous "Travelocity Terminator."

Orbitz found its way on the radar screens of attorneys at the Justice and Transportation Departments, state attorneys general offices, and among various consumer advocacy groups even before going live. Critics felt that Orbitz would collude to set ticket prices and form a monopoly over its rivals. In an interesting twist, Orbitz CEO Jeffrey G. Katz believed much of the lobbying against Orbitz came from supposed consumer alliances that actually represented the interests of Expedia and Travelocity. And there is plenty of evidence that he was at least partially right.

Katz promised that Orbitz would offer consumers a better search engine and many more choices than they currently enjoyed. The immediate benefit of using the Orbitz engine is that it delivered fares from more than 20 major airlines. The results, laid out in a user-friendly manner, could range from a dozen to hundreds of options. The public responded favorably, with 3.7 million unique users visiting in the first month. The company turned these Web surfers into $100 million in reservations. These statistics vaulted Orbitz into third place behind its two main rivals.

Orbitz was a latecomer to the online travel industry, so it had to fight to catch up with the market leaders. To beef up name recognition, each of the site's 35 charter members also committed to spending about $2 million a year on marketing opportunities for Orbitz.

Expedia: Cyberspace Travel Hub

Expedia strengthened its hub strategy by purchasing Travelscape.com and Vacationspot.com for $177 million. The deal gave Expedia access to discount hotel reservations and luxury vacation packages, which broadened the scope of Expedia in important strategic ways, says Blachford. "We decided to act as a retailer rather than as a travel agent and diversified into other areas to decrease our dependency on air. Our business model allows us to make tactical pricing decisions and offer better prices to customers," he explains.[4]

Blachford estimated that technology would remain vital. Just as the banks had to determine how important ATMs would become and then scale to that figure, online sites had to scale to the number of users they forecasted. "One hundred percent of tickets will never be sold online," he says, "but what is the magic number that will? My guess is that it will reach 40 to 50 percent, which means there are still huge opportunities waiting to be realized." That kind of penetration required an ongoing commitment to technological upgrades and innovations, as online firms accounted for only about 14 percent.

The primary benefit of online travel is that people want a one-stop shopping experience and will use the site that can give them the most services in a central location. For example, someone traveling to the snorkeling wonderland of Cozumel, Mexico, wants to reserve airfare and a hotel, but also might want to rent snorkeling gear, plan an excursion to the Mayan ruins at Chichen Itza, and make dinner reservations at several restaurants in Cancun. "In the long run, users will be able to reserve everything on-line," Blachford declares. "They will have an entire itinerary booked and reserved online. Today's world is piecemeal, tomorrow's will present everything all at one place."[5]

Expedia served as Microsoft's first successful spin-off, going public on November 10, 1998, at $14 a share and, like most Net stocks, jumped to $53.44, resulting in a $2 billion market cap, with Microsoft retaining a 70 percent ownership. On July 16, 2001, Microsoft sold Expedia to Barry Diller's USA Networks for $1.5 billion. Diller is a master at convergence; he built USA into a media powerhouse, with tentacles in television (USA), vacation packaging (National Leisure Group), hotel reservations (Hotel Reservation Network), discount shopping (Home Shopping Network), and ticketing (Ticketmaster). He owned a database of about 30 million customers and Microsoft desperately needed access to them. "USA Networks has a broad reach, which Microsoft can leverage to reach consumers," said Microsoft vice president Yusuf Mehdi.[6]

Hilton Books Room on the Web

Bruce Rosenberg vividly remembers the day Hilton Hotels launched its Web site, which enabled customers to make reservations online. "We launched a site that cost $50,000 to build and that was a big bet," he says. "The reservation system concluded with an e-mail sent to the reservation site, but the people there didn't know how to operate e-mail. We set up a bell to alert them an e-mail was coming in."[7] The bell rang three times. Rosenberg was ecstatic. It wasn't the number of orders that got him excited, however; it was where they came from: one each from Europe, Asia, and the United States. A bell then went off in Rosenberg's mind.

The next day he walked in to his boss's office and told him that they got three orders. "You've got to be kidding," his boss replied, not knowing whether to be incredibly happy or extraordinarily sad. Rosenberg had seen the light (and heard the bell). He immediately asked his boss for half-a-million dollars to build out an e-commerce Web site. Luckily, the three orders were enough for him to agree.

Thinking about the Internet, Rosenberg, the senior vice president of e-business, knew the early metrics, but he wondered to himself, "How do you turn it into a real business." From the first day, he decided to follow a single tenet as his guide: leverage the brick and mortar assets to compete online. Hilton focused on customer service and internal discipline, so these values would be kept as the company plunged into e-commerce.

Rosenberg immediately realized that Hilton could have great ambitions on the Web, but he it didn't want it to become a travel agency. He worked internally to set the proper expectations, both for those who expected miracles and others who didn't want to be bothered with the Web. The Web challenge intensified when Hilton acquired the Promus Hotel Corp. in late 1999, which brought Hampton Inn, DoubleTree, and Embassy Suites into the fold. All the disparate brands had to be brought under one umbrella that leveraged the power of the Hilton name.

After conducting numerous user surveys and doing other forms of research, Hilton executives saw that when customers called the Hilton help line via phone, they stayed on an average of only two minutes. On the Web, however, customers initially stayed eight minutes and gradually decreased the time to five minutes. Rosenberg determined that the Hilton homepage had to be the best point of access to the company in the world.

With this idea in mind as a rallying point, bells then started ringing all over Hilton. The company realized that a customer accessing the Web site cost Hilton eight times less than a voice conversation. Using internal tech tools, Rosenberg calculated a return on investment for the homepage and charted it daily. Using the services of a research firm, he then began forecasting how revenue and expenses would change for the site over the next three years. Rather than just trying to grab market share or get big fast—the common mania of pure Web companies—Hilton used statistics and forecasting to guide and reinforce the accuracy of its strategy.

At one point, Rosenberg worried about all the venture capital flowing to competitors and how it would affect Hilton's efforts. In retrospect, he says that it actually kept the company on its toes. "Instead of focusing on competitors, we concentrated on executing on our plan," he explains. "We did not want to overspend or have any write-offs from our e-business efforts." In fact, Rosenberg says that Hilton is already collecting $500 million in revenue from business on its Web site, which will approach 5 percent of the company's total by the end of 2001.[8]

After Hilton built a world-class external site, it then used Web technology to shave costs off its back end, such as having an integrated reservation booking and call center. Tony Nieves, senior vice president of purchasing at Hilton, organized a team to build an internal e-business marketplace to get suppliers hooked directly into the Hilton system. The procurement site began with 500 Hilton hotels and their suppliers, but Nieves expects it to expand to Hilton's 1,600 managed and franchised hotels in the next year. In total, the exchange includes more than 3,500 suppliers, with about 1,000 of these being active participants. Nieves says that the hotels on the system are spending 60 percent of their procurement budgets on the site.

Rosenberg believes the Web is the best place to interact with Hilton. It provides content, personalization, and transaction capabilities across all the company's properties. Hilton's early success on the Web proved that bricks-and-mortar companies could not only compete when it comes to e-commerce, but actually had the infrastructure to dominate.

Today, online travel is a ubiquitous part of consumer culture. Travelocity, Expedia, and others no longer have to spend tens of millions of dollars on marketing campaigns, because people automatically turn to the sites to fulfill their travel needs. The irony of the former upstart online travel companies is that now they are mainstream. In early 2008, Priceline, for instance, sells for $127 a share, whereas Expedia shares are a more modest $25.

In today's Web 2.0 world, the stalwarts of online travel are adapting to consumer demands. Expedia, for example, owns TripAdvisor, a social travel site that features user-generated travel reviews. "The influence of social networking and community services is growing significantly for online travel," explains one industry analyst. "Seeking information and looking for perspective—like-minded experience and judgments—are currently trumping the straightforward hunt for the best price. Services that facilitate a purchasing decision by aggregating or filtering content make [online travel information] relevant to the user."[9]

SEPTEMBER 11

Terrorism and Online Travel

It is clear that Expedia, Travelocity, and Orbitz developed different strategies, despite the similarity of their products. Internet users were trained to expect huge savings online and the travel sites fulfilled this need. With the uncertainties that lingered as a result of the September 11 terrorist attacks, however, the brakes were applied to the phenomenal growth of the online firms. Expedia dropped from trading in the mid-30s per share to the low 20s, lowering its market cap to $1.18 billion, and Travelocity fell from the low 20s down to about $13 a share, which valued the company at $650 million.

The chaos surrounding the airlines resulted in massive layoffs in that business and billions of dollars lost in travel and tourism, which had a ripple effect on the main Web travel sites. Expedia and Travelocity reported that bookings dropped by 50 percent after the attacks. If there were a saving grace for the online firms it was that they had cash in reserve to carry them through the downturn. Expedia, for example, had $225 million in the bank, and as it carried no inventory, could weather the storm better than many of its online brethren.

ECO-FRIENDLY TRAVEL

When checking into a room at the Quorum Hotel-Tampa, guests immediately notice a tag hanging on the back of the door and others strategically placed throughout the suite. The place cards feature beautiful pictures of sandy beaches and sunsets, perfectly appropriate for the Tampa Bay area, which features some of the world's greatest beaches. The message contained on each, however, is more serious: "We invite you to join with us to conserve water by using your towels more than once," the notice reads. "In addition to decreasing water and energy consumption, you help us replace the amount of detergent waste water that must be recycled within our community."[10] The marketing effort to educate guests at the hotel is part of the Southwest Florida Water Management District's (Swiftmud) program to conserve water. Initiated in 2002, the move is one of many nationwide that focuses on reaching people with an eco-friendly message. Consumers in the new millennium demand these types of programs, and the travel industry is one of the most innovative in meeting this need.

As a primary tourist destination, Florida is a leader in the eco-friendly travel movement. The state began a "Green Lodging" program in 2004 within the Florida Department of Environmental Protection's waste management division to promote hotels and motels that meet a number of criteria built around environmental awareness. From 2004 to 2008, the number of hotels participating grew from 10 to more than 100, with another 275 in the application process. Companies achieving the Florida Green Lodging certification have learned that it is also a financial benefit, according to journalist Ted Jackovics, "realizing conservation can become a marketing tool as well as a cost-savings effort."[11]

Nationwide, the eco-friendly movement at hotels began in the 1990s by giving guests the opportunity to opt out of linen and towel service, which saved on water and electricity expenses. The Texas-based Green Hotels Association estimated that hotels could save $6.50 or more a day per room if guests participated. In the Tampa region, since 2002, Swiftmud's plan is estimated to have saved participants about 20 percent to 30 percent in laundry expenses and 1 billion gallons of water.[12]

In addition to Florida, where Governor Charlie Christ signed an executive order requiring state agencies and departments to hold meetings and conferences at Green Lodging companies, similar programs are underway in California, Michigan, North Carolina, Pennsylvania, Vermont, Virginia, and Wisconsin. According to Penny Heudorf, director of sales and marketing at Quorum Hotel-Tampa, businesses are also using the eco-friendly designation in making decisions about where to permit business travel and meetings. "These days, when we go through a process with business clients to negotiate rates, the clients are asking what we are doing in terms of environmental initiatives," she said.[13]

"WHAT HAPPENS IN VEGAS. . ."

In the new millennium, destinations and tourism groups that represent geographic regions banded together in the battle to win travelers in a heated industry based on cutthroat competition. In 2005, Las Vegas, which many people equated with Sinatra's Rat Pack, gambling, and Sin City, embraced its outlaw heritage with a new slogan, "What happens here, stays here." The motto—part of a risky $75 million advertising campaign— strucka chord with adult travelers, who flocked to Vegas, viewing it as a kind of adult playground. The campaign also flew in the face of the city's attempt to mimic Disney with its former "It's anything and everything" family-friendly slogan.[14]

In early 2008, building off the success of "What happens here," Las Vegas tourism executives introduced a complimentary tagline—"Your Vegas is Showing—meant to work with the now-iconic slogan. Erika Pope of the Las Vegas Convention and Visitors Authority explains that Vegas in the new millennium represents the "adult freedom experience." Each year since the original campaign launched, the number of visitors broke the record of the previous year. A total of 38.9 million people visited in 2006, topped by the 39.2 million in 2007.[15]

Although its slogan is catchy, Las Vegas reinvented itself on more than just a catchphrase. At the heart of the transformation is a building boom on the Strip and a steady infusion of celebrities. In early 2008, for example, the gold-covered Trump International hotel opened, capitalizing on "The Donald's" popularity. Rapper and budding business tycoon Jay-Z opened a nightclub (dubbed 40/40) inside The Palazzo, another of Vegas's new hotels. The glitz of potentially rubbing elbows with a real-life celebrity at a new club or at a boxing match draws many tourists to Vegas. At the same time, the average room rate has nearly doubled over five years, from $80 to $139 a night. The new hotels begin rates at $200 and quickly go up from there. Similarly, tickets to shows in Vegas are pricey, from $95 to $250 to see Bette Midler, to $94 to $160 for tickets to Cirque du Soleil's tribute to the Beatles at the Mirage.[16]

LUXURY TRAVEL

For wealthy people, travel means exclusivity and privacy. The difference between these high-end consumers and everyone else is that those who are rich have unlimited resources to pay for those features. For the wealthy, travel is often one of the best ways they can enjoy their money—there are only so many cars, boats, or houses one can own. Milton Pedraza, chief executive officer of the Luxury Institute in New York, explains, "The widening number of affluent travelers around the world are increasingly willing to spend their wealth on *experiences* like travel instead of *things* like cars or second and third homes." From 2005 to 2006, for example, luxury hotel revenue increased 10 percent.[17]

For business travelers on the road, more are opting for higher-end digs and upgrading from the lesser pack of discount chains. In response, some hotels are remodeling and expanding services to lure the corporate money.

According to consulting firm PricewaterhouseCoopers, about 136,500 hotel rooms began construction in 2006, a 64.2 percent increase in one year and the single-biggest jump since 1994.[18]

Little upgrades, such as a larger bed and nicer bathrooms, are enough to get business road warriors hooked. Hampton Hotels designed a program called "Cloud Nine," which attracts people by making sleep more enjoyable with 200-thread-count comforters and jumbo-sized down or foam pillows. Realizing that businesspeople have specific work needs, most hotels offer high-speed Internet access.

12

Visual Arts

I call it the water-park phenomenon. A zillion other things are competing for our leisure time. People might visit a museum to see a Monet
or a toaster or a textile display—what's important is it's getting them
in the door.

—Ford Bell, President/CEO, American
Association of Museums (2008)

The Biennial art show at the Whitney Museum of American Art is a showcase of young talent and presents a kind of state of the union of contemporary art. The 2008 Biennial, according to journalist Leslie Camhi, reveals
the depths in which "we're living at the end of the American empire" and
might make an observer "feel nostalgia for a not-so-distant past when our
nation's art seemed in the vanguard, formally or politically."[1]

The show featured many versions of the trendy "dystopic video art and
sculptural installation," but only one painter, which Camhi claims might
be "a thing of the past, a relic from a preceding generation." Other artists put together works strewn together from pieces of garbage. Phoebe
Washburn built an "ecosystem" of different objects rising up from "beds
of neon-yellow golf balls." Other artists—81 in total—worked in video or
via video screen. Many pondered the dual wars in Iraq and on terror and
the consequences.[2]

Taken as a whole, the 2008 Biennial may not fulfill some grand "vision"
of American art as we near the end of the first decade of the new millennium, but the kinds of work and what is considered art make a statement
about the direction visual arts is charting. Many of the artists featured
video installations, which points to the way art is both following and leading the broader culture. Taking cues from music videos, reality television,
and film, among other factors, artists who work with video are showing

how their work reflects broader societal implications. These artists also point toward a future where art is unfixed, whether in a flat-screen frame or concealed someway within the fabric of a home. Glimpses of this future already sit on mantles in people's homes and on the shelves of retailers in the form of picture frames loaded with digital images that change at the viewer's discretion. How long before this kind of technology transforms art and how people interact with artworks?

Undoubtedly, technology infiltrated the visual arts in the decade as the computer and its peripherals took center stage in American life. For example, computer software and programs enabled graphic artists to create designs that were in some senses more sensual and expressive of the democratic impulse. These works, unlike a static painting, allowed for interaction with the audience and a unique viewer experience. In addition, the visual arts delivered a greater degree of freedom to the art world by making the Internet an important component. With the Web, more people entered into the art world, primarily through purchasing art online or participating in an auction at a site like eBay. Enabling transactions to occur in the virtual world, however, also carried some risk. Art collectors and museums face the real possibility that a rare find purchased through a middleman may actually be a stolen treasure or fake.

Although new artists are breaking onto the scene in the 2000s, few if any have achieved the iconic or popular status of their predecessors, such as Jackson Pollack, Andy Warhol, or Ansel Adams. Artists whose work dominated the art houses of the 1980s and 1990s still receive most of the attention in the world of visual arts. The old masters still receive the lion's share of public attention given to the visual arts, even though traditional paintings are much less influential in today's digital world.

An important trend in the 2000s is that more cultures are now participating in the art world, even if on a local or regional scale. For instance, Native Americans put on arts festivals to showcase their work, as do African Americans and other groups. Most of the smaller programs won't get much more publicity than a blurb in the hometown paper, but the millions of people that flock collectively to these community-building events have the opportunity to gain insight into the artwork of culture's outside their own.

At the Smithsonian Institution's National Museum of the American Indian, for example, the professional staff enlisted "community curators" to help them with framing the last 500 years of native history. These helpers came from different tribes and helped the staff gain a better understanding of artifacts and displays. Kevin Gover, director of the museum and a Pawnee, explained, "Our philosophy is to give voice to the native community, to give them an opportunity to tell their story. In the mind of Indian people, they've never been able to tell their story. Their story is told by others."[3]

ONLINE ART AND AUCTIONS

The Internet revolution extends to the art world and stands poised to increase its importance in the future. The Web offers some critical benefits to potential art buyers: the ability to participate in auctions across physical space and additional research opportunities that did not exist as easily before the wired world. Perhaps the most compelling feature is that the Internet delivers direct access to artists. Collectors are already using this link to buy directly from rising stars. In the near future, such exchanges may eliminate the auction house model, although posthumous sales do necessitate a middleperson role to some degree.

For the larger auctions that generate global interest, Bonhams (bonhams.com), Christie's (Christies.com), and Sotheby's (sothebys.com), all have online sites that attract new audiences who either enjoy the anonymity of the Web experience or may be intimidated by the stuffy atmosphere of an in-person auction.

eBay

Web-based auction site eBay has had a central role as a popular culture phenomenon in the new millennium. Although its traditional auction model waned a bit as the novelty of the site wore off, the company created new revenue streams that simultaneously expanded its influence. In the art world, eBay Live Auctions enabled auctions to take place in the virtual world with or without a simultaneous one in the physical realm. After registering to be an online bidder, a person simply makes bids via the site.

In early 2008, Wildwood Antiques Center near Toledo, Ohio, hosted an auction that included prominent works owned by Owens-Illinois Inc., a local corporation that manufactures glass containers. The auction took place at Wildwood's location, as well the eBay site, with online bids projected onto a 20-foot by 10-foot screen. The onsite bids are also registered on eBay, so both groups have the information simultaneously.[4]

Green Valley Auctions of Mount Crawford, Virginia, sold $368,000 in its annual winter cataloged and uncataloged sale of Eighteenth and Nineteenth Century glass and lighting in January 2008, with more than 3,500 pieces sold over four session. The firm eclipsed its 2007 winter figure, which president and senior auctioneer Jeffrey S. Evans says is due to its online component. "In this auction," he explains, "about 31 percent of the sales over the three days went through eBay Live. We think that's interesting and significant." Using eBay, Evans says, opened the sale globally, with buyers in Egypt, Malta, South America, and the Netherlands, in addition to the firm's traditional European buyers. Others are watching the action via the Internet.[5]

Along with eBay's successes, some gallery owners and observers criticize the company for focusing too much on the bottom line and moving further away from its roots as a place where small businesses and individuals could buy and trade freely. Chuck Hamsher, owner of the Purple Moon gallery in Charleston, West Virginia, had a long and fruitful relationship with the online seller dating back to 1999. By 2001, he opened an eBay store. In 2008, however, he closed the virtual location and stopped doing business with the auctioneer after it lowered listing fees, but increased commission fees. The company also altered its famous feedback/rating system, the backbone of the transaction model.[6]

Hamsher wrote on his blog about why he left eBay and received hundreds of e-mails in response from other small business sellers. With tighter profit margins and cost controls, small businesses have more to lose under eBay's new commission setup. The company bumped its fee from 5.25 percent to 8.75 percent. Perhaps even more debilitating to eBay users is that sellers will no longer be able to post negative feedback to buyers, which opens the site to additional fraud. "The feedback system has worked because it was mutual. The system is worthless without being mutual," Hamsher wrote in his blog.[7]

MUSEUMS

Although most museums focus on displaying great works of art by the acknowledged masters—a distinctly historical outlook—the art world competes with all the other forms of entertainment available to consumers in the modern world. In response, museums launch marketing plans that include family nights, limited-run exhibits that will attract significant attention, and other programs that will draw people off their couches and away from the computer.

Science and technology museums, such as the Museum of Science and Industry (MOSI) in Tampa and the Carnegie Science Center in Pittsburgh, have been particularly successful in marketing to families and children. MOSI has an entire wing designed for kids to interact with science and technology through exhibits that enhance motor skills, logic, and creativity as children play. In some instances, these institutions are willing to take risks to gain exposure. Both centers hosted the controversial "Bodies" traveling exhibit, which featured preserved human bodies and internal organs on display. Despite public outcry from religious organizations and human rights activists, MOSI increased membership and used the money raised from ticket sales to fund operations and new exhibits.

In an attempt to uncover what patrons want from the museum experience, institutions nationwide are using technology. The Museum of Modern Art in New York completed a $450 million expansion in 2005 and simultaneously compiled information on visitors to put into a database.

The Detroit Institute of Arts conducted research into patron preferences and uncovered statistics that overturned common perceptions, including that only 7 percent of visitors actually read wall plaques and spent a mere four or five minutes in any gallery, much less than the 20 minutes that officials assumed. Museum executives realize that these kinds of studies help them determine who visits, why they come, and what will make them return. In implementing the findings, museums are changing everything from the types of music played to hours of operation. Nancy Price from the San Francisco Museum of Modern Art explains, "People want to know that what they're seeing is relevant to their life. This might sound simple, but it's important for us to hear."[8]

The challenge for museums is balancing the presentation of so-called high brow versus low brow exhibits. According to journalist Carol Vogel, "While serving up what audiences want may be a smart business move, there is a fear by curators that things can go too far, that catering to public opinion could dumb down a museum and supplant curatorial wisdom. Are museums for high culture or low? Places to see Ralph Lauren's car collection and *Star Wars* costumes, props and drawings rather than Vermeer and Renaissance tapestries?" This kind of equilibrium remains elusive, yet critical, for museum curators, particularly in an era dominated by digital communications. It is not an easy task to get people into museums.[9]

Michael Govan

In the not-so-distant past, the Los Angeles County Museum of Art (LACMA) had little consequence on the artistic scene—locally or nationally. In 2006, backers brought in Michael Govan to turn around the ailing museum. In the years since, Govan led that transformation, basically turning LACMA into LA's foremost art institution. This is pretty heady stuff for a formerly second-tier museum in a city that is home to Hollywood and the Getty.

Govan represents a new breed of museum chief executive, both strategic and with the artistic flair to make people take notice. Similar to the rock star architects and artists of the last 20 years, Govan takes on high-profile projects and essentially becomes the face of the organization. In 2003, he drew national attention for turning an abandoned biscuit factory into the Dia Art Foundation museum in Beacon, New York.[10]

The first step in the makeover included a physical expansion and upgrade. LACMA opened $56 million Broad Contemporary Art Museum, designed by Italian architect Renzo Piano, to house the collection of its most prominent backer, Eli Broad. The new facility contains 56,000 square feet of exhibition space, which serves as the focal point of the museum's transformation.

But Govan's real strongpoint is in having a knack for exhibit design. Artist Alexis Smith outlined Govan's work in bringing neon artist Dan Flavin to the museum. "The Flavin exhibition was beautifully selected, installed and almost choreographed," Smith explains. "Its level of visual sophistication was doubly interesting because it was done not by a museum curator but by a museum director."[11] Govan also orchestrated the remodeling of the museum's entrance, bringing in artist Robert Irwin to create a garden of palm trees, Chris Burden to install vintage street lamps, and for phase 2 of the renovation, a Jeff Koons-designed 70-foot train replica dangled from a crane.

Today's young museum leaders are able to wow corporate sponsors and celebrities. Govan brought Barbra Streisand into LACMA as a trustee. He also strengthened ties with Hollywood, adding Michael Lynton, the chief executive of Sony Pictures Entertainment, as a director. These ties are critical in running a museum in the new millennium. Govan and his colleagues at other institutions must delicately mix corporate sponsorship and dollars into growth and sustainability plans. For example, the global oil company BP funded the new $25 million solar-powered entrance pavilion and will have its name adorned to the structure. This move led to some criticism, but seems to be a necessity in today's art world. Museums need large endowments and LACMA's $170 million is miniscule compared to better known places like the Museum of Modern Art ($650 million).[12]

Another central figure in the LACMA's renovation is Broad, its benefactor and namesake for the new building. The list of pieces he is donating reads like a who's who of contemporary art: Koons, Cindy Sherman, Roy Lichtenstein, and Robert Rauschenberg. "I'd like to make the largest gift, and I liked to help raise a lot of money," Broad said. "But now that we've got other, younger trustees of some prominence and wealth, I'm delighted that they're very engaged. And we've got a great leader in Michael, so it all feels pretty good to me."[13]

Scams, Fakes, and Fraud

The culmination of a five-year probe into art fraud took place on January 24, 2008, when teams of federal agents from the Internal Revenue Service, National Park Service, and Immigration and Customs Enforcement descended on four California museums—The Mingei International Museum in San Diego, the Los Angeles County Museum of Art, the Pacific Asia Museum in Pasadena, and the Bowers Museum in Santa Ana. The raids came after the agencies investigated possible theft and tax schemes after the institutions allegedly accepted looted cultural treasures from Thailand. According to journalists Jeff McDonald and Jeanette Steele, the action taken in California, "has drawn new attention to an unwelcome fact of the art trade: An increasing amount of pillaged property is finding its way into museums and private collections."[14]

With no federal agency providing oversight into the art theft challenge, even the best museums and collectors in the world face reproach. The stakes are high for all parties involved in complex art purchasing and trades. Often the transactions seem more likely from a James Bond movie than between international dealers and museum representatives. In the 2000s, developing countries are most susceptible to looting.

In the California case, Robert Olson, a Los Angeles smuggler, sold items stolen from grave sites in the Ban Chiang region of northeast Thailand. At the Mingei, federal officials believe that 70 objects were acquired illegally and they seized 23 in the January search. The artifacts in question are mainly earthenware pieces, some that date back to 3000 B.C. Similarly, in 2007, the J. Paul Getty Museum in Los Angeles returned 40 pieces that Italian officials said were stolen. Both The Metropolitan Museum of Art in New York and the Museum of Fine Arts in Boston also returned stolen Italian artwork.[15]

Investigators at Immigration and Customs Enforcement's Office of Investigations conduct extensive analysis of potentially illegal art sales, citing the general political instability in some parts of the world as a catalyst for such crimes. A total of 50 agents watch the Web and investigation international shipping records hoping to minimize illegal trafficking. The office focuses on returning pilfered pieces to their rightful owners, not necessarily convicting the looters and/or middlemen involved in the transactions. Putting the criminals in jail is difficult in these cases, so prosecutors concentrate on getting the items returned.[16]

PHOTOGRAPHY

Ian Allen

Photographer Ian Allen and his friend, documentary filmmaker Jeremy Blakeslee, sneaked into an abandoned Bethlehem steel mill in eastern Pennsylvania to look around and capture images of the empty plant, once teeming with life and hot, molten metal. The building was soon to be demolished and replaced with a casino, so the men dodged security guards and jumped fences to get at the heart of the deserted mill. Of Allen's photography, journalist Jami Attenberg says, "The cavernous images have a mournful air; one can feel the staleness in the place. In some shots, the abandoned machinery looms as if it were wounded. The photos capture what is absent as much as what remains."[17]

Taken from inside and outside the abandoned mill, Allen's photographs underscore desertedness and the immensity of the place. Some of the shots are taken from rooftops as a sheen of snow covers the ground. They reveal depth, represented by the rail lines indicating distance and the blue-gray sky that extends out forever. The rusty buildings preview the work of demolition crews that will pull the plant apart piece by piece. In another shot, a section of the mill's roof in the foreground accentuates the run-down town built on a stark hillside just beyond its gates. These are the people the mill left behind and their homes are multicolored, but worn—a hodgepodge of misshapen buildings filled with people who are as abandoned as the mill itself.

Originally from Seattle, but educated at the School of Visual Arts in New York, the 27-year-old Allen epitomizes the visual arts in the new millennium. He is not limited to one medium, working in both photography and design. Allen also represents the kind of fluid globalization that younger artists embody. On a trip to Asia, Allen contrasted the chaotic street life in Tokyo with the rural solitude of Tibet. Unlike artists of past generations, Allen is focused on his work first, rather than the money he can generate. "At this point in my career, I'd rather be stuffing my portfolio and wait to stuff my wallet later, if ever," he explains. "I'm trying to avoid the ever-increasing salary-equals-success mentality that young designers can get trapped in."[18] Allen's client list represents his interests across popular culture. They range from MTV and HBO to the advertising firm Ogilvy & Mather and *New York* magazine.

Gregory Crewdson

Director, production manager, or choreographer—rather than photographer—might be better labels for what Gregory Crewdson creates on film. Rather than the traditional stereotype of a barren or white room containing little more than a photographer, model, and camera, Crewdson stages elaborate scenes, some on a soundstage and others in the field of often small towns in Massachusetts. Regardless, the result is an image that tells a story of humanity, particularly in the American suburbs. Some of these photographs capture the lurid details people hope to keep from their neighbors; whereas others focus on the elegance in ordinary lives lived.

Born in Brooklyn, New York, in 1962, Crewdson teaches photography at Yale University, where he received his MFA. He gained attention in the 1990s for several series that mixed the mundane and outrageous into a surreal view of life in Lee, Massachusetts, where his family had a cabin when he was a boy. The town serves as the backdrop for many of Crewdson's works. In his artist's biography from the Guggenheim, one gets the sense of the scope and filmic vision of Crewdson's works, which are "decidedly cinematic images reminiscent of the films of Steven Spielberg. These recent photographs have become increasingly spectacular and complex to produce, requiring dozens of assistants, Hollywood-style lighting, and specially crafted stage sets."[19]

One is thrown off when first examining Crewdson's stills. They oblige a second, deeper look, because it is almost impossible to believe that the lush colors aren't from a painting. Crewdson's *Twilight* series (1998–2001), for example, shows typical family scenes, but bathed in deep hues of reds and grays. Then there is an added fantastical aspect of the photograph that completely changes the viewer's perception of the piece. Crewdson explains his fascination with that instant where normal and abnormal collide, saying:

In all my pictures what I am ultimately interested in is that moment of transcendence or transportation, where one is transported into another place, into a perfect, still world. Despite my compulsion to create this still world, it always meets up against the impossibility of doing so. So, I like the collision between this need for order and perfection and how it collides with a sense of the impossible. I like where possibility and impossibly meet.[20]

In a 2006 photo, *Untitled (north by northwest)*, a woman sits in the passenger seat of an automobile, lights still on, stopped in the middle of a desolate street at a yellow light. There is no visible sign of the driver or that the person even existed—the only option is that the character literally ran out of the frame. But, how did the driver get out of the picture before the passenger could react? True to Crewdson's style, the photograph looks like a color movie still, the dawn sky and light mist in the background have sucked the color out of the picture, which allows the faint yellow of a crosswalk in the foreground and the overhead traffic light to sizzle. On first glance, the viewer would be hard pressed to believe that such perfection could be staged.

The tension, however, is always the focus in Crewdson's work. Describing Crewdson's style as a chronicler of suburban America, a recent reviewer said, "Rather than depicting suburbia as a place of expectation, his photographs show the suburbs as a shadowy world where strange and even surreal things happen; in one image showing here, a middle-aged man watches absently as clouds of smoke billow from a backyard shed. You sense that some dark truth lies below the scene's otherwise calm surface." The artist asks the audience to reexamine life both hidden and exposed in the seemingly boring suburbs and perhaps question the stereotypes associated with suburbia.[21]

PAINTING

Mark Bradford

Over a six-year span, Mark Bradford achieved the American Dream. At the beginning of the journey, he ran his mother's hair salon in South Los Angeles with hopes of someday becoming an artist. Fast forward a little more than a handful of years later and his paintings sell for $250,000. He is a featured artist at shows around the country and enjoys global fame, including winning the 2006 Bucksbaum Award, a $100,000 prize given to a participant at the Whitney Biennial.

Like any great American success story, Bradford's did not come without some heartbreak. In 2001, he sold his first piece, titled *Enter and Exit the New Negro,* to the Studio Museum in Harlem. In the next two years, some of his work was met with criticism, including shows at Art Basel Miami and the Whitney Altria space. In 2003, however, Bradford bounced back at a show called "Bounce." Curator Eungie Joo pushed him to "work big" and bought him the canvas to do so. Bradford came back strong, including the piece *Los Moscos,* later one of his works at the 2006 Whitney Biennial.[22]

In September 2007, his first solo show, "Neither New nor Correct," opened at the Whitney. It featured scenes from his hometown Leimert Park neighborhood in Los Angeles. Bradford's influences extend beyond his African American roots to include his place as a third generation small business owner. He explains:

Early on, I was interested in using material that came from my merchant roots. My mother was a hair stylist; I was a hair stylist. But then I started thinking, "Where is what I do?" It doesn't sound right, but that was my question. And the answer to where? was community. Once I looked out of the hair salon and became interested in the environment around me—and the language of that environment—everything that I had been trying to talk about was already there . . . I wanted to engage that material more directly. The conversations I was interested in were about community, fluidity, about a merchant dynamic, and the details that point to a genus of change. The species I use sometimes are racial, sexual, cultural, stereotypical. But the genus I'm always interested in is change.[23]

Like many other twenty-first century artists, Bradford works across many forms of media, not just painting. He is well regarded as a "found" artist, or one who takes things he finds on the streets (in Bradford's case, signage and advertising) and turns it into art. "Bradford incorporates elements from his daily life into his canvases: remnants of found posters and billboards, graffitied stencils and logos, and hairdresser's permanent endpapers he's collected from his other profession as a stylist," the experts at The Saatchi Gallery proclaim. "In *The Devil is Beating His Wife,* Bradford consolidates all these materials into a pixelized eruption of cultural cross-referencing. Built up on plywood in sensuous layers ranging from silky and skinlike to oily and singed, Bradford offers abstraction with an urban flair that's explosively contemporary."[24]

Cost of Products in the 2000s

Food

Chicken breast	$2.99 per lb.
Prime rib	$4.99–$7.99 per lb.
Cooked deli ham	$5.99 per lb.
Butter	$3.49 per lb.
Eggs	$2.29 per dozen
Milk	$3.19 per half gallon
Bread	$1.99–$3.69 per loaf
Canned tomatoes	$1.59 for a 14.5 oz can
Oranges	$0.89–$1.99 per lb.
Potatoes	$0.69 per lb.
Premium tomatoes	$0.99 per lb.
Red Baron Pizza Bread (frozen)	$4.29 per package
Coffee	$7.99 per lb.
Stouffers Macaroni & Cheese Dinner (frozen)	$3.79
Tombstone Pizza (frozen)	$5.49
Kendall-Jackson Wine (per bottle)	$15.99
Coke products (sale, per 12-pack)	$2.50–$3.50

Clothing

Men's dress shoes	$90–$150
Lauren by Ralph Lauren 2-button Blazer	$300.00
Calvin Klein 3-button Black Wool Suit	$495.00
Woman's coat	$100–$250
Nine West V-Neck Button Front Dress	$134.00
Jones New York Beaded Black Evening Dress	$180.00
Woman's designer shoes	$79.99–$450

Guess? Lila Short-Sleeved Cardigan (Juniors)	$69.00
Children's wear (average per outfit)	$70–$80
Sesame Street Baby Girl Abby Bermuda Shorts Set	$24.00

Shelter/Furnishings

Single-family home price (2007 average)	$266,200
All types of housing (2008 average)	$200,700
Rent and utilities (2001 national average)	$633
Bedroom suite	$1,500–$1,999.99
Dining room set	$800–$999.99
Living room suite	$1,500–$2,499.99
Stove	$499.99–$749.99
Washing machine	$499.99

Personal Items

Toilet tissue (12-pack)	$6.50
Toothpaste	$3.79 per tube
Cigarettes	$3.00+per pack
Wrist watch	$25–$250
Deodorant	$2.79
Crest teeth whitening strips	$39.99

Transportation

Gasoline	$4.10+pergallon—unleaded regular (July 4, 2008 national average)
2008 BMW 5 Series (MSRP)	$49,400
2008 Toyota Camry LE, 4dr Sedan	$21,075
2008 Cadillac Escalade, 4dr SUV	$58,490
2008 Toyota Prius, 4dr hybrid	$22,875

Entertainment and Leisure

Mass magazine	$0.99–$6.99
Newspaper	$0.25–$1.25 per issue
X Box 360	$349.99
CD (retail price)	$9.99–$15.99
DVD (retail price)	$15.99–$23.99
iPod Classic, 80 GB	$249.00
Digital song download, iTunes	$0.99 per song
Cell phone (with a two-year service contract)	$49.99–$500
Movie ticket	$5.50–$9.00
Nintendo Wii game cartridge	$49.99
Panasonic 46" 1080p Plasma HDTV	$2,799.99
Apple MacBook (laptop)	$1,099.99
Dell AMD Turion Dual-Core laptop	$599.99

Notes

INTRODUCTION

1. Stanley J. Baran and Dennis K. Davis, *Mass Communications Theory: Foundations, Ferment, and Future*, 4th ed. (Belmont, CA: Thomson Wadsworth, 2006), 2.

2. Lev Grossman, "Time's Person of the Year: You," *Time*, December 13, 2006, http://www.time.com/time/magazine/article/0,9171,1569514,00.html (accessed November 15, 2007).

3. David Samuels, "Shooting Britney," *The Atlantic*, April 2008, 37.

CHAPTER 1

1. Jack Loechner, "It's a Wrap: The Internet Year 2007," *Research Brief*, Center for Media Research, February 6, 2008, http://blogs.mediapost.com/research_brief/?p=1634 (accessed February 6, 2008).

2. Ibid.

3. Associated Press, "Data Breaches Climb in '07," *St. Petersburg Times*, December 31, 2007, 5A.

4. "The $1.7 Trillion Dot.Com Lesson," *CNNMoney*, November 9, 2000, http://money.cnn.com/2000/11/09/technology/overview (accessed November 15, 2000).

5. "UN Report Cites Global Internet Growth Despite Economic Woes," *USA Today*, 18 November 2002, http://www.usatoday.com/tech/news/2002–11–18-global-net_x.htm (accessed November 19, 2002).

6. Samantha Levine, "News in the Hands of Too Few?" *U.S. News & World Report*, 144, 1(2008): 23–25. Academic Search Premier, EBSCOhost (accessed March 22, 2008).

7. Jim Hu, "Case Accepts Blame for AOL-Time Warner Debacle," CNET News. com, January 12, 2005, http://news.cnet.com/Case-accepts-blame-for-AOL-Time-Warner-debacle/2100-1030_3-5534519.html (accessed July 15, 2008).

8. Quoted in "Business: The Anti-Mogul," *The Economist*, November 10, 2007, http://www.proquest.com.proxy.usf.edu (accessed March 20, 2008).

9. Quoted in Matt Smith, "Bush: I Will Work to Earn Your Respect," *CNN.com Election 2000*, December 13, 2000, http://archives.cnn.com/2000/ALLPOLITICS/stories/12/13/bush.ends.campaign/index.html (accessed December 14, 2000).

10. "Looking Back, Looking Forward: A Forum," *The Nation*, December 2, 2004, http://www.thenation.com/doc/20041220/forum/3 (accessed December 2, 2004).

11. Sean Wilentz, "The Worst President in History?" *Rolling Stone*, May 4, 2006, 32–33; Robert S. McElvaine, "Historians vs. George W. Bush," *History News Network*, August 20, 2005, http://hnn.us/comments/66933.html (accessed August 20, 2005).

12. Richard Willing, "Ex-CIA Spy's Account Unveiled," *USA Today*, October 21, 2007, http://www.usatoday.com/news/washington/2007–10–21-plame-book_n.htm (accessed April 18, 2008).

13. "President Bush—Overall Job Rating in National Polls," *PollingReport.com*, http://www.pollingreport.com/BushJob.htm (accessed March 15, 2008).

14. Wilentz, "Worst President," 34.

15. Richard Wolf, "Bush Has Big Plans for His Last Year," *USA Today*, January 29, 2008, Academic Search Premier, EBSCOhost, http://search.ebscohost.com/login.aspx?direct=true&db=aph&AN=J0E332403812708&site=ehost-live (accessed March 17, 2008).

16. Ibid.

17. Wilentz, "Worst President," 35.

18. James Poniewozik. "The Big Fat Year in Culture: So much for the post-9/11 Warm-and-Fuzzies. In 2002 the Pop World got Weird Again." *Time*, December 30, 2002, Expanded Academic ASAP. Thomson Gale. University of South Florida. http://find.galegroup.com.proxy.usf.edu/itx/infomark.do?&contentSet=IAC-Documents&type=retrieve&tabID=T003&prodId=EAIM&docId=A95739763&source=gale&srcprod=EAIM&userGroupName=tamp59176&version=1.0 (accessed June 9, 2007).

19. *The Complete 9/11 Commission Report* is available at http://govinfo.library.unt.edu/ 911/report/index.htm.

20. Jack Devine, "An Intelligence Reform Reality Check," *Washington Post*, February 18, 2008, http://www.washingtonpost.com/wp-dyn/content/article/2008/02/17/AR2008021701733.html (accessed March 30, 2008).

21. "Bush's 'Bannergate' Shuffle," *Time*, November 1, 2003, http://www.time.com/time/columnist/ dickerson/article/0,9565,536170,00.html (accessed November 15, 2005).

22. "Public Attitudes Toward the War in Iraq: 2003–2008," Pew Research Center, March 19, 2008, http://pewresearch.org/pubs/770/iraq-war-five-year-anniversary (accessed April 17, 2008).

23. Lizette Alvarez and Andrew W. Lehren, "Six of the Fallen, in Words They Sent Home," *The New York Times*, March 25, 2008, http://www.nytimes.com/2008/03/25/us/25dead.web.html?pagewanted=all (accessed March 30, 2008); "U.S. And Coalition Casualties," Forces: U.S. & Coalition/Casualties, Special Reports from CNN.com, http://www.cnn.com/SPECIALS/2003/iraq/forces/casualties (accessed March 30, 2008).

24. "Public Attitudes Toward the War," Pew Research Center.

25. Dana Priest and Anne Hull, "Soldiers Face Neglect, Frustration At Army's Top Medical Facility," *Washington Post*, February 18, 2007, http://www.washingtonpost.com/wp-dyn/content/article/2007/02/17/AR2007021701172.html (accessed March 30, 2007).

26. Ibid.

27. Paul Elias, "Veterans Accuse Government of Mishandling Medical Care," *The Mercury News* (San Jose), April 19, 2008, http://www.mercurynews.com/breakingnews/ci_8984799 (accessed April 19, 2008).

28. Quoted in Bob Batchelor, "Unspeakable Tragedy: Race and Katrina," *PopMatters*, August 29, 2006, http://www.popmatters.com/features/060829-katrina.shtml (accessed August 29, 2006).

29. George Bush, President Bush Addresses NAACP Annual Convention, July 20, 2006, http://www.whitehouse.gov/news/releases/2006/07/20060720.html (accessed July 21, 2006).

30. Pat Regnier, "Are You Better Off?" *Money: 35th Anniversary Special*, October 1, 2007, 110. http://www.proquest.com.proxy.usf.edu (accessed November 3, 2007).

31. Yang Yang, "Social Inequalities in Happiness in the United States, 1972 to 2004: An Age-Period-Cohort Analysis," *American Sociological Review* 73.2 (2008): 204–26, http://news.uchicago.edu/images/ assets/pdf/Happinesspaper.pdf.

32. Ibid.

33. Darla Mercado, "Foreclosure Filings Up 93% this Year," *InvestmentNews*, August 21, 2007.

34. Regnier, "Are You Better Off?"

35. Quoted in Jeannine Aversa, "Many Believe US Already in a Recession," *Associated Press*, February 10, 2008, http://ap.google.com/article/ALeqM5hJjzb-73g6-mEmgvyixbf7Vzw2lgD8UNNUBO2 (accessed February 11, 2008).

36. Ibid.

37. Ibid.

38. "Outsourcing Trends to Watch in 2007," *Fortune*, September 3, 2007, S2.

39. Bethany McLean and Peter Elkind, "The Guiltiest Guys in the Room," *Fortune*, July 5, 2006, http://money.cnn.com/2006/05/29/news/enron_guiltyest/index.htm (accessed September 15, 2006).

40. Penelope Patsuris, "The Corporate Scandal Sheet," *Forbes.com*, August 26, 2002, http://www.forbes.com/2002/07/25/accountingtracker.html (accessed November 15, 2007).

41. Quoted in "CEOs Defend Their Paychecks," *St. Petersburg Times*, March 8, 2008, 2D.

42. "You've Got Mail (Lots of It)," *St. Petersburg Times*, January 27, 2008, 1F.

43. Bobby White, "The New Workplace Rules: No Video-Watching," *The Wall Street Journal*, March 4, 2008, B1.

44. Ibid.

45. Quoted in ibid.

46. Ibid.

47. Jeannine Aversa, "Employers Slash Jobs by Most in 5 Years," *AP*, March 7, 2008, http://biz.yahoo.com/ap/080307/economy.html (accessed March 7, 2008).

48. Ibid.

49. Quoted in Tim Paradis, "Stocks Turn Mixed in Early Trading," *AP*, March 7, 2008, http://biz.yahoo.com/ap/080307/wall_street.html?.v=19 (accessed March 7, 2008).

50. "Empty-Nesters, Unite," *Atlantic Monthly*, October 2007, 33.

51. Quoted in ibid.

52. Jerry Adler, "The Boomer Files; Hitting 60." *Newsweek* (November 14, 2005): 50. Expanded Academic ASAP. Thomson Gale. University of South Florida. http://find.galegroup.com.proxy.usf.edu/ itx/infomark.do ?&contentSet=IAC-Documents&type=retrieve&tabID=T003&prodId=EAIM&docId=A138452122& source=gale&srcprod=EAIM&userGroupName=tamp59176&version=1.0 (accessed June 9, 2007).

53. Lorne Manly, "TV's Silver Age," *The New York Times Magazine*, May 6, 2007 http://www.nytimes.com/2007/05/06/magazine/06tvland-t.html?pagewanted=1&_r=1 (accessed February 10, 2008).

54. Quoted in William Hupp, "The Misunderstood Generation," *Advertising Age*, February 5, 2008, http://adage.com/sendopinion?article_id=124865 (accessed February 5, 2008).

55. Chad Lorenz, "The Death of E-Mail," *Slate*, November 14, 2007, http://www.slate.com/id/2177969/pagenum/all/#page_start (accessed November 18, 2007).

56. Ibid.

57. "Summary of Key Findings," *U.S. Religious Landscape Survey*, Pew Forum on Religion & Public Life, http://religions.pewforum.org/reports (accessed March 20, 2008).

58. Ibid.

59. Ibid.

CHAPTER 2

1. Sam Roberts, *Who We Are Now: The Changing Face of America in the Twenty-first Century*. New York: Henry Holt, 2004, 24.

2. Quoted in Laura M. Holson, "Text Generation Gap: U R 2 Old (JK)," *The New York Times*, March 9, 2008, http://www.nytimes.com/2008/03/09/business/09cell.html?ei=5070&en=32991e 7da51dece2& ex=1205643600&emc=eta1&pagewanted=all (accessed March 9, 2008).

3. Quoted in ibid.

4. The Pew Research Center for The People & The Press, *A Portrait of "Generation Next:" How Young People View Their Lives, Futures and Politics*, Pew Research Center, January 9, 2007, 2, 13–14.

5. Quoted in Dan Zak, "Me," *Washington Post*, March 2, 2008, http://www.washingtonpost.com/wp-dyn/content/article/2008/02/28/AR2008022803315.html?sid=ST2008022901519 (accessed March 10, 2008).

6. Tara Parker-Pope, "Peeking Inside the Mind of the Boy Dating Your Daughter," *The New York Times*, February 24, 2008, http://www.nytimes.com/2008/02/24/weekinreview/24parker-ART.html?pagewanted=all (accessed March 8, 2008).

7. Quoted in ibid.

8. Quoted in Lori Aratani, "Catching Up to the Boys, in the Good and the Bad, *Washington Post,* February 10, 2008, http://www.washingtonpost.com/wp-dyn/content/article/2008/02/09/ AR2008020901324.html (accessed February 28, 2008).

9. Ibid.

10. Pamela M. Prah, "Teen Spending," *CQ Researcher,* May 26, 2006, 457, 459.

11. Quoted in ibid., 459.

12. Ibid., 464.

13. Quoted in ibid., 471.

14. Office of National Drug Control Policy, *Youth Drug Use Declines,* Fact Sheet, December 2007, 1.

15. Tom A. Peter, "Montana Leads the Way in U.S. Success in Curbing Meth," *The Christian Science Monitor,* March 27, 2008, http://www.csmonitor.com/2008/0327/p02s01-usgn.html (accessed March 30, 2008).

16. "Fast Food Ads Fueling Obesity Among Hispanic Kids," *Washington Post,* February 21, 2008, http://www.washingtonpost.com/wp-dyn/content/article/2008/02/21/AR2008022101093.html (accessed February 22, 2008).

17. Steven K. Galson, "Prevention of Childhood Overweight and Obesity," Speech, Presented at the National Childhood Obesity Congress (Miami), March 19, 2008, http://www.surgeongeneral.gov/news/speeches/03192008.html (accessed April 17, 2008).

18. Ibid.

19. Rebecca Keister, "Teens Butting Out," *Sun Chronicle* (MA), March 2, 2008, http://www.thesunchronicle.com/articles/2008/03/03/news/news01.txt (accessed March 8, 2008).

20. Sewell Chan, "Study Says Teenagers are Avidly Shunning Cigarettes," *The New York Times,* March 10, 2006, http://www.nytimes.com/2006/03/10/nyregion/10smoking.html?emc=eta1# (accessed October 10, 2007).

21. Quoted in ibid.

22. Office of National Drug Control Policy, *Teens, Drugs & Violence: A Special Report,* June 2007, 1.

23. Ibid., 2.

24. Larry D. Rosen, "Adolescents in MySpace: Identity Formation, Friendship and Sexual Predators," California State University, Dominguez Hills, June 2006, http://www.csudh.edu/psych/Adolescents%20in%20MySpace%20-%20Executive%20Summary.pdf (accessed February 3, 2008), 5–6.

25. Ibid.

26. Quoted in Ellen Lee, "MySpace Suit Dismissed by Judge in Texas," *San Francisco Chronicle,* 15 February 2007, http://www.sfgate.com/cgi-bin/article.cgi?file=/chronicle/archive/2007/02/15/BUGEKO4VU01.DTL&type=business (accessed January 31, 2008).

27. Quoted in Dan Herbeck, "How a Sinister MySpace Predator Targeted Teen Girls," *The Buffalo News,* January 6, 2008, http://www.buffalonews.com/home/story/244627.html (accessed February 3, 2008).

28. Quoted in Marcia Clemmitt, "Cyber Socializing." *CQ Researcher,* July 28, 2006, 628.

29. Roberts, *Who We Are Now,* 198–99.

30. Ibid.

31. Claudia Willis, "How to Make Great Teachers," *Time,* February 13, 2008, http://www.time.com/time/printout/0,8816,1713174,00.html (accessed February 21, 2008).

32. Matt Miller, "First, Kill All the School Boards," *The Atlantic,* January/February 2008, 94.

33. Quoted in Claudia Wallis and Sonja Steptoe, "How to Fix No Child Left Behind," *Time,* May 24, 2007, http://www.time.com/time/printout/0,8816,1625192,00.html (accessed February 25, 2008).

34. Theoni Soublis Smyth, "Who Is No Child Left Behind Leaving Behind?" *The Clearing House,* January/February 2008, 133.

35. Ibid., 135–36.

36. Linda Jacobson, "NCLB Restructuring Found Ineffectual in California," *Education Week,* February 20, 2008, EBSCO Host Research Databases, Academic Search Premier (accessed March 17, 2008).

37. Marcia Clemmitt, "Students Under Stress," *CQ Researcher,* July 13, 2007, 577, 580.

38. Ibid., 579.

39. Quoted in ibid., 581.

40. Andrew Delbanco, "Academic Business," *The New York Times Magazine,* September 30, 2007, http://www.nytimes.com/2007/09/30/magazine/30wwln-lede-t.html?_r=1&sq=andrew%20delbanco&st=nyt&adxnnl=1&oref=slogin&scp=2&pagewanted=all&adxnnlx=1206591298-AIngwEOa9ffjRBBjfIMR0w (accessed March 24, 2008).

41. Alan Fram and Trevor Tompson, "College Students Often Stressed Out, Worried Study Says," *Associated Press,* March 19, 2008, http://www.ajc.com/news/content/news/stories /2008/03/18/stress_0319.html (accessed March 20, 2008).

42. Ibid.

43. Pew Research Center, *A Portrait of "Generation Next,"* 24–25.

44. Ibid., 25.

45. Quoted in Kyla King, "College-Age Voters Get Involved in Presidential Politics Via New Media," The *Grand Rapids Press,* April 20, 2008, http://www.mlive.com/news/index.ssf/2008/04/collegeage_voters_get_involved.html (accessed April 20, 2008).

46. Ibid.

47. King, "College-Age Voters."

48. Eve Tahmincioglu, "E-schooling Grows, But Where are the Teachers?" *The International Herald Tribune,* March 10, 2008, LexisNexis Academic database (accessed March 14, 2008).

CHAPTER 3

1. Robert W. McChesney, *The Problem of the Media: U.S. Communication Politics in the Twenty-First Century* (New York: Monthly Review Press, 2004) 161.

2. Christopher Lasch, *The Culture of Narcissism: American Life in an Age of Diminishing Expectations* (New York: W. W. Norton, 1979) 137–38.

3. McChesney, 166.

4. Quoted in McChesney, 149.

5. Irene Costera Meijer, "Advertising Citizenship: An Essay on the Performative Power of Consumer Culture," *Media, Culture & Society* 20 (1998): 242.

6. Ibid.

7. Ibid., 247.

8. Stuart Elliott, "This Year's Super Bowl Ads to Be Gentle and Sweet," *The New York Times,* January 31, 2008, http://www.nytimes.com/2008/01/31/business/media/31adco.html?fta=y (accessed January 31, 2008).

9. Quoted in Gavin O'Malley, "Snickers Scrubs Super Bowl Ad Site," *Media-Post Publications* February 7, 2007, http://publications.mediapost.com/index.cfm?fuseaction=Articles.showArticle&art_aid=55165&passFuseAction=PublicationsSearch.showSearchReslts&art_searched=snickers&page_number=0 (accessed February 7, 2007).

10. Jerry Kirkpatrick, "A Philosophic Defense of Advertising," *Advertising in Society: Classic and Contemporary Readings on Advertising's Role in Society,* eds. Roxanne Hovland and Gary B. Wilcox (Lincolnwood, IL: NTC, 1989): 517.

11. Jib Fowles, *Advertising and Popular Culture* (Thousand Oaks, CA: Sage, 1996): 49.

12. Hartley, 352.

13. Patricia Sellers, "MySpace Cowboys," *Fortune,* September 4, 2006: 73–74.

14. Quoted in ibid.

15. Brian Morrissey, "Inside the Promise and Peril of YouTube," *ADWEEK,* January 29, 2007: 10.

16. Ron Ruggless, "Students' Low-Cost Chipotles Ads Draw 18 Million Online Viewers," *Nation's Restaurant News,* December 4, 2006: 4.

17. Paul Gillin, "The World's Watching: So Why Aren't PR Pros Using Viral Video?" *Bulldog Reporter's Daily Dog,* March 29, 2007, http://www.bulldogreporter.com/dailydog/issues/1_1/dailydog_barks_bites/ index.html (accessed March 29, 2007).

18. Ibid.

19. Fowles, 165.

20. Leslie Wayne, "McCain Reports Improved Fund-Raising, but Still Lags," *The New York Times,* 21 April 21, 2008, http://www.nytimes.com/2008/04/21/us/politics/21campaign.html (accessed April 21, 2008).

21. Chuck Todd, "Campaign by the Numbers," *The New York Times,* November 3, 2004, http://www.nytimes.com/2004/11/03/opinion/03todd.html?scp=103&sq=campaign+advertising+bush+kerry&st=nyt (accessed March 30, 2005).

22. Ibid.

23. Don Van Natta Jr. and John M. Broder, "With Finish Line in Sight, An All-Out Race for Money," *The New York Times,* November 3, 2000, http://query.nytimes.com/gst/fullpage.html?res=9901E5D61F30F930A35752C1A9669C8B63&sec=&spon= (accessed April 20, 2008).

24. Ibid.

25. Omnicom, 2006 Annual Report, Omnicom Group, April 2007, http://www.omnicomgroup.com/investorrelations/financialoverview/financialperformance.

26. Andrew McMains, "OMC Shows New Creative Tactics," *AdWeek,* December 5, 2007, http://www.adweek.com/aw/national/article_display.jsp?vnu_content_id=1003681472 (accessed December 20, 2007).

27. Omnicon, 2006 Annual Report.

28. Quoted in Nicola Ruiz, "Can A Star Sell You Style," *Forbes,* April 18, 2008, http://www.forbes.com/style/2008/04/18/style-star-ad-forbeslife-cx_nr_ 0418style.html (accessed April 21, 2008).

29. Ibid.

30. Ibid.

31. Elliott, "Forecasters Say Madison Avenue Will Escape a Recession, Just Barely," *The New York Times,* December 4, 2007, http://proquest.umi.com/pqd web?did=1392567101&sid=4&Fmt=3&clientId=20178&RQT=309&VName=PQD (accessed January 8, 2008).

32. Quoted in ibid.

CHAPTER 4

1. Quoted in Russell Fortmeyer, "The State of American Architecture: Chicago," *BusinessWeek,* February 11, 2008, http://www.businessweek.com/innovate/ content/feb2008/id20080213_872885.htm (accessed March 1, 2008).

2. Quoted in Clifford A. Pearson, "The State of American Architecture: Atlanta," *BusinessWeek,* February 11, 2008, http://www.businessweek.com/innovate/ content/feb2008/id20080213_006669.htm (accessed March 1, 2008).

3. Quoted in ibid.

4. Joint Center for Housing Studies of Harvard University, *The State of the Nation's Housing: 2007,* Cambridge, MA: Harvard College, 2007, 1.

5. Ibid.

6. Ibid., 4.

7. Ibid., 5.

8. Ibid., 6–7.

9. "Freedom Tower," World Trade Center Web site, Silverstein Properties, http://www.wtc.com/about/freedom-tower (accessed March 31, 2008).

10. Quoted in Clifford A. Pearson, "The State of American Architecture: New York," *BusinessWeek,* February 11, 2008, http://www.businessweek.com/ innovate/content/feb2008/id20080211_678597.htm (accessed March 1, 2008).

11. Nicolai Ouroussoff, "Medieval Modern: Design Strikes a Defensive Posture," *The New York Times,* March 4, 2007, http://www.nytimes.com/2007/03/04/ weekinreview/04ouroussoff.html?_r=1&scp=2&sq=%22david+childs%22&st=nyt& oref=slogin (accessed March 1, 2008).

12. Bill Saporito, "Inside the New American Home," *Time,* October 14, 2002, http://www.time.com/time/magazine/article/0,9171,1003432,00.html (accessed January 29, 2008).

13. Quoted in ibid.

14. "The Redesigning Of America," *Time* 155.11 (March 20, 2000), http://find. galegroup.com.proxy.usf.edu/itx/infomark.do?&contentSet=IAC-Documents& type=retrieve&tabID=T003&prodId=EAIM&docId=A60588201&source=gale&srcp rod=EAIM&userGroupName=tamp59176&version=1.0/ (accessed June 9, 2007).

15. Quoted in ibid.

16. Quoted in Candace Ord Manroe, "Hot Home Trends 2008," *At Home with Century 21,* January/February 2008, 17.

17. Ibid., 18.

18. Judy Stark, "Remodeling Makeover," *St. Petersburg Times,* March 1, 2008. 5F.

19. Quoted in ibid.

20. Nicolai Ouroussoff, "Gehry's New York Debut: Subdued Tower of Light," *The New York Times,* March 22, 2007, http://www.nytimes.com/2007/03/22/arts/design/22dill.html?pagewanted=1&_r=1&hp (accessed January 31, 2008).

21. Jamie Reno, "Scenes From a New Mall," *Newsweek,* October 15, 2007, http://www.newsweek.com/id/43924 (accessed February 1, 2008).

22. Ibid.

23. Quoted in Stephanie Hacke, "Town Centers Help Create Sense of Community," *Woodland Progress,* February 27, 2008, http://www.gatewaynewspapers.com/woodlandprogress/92658 (accessed March 7, 2008).

24. Quoted in ibid.

CHAPTER 5

1. Sharon Fink, "As the Fashion World Churns," *St. Petersburg Times,* February 2, 2008, E1.

2. Ibid., E3.

3. Paco Underhill, *Why We Buy: The Science of Shopping* (New York: Simon & Schuster, 1999), 31.

4. "Wal-Mart Reports Record Fourth Quarter Sales and Earnings," Wal-Mart Stores Web site, February 19, 2008, http://www.walmartstores.com/FactsNews/NewsRoom/7950.aspx (accessed February 25, 2008).

5. Quoted in Anthony Bianco and Wendy Zellner, "Is Wal-Mart Too Powerful?" *BusinessWeek,* October 6, 2003, 102.

6. Alex Kuczynski, "Now You See It, Now You Don't," *The New York Times,* September 12, 2004, http://www.nytimes.com/2004/09/12/fashion/12THON.html (accessed January 5, 2005).

7. Quoted in Marc Karimzadeh, "The Delebrities," *Women's Wear Daily,* December 11, 2007, http://www.wwd.com/article/print/120803 (accessed February 20, 2008).

8. Quoted in Angela Phipps Towle, "Celebrity Branding," *The Hollywood Reporter,* November 18, 2003, http://www.hollywoodreporter.com/hr/search/article_display.jsp?vnu_content_id=2030984 (accessed July 2, 2007).

9. Jane Friedman, "Cosmetic Surgery." *CQ Researcher,* April 15, 2005, 319.

10. Quoted in Kirsten Sharnberg, "After Plastic Surgeries, More Do An About-Face," *Chicago Tribune,* January 21, 2008, http://www.chicagotribune.com/news/nationworld/chi-plastic_regrets_21jan21,0,506282.story?coll=chi_tab01_layout (accessed January 21, 2008).

11. Friedman, 323.

12. Ibid., 332.

13. Jeanne Huff, "Botox: In Search of Youth," *Idaho Statesman,* January 12, 2008, http://www.idahostatesman.com/life/story/261770.html (accessed January 21, 2008).

14. Natasha Singer, "The Little Botox Shop Around the Corner," *The New York Times,* April 19, 2007, http://www.nytimes.com/2007/04/19/fashion/19skin.html?pagewanted=1 (accessed January 21, 2008).

CHAPTER 6

1. *Super Size Me,* DVD, directed by Morgan Spurlock (New York: Showtime Networks, 2004).

2. Richard Schickel, "Pigging Out to Make a Point," *Time,* June 7, 2004, http://www.time.com/time/magazine/article/0,9171,994386,00.html (accessed February 18, 2008).

3. George Will, "Make Big Macs and Millionaires," *The Tampa Tribune,* December 30, 2007, C2.

4. Press Release, "McDonald's Business Momentum Drives Strong Results for 2007," McDonald's Corporation, http://www.mcdonalds.com/corp/news/fnpr/2008/fpr_012808.html (accessed February 25, 2008).

5. Will, "Make Big Macs and Millionaires," C2.

6. National Center for Health Statistics, "Health, United States, 2007 With Chartbook on Trends in the Health of Americans," Hyattsville, MD: 2007, 40.

7. Quoted in Nanci Hellmich, "Portion Distortion," *USA Today,* June 23, 2005, 8B.

8. Kim Painter, "A Gluttony of Glug-Glugging," *USA Today,* April 10, 2006, 6D.

9. Leslie Goldman, "Our Dirty Little Secret? We Can't Stop Bingeing," *Health,* June 2007, 129–30.

10. Quoted in ibid., 130.

11. Ibid., 131, 194.

12. Quoted in Christina Le Beau, "Diets Compared," *Better Nutrition,* 66 (2004): 37.

13. Katherine Hobson, "Still No Perfect Diet," *U.S. News and World Report,* March 19, 2007, 59.

14. Le Beau, 38–39.

15. Gail Gorman, "The Big Fat Lie," *The Consumer's Medical Journal,* 2005, 2.

16. Ibid., 4.

17. Conor Clarke, "Hill of Beans," *The New Republic,* November 20, 2006, 8.

18. Maria Bartiromo, "Howard Schultz on Reinventing Starbucks," *Business-Week,* April 21, 2008, Academic Search Premier, (accessed April 28, 2008).

19. Ibid.

20. Kenneth Hein, "PepsiCo Positions Amp as Everyman's Drink," *Brandweek,* January 21, 2008, Academic Search Premier (accessed April 20, 2008).

21. Quoted in Gerry Khermouch, "Canned Heat," *Brandweek,* October 8, 2007, Academic Search Premier (accessed March 30, 2008).

22. Hein, "PepsiCo."

23. Khermouch, "Canned Heat."

24. Quoted in Jen Haley, "Consumers Pinching their Pennies," *CNN,* March 10, 2008, http://www.cnn.com/2008/LIVING/personal/03/07/consumer.spending (accessed March 11, 2008).

25. Janelle Barlow, "Top Brands," *Fast Casual,* 14 (2007/2008): 7.

26. Valerie Killifer, "Chipotle Sizzles at No. 1," *Fast Casual,* 14 (2007/2008): 18.

27. Quoted in ibid.

28. David Brown, "USDA Orders Largest Meat Recall in U.S. History," *Washington Post,* February 18, 2008, A01.

29. Quoted in ibid.

30. Quoted in Brian Stelter, "Celebrity Chef Sells His TV Shows and Products to Martha Stewart," *The New York Times*, February 20, 2008, http://www.nytimes.com/2008/02/20/business/media/20martha.html?_r=1&ref=media&oref=slogin (accessed March 11, 2008).

31. "Rachael Ray's Official Biography," Rachael Ray's Official Web site, http://www.rachaelray.com/bio.php (accessed March 1, 2008).

32. Ibid.

33. Alec Foege, "The Rachael Way," *Brandweek* 48, Academic Search Premier, EBSCOhost, http://search.ebscohost.com.proxy.usf.edu/login.aspx?direct=true&db=aph&AN=24269226&site=ehost-live (accessed March 11, 2008).

34. Quoted in Jill Hunter Pellettieri, "Rachael Ray," *Slate*, July 13, 2005, http://www.slate.com/id/2122085 (accessed March 11, 2008).

35. Florence King, "Our Last Nerve," *National Review*, March 5, 2007, 42.

36. Jenny Allen, "Martha Comes Clean," *Good Housekeeping*, 244, 9: 152–232. Academic Search Premier, EBSCOhost, http://search.ebscohost.com.proxy.usf.edu/login.aspx?direct=true&db=aph&AN=27047795&site=ehost-live (accessed March 11, 2008).

37. Quoted in ibid.

38. Ibid.

39. Diane Brady, "The Reinvention of Martha Stewart," *BusinessWeek*, 4008 (2006): 76–80. Academic Search Premier, EBSCOhost, http://search.ebscohost.com.proxy.usf.edu/login.aspx?direct=true&db=aph&AN=22910974&site=ehost-live (accessed March 11, 2008).

40. Ibid.

CHAPTER 7

1. Laura M. Holson, "Lights, Camera, Pixels . . . Action!" *The New York Times*, October 24, 2005, C1.

2. Mike Vorhaus, "Favorite Leisure Activities Among Females," *Advertising Age*, February 11, 2008, Academic Search Premier (accessed April 27, 2008).

3. Ibid.

4. Brian Stelter, "From MySpace to YourSpace," *The New York Times*, January 21, 2008, http://www.nytimes.com/2008/01/21/technology/21myspace.html?_r=2&pagewanted=1&oref=slogin (accessed January 23, 2008).

5. Quoted in Ibid.

6. Michael Hirschorn, "About Facebook," *The Atlantic Monthly*, October 2007, 155.

7. Erick Schonfeld, "MySpace May Still Dominate in the U.S., But (Surprise!) Facebook is Catching Up Fast Worldwide," *TechCrunch*, January 16, 2008, http://www.techcrunch.com/2008/01/16/myspace-may-still-dominate-in-the-us-but-surprise-facebook-is-catching-up-fast-worldwide/ (accessed January 16, 2008).

8. Ibid.

9. Gavin O'Malley, "YouTube Continues to Grow Video Share," *Online Media Daily*, January 18, 2008, http://publications.mediapost.com/index.cfm?fuseaction=Articles.showArticle&art_aid=74597 (accessed January 18, 2008).

10. "Video Sharing Web Site Audience Doubles in a Year," *Research Brief,* Center for Media Research, January 22, 2008, http://blogs.mediapost.com/research_brief/?p=1623 (accessed February 1, 2008).

11. Ibid.

12. "10 Billion Video Views Online in December," *Research Brief,* Center for Media Research, February 22, 2008, http://blogs.mediapost.com/research_brief/?p=1646 (accessed February 26, 2008).

13. Seth Schiesel, "As Gaming Turns Social, Industry Shifts Strategies," *The New York Times,* February 28, 2008, http://www.nytimes.com/2008/02/28/arts/television/28game.html?sq=&pagewanted=all (accessed February 28, 2008).

14. Schiesel, "In the List of Top-Selling Games, Clear Evidence of a Sea Change," *The New York Times,* February 1, 2008, http://www.nytimes.com/2008/02/01/arts/01game.html?fta=y (accessed February 1, 2008).

15. Ibid.

16. John B. Horrigan, *Online Shopping,* Pew Internet & American Life Project, February 13, 2008, i.

17. Ibid., iii, iv.

18. David Samuels, "Shooting Britney," *The Atlantic,* April 2008, 37.

19. David M. Halbfinger and Geraldine Fabrikant, "In the Drama of Britney Spears, a Show Business Fortune Is at Risk," *The New York Times,* February 25, 2008, http://www.nytimes.com/2008/02/25/business/media/25britney.html?sq= (accessed February 26, 2008).

20. Quoted in ibid.

21. Hilary Hylton, "Anna Nicole Smith, 1967–2007," *Time,* February 8, 2007, http://www.time.com/time/arts/article/0,8599,1587535,00.html (accessed September 15, 2007).

22. Ruth La Ferla, "A Glossy Rehab for Tattered Careers," *The New York Times,* March 9, 2008, http://www.nytimes.com/2008/03/09/fashion/09magazines.html?_r=2&pagewanted=all&oref=slogin (accessed March 30, 2008).

23. Matt Higgins, "Dramatic Fall Exposes the Risk in Extreme Sports," *The New York Times,* August 4, 2007, http://www.nytimes.com/2007/08/04/sports/othersports/04xgames.html ?scp=5&sq=extreme+sports&st=nyt (accessed September 15, 2007).

24. Jodai Saremi, "Leisure Fun Facts," *American Fitness,* March/April 2008, 41.

25. Ibid.

26. Quoted in John Goff, "A Wild Ride," *CFO,* August 2007, 41.

27. Ibid., 45.

28. Juliet Macur, "Vick Receives 23 Months and a Lecture," *The New York Times,* December 11, 2007, http://www.nytimes.com/2007/12/11/sports/football/11vick.html?_r=1&oref=slogin (accessed December 25, 2007).

29. Joe Drape, "The Official Line vs. the Betting Line," *The New York Times,* January 31, 2008, http://www.nytimes.com/2008/01/31/sports/football/31gambling.html?scp=9&sq=football+popularity&st=nyt (accessed January 31, 2008).

30. Grant Wahl, "Ahead of his Class," *Sports Illustrated,* February 18, 2002.

31. Tom Friend, "Next: LeBron James," *ESPN The Magazine,* December 23, 2002.

32. Marc Stein, "Breaking Down LeBron James' Game," *ESPN.com,* December 12, 2002.

33. Ibid.

34. Howard Beck, "Ready for N.B.A. Throne, but Not Like Mike," *The New York Times,* June 6, 2007, http://www.nytimes.com/2007/06/06/sports/basketball/06lebron.html?_r=1&oref=slogin&pagewanted=all (accessed June 6, 2007).

35. Jay Mariotti, "Sorry, MJ, but Tiger has Trumped You," *Chicago Sun-Times,* February 26, 2008, http://www.suntimes.com/sports/mariotti/812610,mariotti022608.article (accessed March 12, 2008).

36. "Tiger Woods Profile," Official Website for Tiger Woods, http://www.tigerwoods.com/defaultflash.sps (accessed February 26, 2008).

37. Quoted in Paul Vitello, "American Players are Abandoning the Courses," *International Herald Tribune,* February 25, 2008, http://www.iht.com/articles/2008/02/25/sports/GLUT.php (accessed March 13, 2008).

38. Ibid.

39. Quoted in Gary Stoller, "More Hotels Give Guests Opportunity to go Ahhh," *USA Today,* September 26, 2006, Academic Search Premier, EBSCOhost (accessed July 9, 2008).

40. Quoted in ibid.

41. *"Yoga Journal* Releases 2008 'Yoga in America' Market Study; Practitioner Spending Grows to Nearly $6 Billion a Year," Press Release, February 26, 2008.

42. "IHRSA Releases 2008 IHRSA Global Report: The State of the Health Club Industry," Press Release, June 3, 2008.

43. Jessica Severs, "Review: 'Wii Fit' Gives Gamers a True Physical Challenge," The *Pittsburgh Tribune-Review*, May 29, 2008, Gale General OneFile (accessed July 8, 2008).

44. "Poll: Majority of Fans Think Clemens is Lying," *USA Today,* February 27, 2008, S1.

45. Tom Verducci, "Believe Him or Not," *Sports Illustrated,* 108 (2008): 38–41, Academic Search Premier, EBSCOhost (accessed March 24, 2008).

46. Abraham Socher, "No Game for Old Men," *Commentary,* March 2008, 56.

47. Michael Hiestand, "Mixed-Martial Arts Gets Fighting Chance on CBS," *USA Today,* February 29, 2008, S3.

48. Paula Lehman, "Offbeat Thrills Now, Big Money Later?" *Business Week,* 4049 (2007): 64–66, Academic Search Premier, EBSCOhost (accessed March 17, 2008).

49. Greg Beato, "Bleeding Into the Mainstream," *Reason,* 39 (2007): 16–18, Academic Search Premier, EBSCOhost (accessed March 17, 2008).

50. Christa Case Bryant and Mark Sappenfield, "For Extreme Sports Fans, Olympics Adds Jumping Cyclists," *The Christian Science Monitor*, July 7, 2008, http://www.csmonitor.com/2008/0707/p01s01-wogn.html (accessed July 8, 2008).

51. Edward Iwata, "Tony Hawk Leaps to Top of Financial Empire," *USA Today*, March 10, 2008, Academic Search Premier, EBSCOhost (accessed July 9, 2008).

CHAPTER 8

1. Jordan E. Rosenfeld, "Shock and Awe," *Writer's Digest,* October 2007, 47.

2. Julie Watson and Tomas Kellner, "J. K. Rowling and the Billion-Dollar Empire," *Forbes.com,* February 26, 2004, http://www.forbes.com/maserati/billionaires2004/cx_jw_0226rowlingbill04.html (accessed September 15, 2005).

3. "Pottermania Unleashed," *Forbes.com,* July 20, 2007, http://www.forbes.com/business/2007/07/20/potter-scholastic-books-biz-cx_0720potter.html (accessed September 15, 2008).

4. Quoted in "New Study Finds that the Harry Potter Series has a Positive Impact on Kids' Reading and their School Work," Press Release, July 25, 2006, Scholastic Web site, http://www.scholastic.com/aboutscholastic/news/press_07252006_CP.htm (accessed April 1, 2008).

5. Quoted in Julie Bick, "Seattle Helps Shape What Nation Reads," *The Seattle Times,* March 11, 2008, http://seattletimes.nwsource.com/html/businesstechnology/2004273751_seattlebookczars.html (accessed March 15, 2008).

6. Quoted in Liz Ruiz, "Coben Tried to 'Grab You on Page One,'" *The State* (South Carolina), February 17, 2008, E2.

7. Chuck Leddy, "Loot vs. Literature: Genre and Literary Fiction," *Writer* 121 1(2008): 8–9.

8. Rachel Donadio, "Promotional Intelligence," *The New York Times,* May 21, 2006, http://www.nytimes.com/2006/05/21/books/review/21donadio.html?sq=&pagewanted=all (accessed September 15, 2006).

9. Ibid.

10. Ibid.

11. "Meghan Holohan, "An Active Voice," *Pitt Magazine,* Summer 2003, 29.

12. Craig Offman, "Tom Wolfe Calls Irving, Mailer and Updike 'the Three Stooges,'" Salon.com, January 21, 2000, http://archive.salon.com/books/log/2000/01/21/wolfe/index.html (accessed August 29, 2001).

13. Richard Lacayo, "Oprah Turns the Page," *Time,* April 15, 2002, http://www.time.com/time/magazine/article/0,9171,1002228,00.html (accessed November 15, 2002).

14. David Carr, "How Oprahness Trumped Truthiness," *The New York Times,* January 30, 2006, http://www.nytimes.com/2006/01/30/business/media/30carr.html?ex=1296277200&en=1c0e8843da5b43d6&ei=5088&partner=rssnyt&emc=rss (accessed April 27, 2006).

15. Randy Dotinga, "Iraq War Books Do A Quickstep into Print," *The Christian Science Monitor,* http://www.csmonitor.com/2005/1130/p14s03-bogn.html (accessed April 1, 2008).

CHAPTER 9

1. Brian Hiatt, "How to Sell a Smash Hit," *Rolling Stone,* September 7, 2006, 19.

2. Hiatt, "Rock Games Strike A Chord," *Rolling Stone,* October 18, 2007, 19–20.

3. Dan Barkin, "He Made the iPod: How Steve Jobs of Apple Created the New Millennium's Signature Invention," *Knight Ridder Tribune Business News,* 3 December 2006, ProQuest Database (accessed January 1, 2007).

4. Grace Wong, "Apple's iPod is Turning 5," CNNMoney.com, October 20, 2006, http://money.cnn.com/2006/10/20/technology/apple_ipod/index.htm (accessed October 25, 2006).

5. Dean Goodman, "Album Sales Plunge in '07 as Digital Growth Slows," *Reuters Online,* January 3, 2008, http://www.reuters.com/article/internetNews/idUSN3053893220080104 (accessed January 4, 2008).

6. Steve Knopper, "2007: From Bad to Worse," *Rolling Stone,* February 7, 2008, 15.

7. Quoted in Shirley Halperin, "American Dreams," *Entertainment Weekly,* July 27, 2007, Lexis-Nexis Academic (accessed January 1, 2008).

8. Brian Hiatt, "Lost in the Flood," *Rolling Stone,* September 22, 2005, 13–14.

9. *Blacks See Growing Values Gap Between Poor and Middle Class,* Pew Research Center, November 13, 2007, 6, 42.

10. Ibid., 42.

11. Peter Katel, "Debating Hip-Hop," *CQ Researcher,* June 15, 2007, 531.

12. Quoted in "Hip-Hop Comes Alive at Smithsonian Exhibit," Newsday, March 21, 2008, http://www.newsday.com/travel/ny-f5619682mar23,0,7919095.story (accessed March 21, 2008).

13. Katel, "Debating," 532.

14. "Apple Introduced the U2 iPod," Apple Press Release, October 26, 2004.

15. Ibid.

16. Quoted in Jann S. Wenner, "Bono: The *Rolling Stone* Interview," *Rolling Stone,* November 3, 2005, 61.

17. Mark Binelli, "The Guru," *Rolling Stone,* September 22, 2005, 74, 76.

18. Ibid., 76.

19. Josh Tyrangiel, "The Dude," *Time,* 169 (2007): 62–65, Academic Search Premier, EBSCOhost (accessed March 1, 2008).

20. Quoted in ibid.

CHAPTER 10

1. Sarah Mahoney, "Super Bowl-Related Sales Approach $10 Billion," *Media-Post Publications,* January 24, 2008, http://publications.mediapost.com/index.cfm?fuseaction=Articles.showArticle&art_aid=74959 (accessed February 1, 2008).

2. Paul Thomasch, "Giants and Patriots Draw Record Super Bowl Audience," *Reuters,* February 4, 2008, http://www.reuters.com/article/topNews/idUSN04 20266320080204?pageNumber=1&virtualBrandChannel=0 (accessed February 6, 2008).

3. "TV Basics: Television Households," *TV Basics: An Online Brochure,* Television Bureau of Advertising, http://www.tvb.org (accessed February 8, 2008).

4. Ibid.

5. *2006 Media Comparisons Study,* Television Bureau of Advertising, http://www.tvb.org (accessed February 9, 2008).

6. Ibid.

7. Bill Carter, "How a Hit Almost Failed Its Own Audition," *The New York Times,* April 30, 2006, http://www.nytimes.com/2006/04/30/business/yourmoney/30idol.html?pagewanted=all (accessed April 30, 2006).

8. Ken Barnes, "Long Live 'American Idol,'" *USA Today,* March 10, 2008, L3.

9. Richard M. Huff, *Reality Television.* Westport, CT: Praeger, 2006, 2–3.

10. Ibid., 6.

11. Ibid., 7.

12. Derek Foster, "Jump in the Pool: The Competitive and Collegial Culture of Survivor Fan Communities," in *Understanding Reality Television,* eds. Su Holmes & Deborah Jermyn (London: Routledge, 2004), 280.

13. "We Like To Watch: Led by the Hit *Survivor*, Voyeurism has become TV's Hottest Genre," *Time*, June 26, 2000, Expanded Academic ASAP. Thomson Gale. http://find.galegroup.com.proxy.usf.edu /itx/infomark.do?&contentSet=IAC-Documents&type=retrieve&tabID=T003&prodId=EAIM&docId=A62880218&source=gale&srcprod=EAIM&userGroupName=tamp59176&version=1.0 (accessed June 9, 2007).

14. Ibid.

15. Yinka Adegoke, "Cable Loses Subscribers, Satellite Gains in Q1," *Reuters*, April 28, 2008, http://www.reuters.com/article/marketsNews/idUSN28461999 20080428?sp=true (accessed April 29, 2008).

16. Chuck Bell, "Time for New Yorkers to Strike Back Against Big Cable," *NYDailyNews.com*, April 16, 2008, http://www.nydailynews.com/opinions/2008/04/16/2008-04-16_time_for_new_yorkers_ to_strike_back_agai.html (accessed April 28, 2008).

17. Tim Goodman, "TV's Best of 2007," *San Francisco Chronicle*, December 31, 2007, http://www.sfgate.com/cgi-bin/article.cgi?file=/c/a/2007/12/31/DDDGU66SJ.DTL (accessed April 1, 2008).

18. Quoted in Ronald Grover and Tom Lowry, "Spending Like Mad Men on Cable TV," *BusinessWeek*, April 24, 2008, http://www.businessweek.com/magazine/content/08_18/b4082054975746.htm? chan=top+news_top+news+index+businessweek+exclusives (accessed April 30, 2008).

19. Ibid.

20. Jeff Zucker, "A Time for Change," *Vital Speeches of the Day*, May 2008, 205.

21. Ibid., 207.

22. "Prime Time is Anytime," Digital Life America survey, Solutions Research Group, February 4, 2008, 1.

23. Ibid.

24. David M. Halbfinger and Michael Cieply, "*No Country for Old Men* Wins Oscar Tug of War," *The New York Times*, February 25, 2008, http://www.nytimes.com/2008/02/25/movies/awardsseason /25osca.html?ref=awardsseason (accessed March 30, 2008).

25. David Carr, "In Oscars, No Country For Hit Films," *The New York Times*, March 3, 2008, http://query.nytimes.com/gst/fullpage.html?res=9C01E3D6143BF930A35750C0A96E9C8B63 (accessed March 30, 2008).

26. Brooks Barnes and Matt Richtel, "Studios Are Trying to Stop DVDs From Fading to Black," *The New York Times*, February 25, 2008, http://www.nytimes.com/2008/02/25/business/media/25dvd.html (accessed February 25, 2008).

27. Caryn James, "A Movie Star for All Eras, Even the Present," *The New York Times*, January 6, 2008, http://www.nytimes.com/2008/01/06/movies/awardsseason/06jame.html (accessed February 1, 2008).

28. Michelle Tauber, et al., "And now . . . Brangelina," *People* 63 (2005): 56–61, Academic Search Premier, EBSCOhost (accessed February 26, 2008).

29. Alec Appelbaum, "Pitt Unveils Sustainable Housing for New Orleans," *Architectural Record*, 196 (2008): 12, Academic Search Premier, EBSCOhost (accessed February 26, 2008).

30. Quoted in Robin Pogrebin, "Brad Pitt Commissions Designs for New Orleans," *The New York Times*, December 3, 2007, http://www.nytimes.com/2007/12/03/arts/design/03pitt.html?sq= (accessed December 3, 2007).

31. James Poniewozik, "The Day That Changed . . . Very Little," *Time,* August 7, 2006, Expanded Academic ASAP, Thomson Gale, (accessed January 24, 2007).

32. "What's Entertainment Now?" *Time,* October 1, 2001, Expanded Academic ASAP, Thomson Gale (accessed June 9, 2007).

33. Richard Corliss, "Why the Iraq Films Are Failing," *Time,* November 15, 2007, http://www.time.com/time/magazine/article/0,9171,1684509,00.html (accessed February 21, 2008).

34. Miriam Kreinin Souccar, "Broadway Strike Shows No Lasting Effects," *Crain's New York Business,* January 14, 2008, LexisNexis Academic (accessed May 1, 2008).

35. Quoted in ibid.

36. "Seasons Greeting B'Way," *Variety,* April, 7–13, 2008, LexisNexis Academic (accessed May 1, 2008).

CHAPTER 11

1. Ben Cutler, "Online Travel: The Internet's Biggest Retail Sector Gets Even Bigger," *Internet Consumer Trend Report,* 2001.

2. Erik Blachford, interview by Bob Batchelor, April 15, 2001.

3. Ibid.

4. Ibid.

5. Ibid.

6. Jay Greene, "Microsoft's First-Class Deal," *BusinessWeek,* July 30, 2001, 37.

7. Bruce Greenberg, interview by Bob Batchelor, May 20, 2001.

8. Ibid.

9. Wendy Tanaka, "Travel Web Sites Get Personal," Forbes.com, March 28, 2008, http://www.forbes.com/technology/2008/03/27/social-network-travel-tech-personal-cx_wt_0328travel.html (accessed March 28, 2008).

10. Quoted in Ted Jackovics, "Accommodations for the Environment," *The Tampa Tribune,* February 24, 2008, B8.

11. Ibid.

12. Ibid., B7.

13. Ibid.

14. Michael McCarthy, "Vegas Goes Back to Naughty Roots," *USA Today,* April 11, 2005, 6B.

15. Kitty Bean Yancey, "$40B Thrown into Vegas Development Kitty," *USA Today,* January 18, 2008, 7D.

16. Ellen Creager, "New Glitter Adds Gold to Vegas," *St. Petersburg Times* (FL), April 13, 2008, 4L.

17. Quoted in Chris McGinnis, "The Pampered Traveler," *Fortune,* October 29, 2007, S2.

18. Ibid., S6.

CHAPTER 12

1. Leslie Camhi, "The 2008 Whitney Biennial and the Failure of an Empire," *Village Voice,* March 11, 2008, http://www.villagevoice.com/art/0811,374042,374042,13.html (accessed March 12, 2008).

2. Ibid.

3. Quoted in Robin Pogrebin, "For American Indians, A Chance to Tell Their Own Story," *The New York Times,* March 12, 2008, http://www.nytimes.com/2008/03/12/arts/artsspecial/12indian.html?ex=1206072000&en=409ca01d c3bc767f&ei=5070&emc=eta1 (accessed March 12, 2008).

4. Tahree Lane, "Diverse Collection to be Sold on Sunday," *Toledo Blade,* February 21, 2008, http://toledoblade.com/apps/pbcs.dll/article?AID=/20080221/ART03/802210318 (accessed March 1, 2008).

5. Quoted in W. A. Demers, "Galle Vase Emerges at $20,340 at Green Valley Auction," *Antiques and The Arts Online,* February 26, 2008, http://antiquesandthearts.com/Antiques/AuctionWatch/2008-02-26__11-47-50.html (accessed March 11, 2008).

6. Sarah K. Winn, "Local Retailer Boycotts eBay," *The Charleston Gazette,* March 2, 2008, http://sundaygazettemail.com/News/Business/200803010319 (accessed March 12, 2008).

7. Quoted in ibid.

8. Quoted in Carol Vogel, "Museums Refine the Art of Listening," *The New York Times,* March 12, 2008, http://www.nytimes.com/2008/03/12/arts/artsspecial/12visitors.html?ex=1206072000&en=4173627bbdd5b2a7&ei=5070&emc=eta1 (accessed March 12, 2008).

9. Ibid.

10. Barbara Isenberg, "Thinking Out of the Box," *Time,* November 19, 2007, http://www.time.com/time/magazine/article/0,9171,1685661,00.html (accessed February 22, 2008).

11. Quoted in Ibid.

12. Edward Wyatt, "To Have and Give Not," *The New York Times,* February 10, 2008, http://www.nytimes.com/2008/02/10/arts/design/10wyat.html?scp=8&sq=govan+los+angeles&st=nyt (accessed February 22, 2008).

13. Quoted in ibid.

14. Jeff McDonald and Jeanette Steele, "Balancing Art, Ethics," *The San Diego Union-Tribune,* February 17, 2008, http://www.signonsandiego.com/news/metro/20080217-9999-1m17art.html (accessed March 12, 2008).

15. Ibid.

16. Ibid.

17. "New Visual Artists 2008," *Print,* April 2008, 109.

18. Quoted in ibid., 111.

19. "Gregory Crewdson Biography," Guggenheim Museum, http://www.guggenheimcollection.org/site/artist_bio_172.html (accessed March 15, 2008).

20. "Crewdson Interview," Egg The Arts Show, n.d., http://www.pbs.org/wnet/egg/210/crewdson/ interview.html (accessed March 15, 2008).

21. Benjamin Genocchio, "The Soul of Suburbia, Captured on Film," *The New York Times,* http://query.nytimes.com/gst/fullpage.html?res=9B0CE5DF1F3BF930A25752C0A96E9C8B63&sec=&spon=&pagewanted=2 (accessed March 15, 2008).

22. Brian Keith Jackson, "How I Made It: Mark Bradford," *New York Magazine,* September 24, 2007, http://nymag.com/arts/art/features/37954/ (accessed March 1, 2008).

23. "Interview: 'Market > Place,'" *Paradox*, Season 4, 2007, Art:21–Art in the Twenty-First Century, PBS, http://www.pbs.org/art21/artists/bradford/clip1.html (accessed March 15, 2008).

24. "Selected Works by Mark Bradford," The Saatchi Gallery: London Contemporary Art Gallery, http://www.saatchi-gallery.co.uk/artists/mark_bradford.htm (accessed March 15, 2008).

Further Reading

Batchelor, Bob, ed. *Basketball in America: From the Playgrounds to Jordan's Game and Beyond*. Binghamton, NY: Haworth Press, 2005.

Battelle, John. *The Search: How Google and Its Rivals Rewrote the Rules of Business and Transformed Our Culture*. New York: Portfolio, 2005.

Benedict, Jeff. *Out of Bounds: Inside the NBA's Culture of Rape, Violence, & Crime*. New York: HarperCollins, 2004.

Berman, Morris. *Dark Ages America: The Final Phase of Empire*. New York: W. W. Norton, 2006.

Biagi, Shirley. *Media/Impact: An Introduction to Mass Media*. 8th ed. Boston: Wadsworth Cendage Learning, 2009.

Brooks, David. *Bobos in Paradise: The New Upper Class and How They Got There*. New York: Simon & Schuster, 2000.

Browne, Ray B., ed. *Profiles of Popular Culture: A Reader*. Madison: The University of Wisconsin Press, 2005.

Cusic, Don. *Baseball and Country Music*. Madison: University of Wisconsin Press; Popular Press, 2003.

Duncan, Russell and Joseph Goddard. *Contemporary America*. 2nd ed. London: Palgrave Macmillan, 2005.

Dylan, Bob. *Chronicles: Volume One*. New York: Simon & Schuster, 2004.

Dyson, Michael Eric. *The Michael Eric Dyson Reader*. New York: Basic Civitas Books, 2004.

Faludi, Susan. *The Terror Dream: Fear and Fantasy in Post-9/11 America*. New York: Metropolitan Books, 2007.

Fight Club. Directed by David Fincher. 139 minutes. Distributed by 20th Century Fox, 2000. DVD.

Fishwick, Marshall William. *Probing Popular Culture: On and Off the Internet*. New York: Haworth Press, 2004.

Franklin, John Hope. *Mirror to America: The Autobiography of John Hope Franklin*. New York: Farrar, Straus and Giroux, 2005.

Friedman, Thomas L. *The World is Flat: A Brief History of the Twenty-First Century*. New York: Farrar, Straus and Giroux, 2005.

Gitlin, Todd. *The Bulldozer and the Big Tent: Blind Republicans, Lame Democrats, and the Recovery of American Ideals*. Hoboken, NJ: John Wiley & Sons, 2007.

Gray-Rosendale, Laura, ed. *Pop Perspectives: Readings to Critique Contemporary Culture*. New York: McGraw-Hill, 2008.

Heller, Dana, ed. *The Great American Makeover: Television, History, Nation*. New York: Palgrave Macmillan, 2006.

Hoyle, Russ. *Going to War: How Misinformation, Disinformation, and Arrogance Led America into Iraq*. New York: Thomas Dunne Books, 2008.

Johnson Woods, Toni. *Blame Canada!: South Park and Popular Culture*. New York: Continuum, 2007.

Kaufman, Robert Gordon. *In Defense of the Bush Doctrine*. Lexington: University Press of Kentucky, 2007.

Leavy, Patricia. *Iconic Events: Media, Politics, and Power in Retelling History*. Lanham, MD: Lexington Books, 2007.

Levitt, Steven D. and Stephen J. Dubner. *Freakonomics: A Rogue Economist Explores the Hidden Side of Everything*. New York: William Morrow, 2005.

Mackiewicz Wolfe, Wojtek. *Winning the War of Words: Selling the War on Terror from Afghanistan to Iraq*. Westport, CT: Praeger, 2008.

McGraw, Phillip C. *Self Matters: Creating Your Life from the Inside Out*. New York: Free Press, 2001.

Montgomery, Bruce P. *The Bush-Cheney Administration's Assault on Open Government*. Westport, CT: Praeger, 2008.

Mooney, Chris. *Storm World: Hurricanes, Politics, and the Battle Over Global Warming*. Orlando: Harcourt, 2007.

Roberts, Sam. *Who We Are Now: The Changing Face of America in the Twenty-first Century*. New York: Henry Holt, 2004.

Sammon, Bill. *Fighting Back: The War on Terrorism from Inside the Bush White House*. Lanham, MD: Regnery, 2002.

———. *Misunderestimated: The President Battles Terrorism, John Kerry, and the Bush Haters*. New York: Regan Books, 2004.

Searching for the Roots of 9/11: Thomas L. Friedman Reporting. Produced by Edward Gray. 50 minutes. Distributed by Discovery Channel, 2003. DVD.

Star Wars. Episode III, Revenge of the Sith. Directed by George Lucas. 140 minutes. Distributed by 20th Century Fox Home Entertainment, 2005. DVD.

Stewart, Jon, David Javerbaum, and Ben Karlin. *America (the Book): A Citizen's Guide to Democracy Inaction*. New York: Warner Books, 2004.

Super Size Me. Directed by Morgan Spurlock. 100 minutes. Distributed by Samuel Goldwyn Films and Showtime Independent Films, 2004. DVD.

Vise, David A. and Mark Malseed. *The Google Story*. New York: Delacorte, 2005.

Yeffeth, Glenn, ed. *The Man from Krypton: A Closer Look at Superman*. Dallas: BenBella Books, 2005.

Zegart, Amy B. *Spying Blind: The CIA, the FBI, and the Origins of 9/11*. Princeton: Princeton University Press, 2007.

Index

About the Author

BOB BATCHELOR teaches Public Relations in the School of Mass Communications at the University of South Florida in Tampa. A noted popular culture expert, Bob is the author of *The 1900s* (Greenwood Press, 2002); editor of *Basketball in America: From the Playgrounds to Jordan's Game and Beyond* (2005); and co-author with Thomas Heinrich of *Kotex, Kleenex, and Huggies: Kimberly-Clark and the Consumer Revolution in American Business* (2004).